Intelligent Java™ Applications for the Internet and Intranets

Mark Watson

Morgan Kaufmann Publishers
San Francisco, California

Senior Editor	Diane D. Cerra	Copyeditor	Ken DellaPenta
Production Manager	Yonie Overton	Proofreader	Jennifer McClain
Production Editor	Elisabeth Beller	Indexer	Steve Rath
Cover Design	Ross Carron Design	Cover Photo	© The Field Museum
Printer	Courier Corporation		Cat# 36098, Chicago
			Photo by James Balodimas
			and Julie Pitzen

This book was author-typeset in Microsoft Word 7.0.

Designations used by companies to distinguish their products are often claimed as trademarks or registered trademarks. In all instances where Morgan Kaufmann Publishers, Inc. is aware of a claim, the product names appear in initial capital or all capital letters. Readers, however, should contact the appropriate companies for more complete information regarding trademarks and registration.

Morgan Kaufmann Publishers, Inc.
Editorial and Sales Office
340 Pine Street, Sixth Floor
San Francisco, CA 94104-3205
USA

Telephone	415/392-2665
Facsimile	415/982-2665
E-mail	mkp@mkp.com
WWW	http://www.mkp.com

Order toll free 800/745-7323

01   00   99   98   97   5   4   3   2   1

Library of Congress Cataloging-in-Publication Data

Watson, Mark.
    Intelligent Java applications for the internet and intranets /
  Mark Watson.
      p.   cm.
    Includes bibliographical references and index.
    ISBN 1-55860-420-0 (pbk.)
    1. Java (Computer program language) 2. Intelligent agents
  (Computer software) 3. Internet programming. 4. Intranets
  (Computer networks) I. Title.
QA76.73.J38W38 1997
005.2'762--dc21   97-10626
                                   CIP

Intelligent Java™ Applications for the Internet and Intranets

To Carol, love always

Contents

Preface

I have been fascinated by the concept of artificial intelligence (AI) for the last 20 years, and I have had the good fortune to work in this exciting field for the last 10 years. I have applied AI technology to commercial and military applications, have written commercial AI tool products for the Hardware LISP machine and Macintosh and Windows environments, and have written eight books, most of which have, at least peripherally, dealt with AI. I was the technical lead on developing a real-time distributed expert system that is in use by most regional telephone companies to detect fraud. I presently write AI game agents for Nintendo and Windows 95 games, and virtual-reality-based entertainment systems.

The most compelling application for AI in the next decade will be the development of intelligent agents for both entertainment and practical knowledge-processing applications. This book lays out a theoretical foundation for AI and provides many complete example programs and Java classes/packages that can be reused without restriction *in compiled form* without royalty payments to the author. I ask you not to distribute the source code for the libraries contained in this book without permission.

There are three types of Java interfaces and classes developed in this book:

1. Low-level AI classes (e.g., frames with inheritance, natural language processing, neural network simulations, genetic algorithm tools)
2. User interface frameworks (e.g., Java applet classes for containing AI classes and supporting text and graphics fields)
3. Distributed AI frameworks (i.e., client/server classes to facilitate writing distributed agents)

These three types of interfaces and frameworks are all used for building the following complete example programs in the third part of this book:

- An arcade-style game that uses genetic algorithms to evolve new opponent strategies.
- A handwriting recognition system that uses neural networks.
- Genetic-algorithm-based tools for improving training data for neural networks.
- A distributed natural language demonstration system that answers questions about ancient and medieval history. Knowledge of people, places, and events is provided

by a separate server program that can run on the same computer as the natural language processing client application or on any other computer on the same Intranet or the Internet.

- An information-gathering application that can access remote Web sites and remote POP electronic mail servers.

I chose the new Java programming language developed by Sun Microsystems for the examples in this book for these reasons:

- Java is freely available for most popular computer systems.
- Java is a modern language supporting object-oriented design and programming.
- Java uses a built-in garbage collector, so we will not have to worry about memory management of complex data structures.
- Java supports dynamic multiple-dimensional arrays, hash tables, dictionaries, and other useful complex data types.
- Java has built-in support for threads and Internet programming; many of the most interesting applications of AI are in distributed systems.

There are no systems today that anyone should consider to be artificially intelligent. Many of the AI demonstration systems are, I believe, on the wrong track. The authors of these systems sometimes make outrageous claims regarding the underlying knowledge built into their systems when these systems are, in fact, symbol-processing systems, in which the symbols are given labels that have deep connotations for human readers but that could be substituted for by simple algebraic variables for all the AI systems care.

It is not my intention to "flame" these researchers; rather, I will briefly discuss representative samples of work of those researchers who I feel are on the correct path. After providing a brief history and survey of AI, in Chapters 2 through 7, I develop utility classes that are used to create complete Java program examples in Chapters 9 through 12 to ground the theory in real code. Chapter 8 stands on its own as an introduction to writing expert systems.

You will find that the program miniatures provide new perspectives on problem solving and are readily reusable in your programs.

I use a simplified Booch object-modeling notation in this book. Figure P.1 shows a typical Booch class diagram.

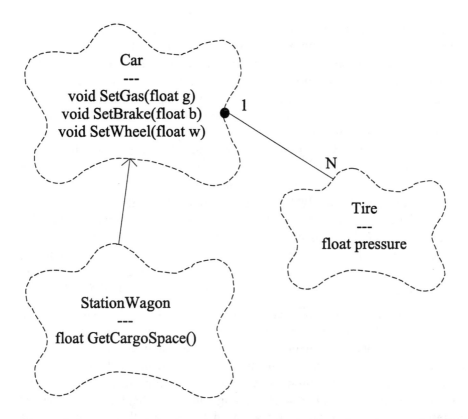

Figure P.1   A Booch class diagram showing a base class **Car**, a class **StationWagon** derived from class **Car**, and a class **Tire** contained in class **Car**. This containment is 1 to N; that is, one car contains many tires. Each class is represented as a "cloud" containing the class name and the public class interface.

The Booch notation shown in Figure P.1 is a great notation for expressing object-oriented designs. A software library or Java class consists of three related assets:

1. A short description of the requirements for the library or class. Answer the question, Why was this class written?
2. A short description of the design decisions used for creating the library or class. Booch class, object interaction, and Harel state diagrams can be useful for describing a design.
3. The source code for the library or class.

Libraries consisting of all three of these component assets are, I believe, much more valuable than simply maintaining source code.

You do not need to read this book in a linear fashion. Chapter 2 describes the design and implementation of a portable user interface class **GUI,** used in all of the example programs in this book. You can skip Chapter 2 if you are not particularly interested in user interface programming. Chapter 3 describes the design and implementation of flexible frame data structures that are used in many of the examples in the book. Chapter 3 also describes the design and implementation of client and server classes that make it much easier to break programs into more manageable pieces that can be run on different machines on a local area network or the Internet. Chapter 4 describes the theory and implementation of neural network simulation classes. Chapter 5 describes the theory and implementation of Java classes for implementing genetic algorithms. Chapter 6 describes different approaches to natural language processing and implements Java classes supporting conceptual dependency theory. Chapter 7 provides a wide range of tools for writing software agents, including classes for object servers (for maintaining and sharing frame data structures), accessing information on the World Wide Web, and for automatically sending and receiving electronic mail. Chapter 8 is a general introduction and tutorial for writing expert systems using the Java Jess implementation of OPS5/CLIPS.

Chapters 9 through 14 describe projects that use the Java class libraries developed in the first half of the book. Chapter 9 uses the Gamelet arcade game tool kit to implement an arcade game; enemy ships are controlled by machine language control programs that are evolved using genetic algorithms. Chapter 10 uses the neural network classes to implement a handwriting recognition program. Chapter 11 provides an example of using a greedy algorithm to improve neural network training data sets. Chapter 12 uses genetic algorithms to improve both neural network training data sets and the structure of the neural network handwriting recognition program that was developed in Chapter 10; this program is extended to recognize all characters in the alphabet. Chapter 13 uses the natural language processing classes developed in Chapter 6 for a program to answer history questions; the frame data structures developed in Chapter 2 are used to store data dealing with historical events and people, and the object (frame) server developed in Chapter 4 is used to place the history database in a separate server program that can run on any computer in a local area network or the Internet. Chapter 14 provides the design and implementation of a complete agent-based information retrieval program for the Internet.

Acknowledgments

I would like to thank my wife Carol for her encouragement of this writing project and for proofreading several versions of the manuscript; Mark Tacchi of NeXT, for writing and making freely available the Java Gamelet tool kit that is used in a sample program in this book; Harm Verbeek, for writing and making freely available the Java classes for sending and receiving electronic mail; Ernest Friedman-Hill of Sandia National Laboratories, for developing the Jess Java implementation of the OPS5 expert system tool that is used in the example expert systems developed in this book; my agent, Matt Wagner; my editor, Diane Cerra; my copy editor, Ken DellaPenta; and my production editor, Elisabeth Beller. I would also like to thank Borland for providing their Java development tools, TGV Software/CISCO Systems for providing their Cheetah Web server for use in preparing this book, and Gold Software for providing their WithClass Object Modeling Tool.

I am grateful for the creative work environment provided by my bosses at Angel Studios: Diego Angel, Steve Rotenberg, Brad Hunt, Jill Hunt, Michael Limber, and Harry Benham. I would also like to thank my friends and colleagues who I both learn from and receive encouragement from for my writing projects, especially: Brad Merril, David and Sharon Casey, Will Scarvey, Mike Street, Mark Rotenberg, Max Loeb, Tom and Cheryl Munnecke, Tim and Kathy Kraft, Dave Bond, Gady Costeff, Betty Torano, Steve Reed, Jim McLeod, Chris Fodor, Michelle Simon, Chris Ryan, David Etherton, Michael Romero, Curtis Bradley, Frederic Marcus, Jeff Roorda, Michael Kelley, John Thompson, Michael Knepp, Ryan Camoras, and Clint Keith.

Introduction

Most people are skeptical when they hear the phrase "artificial intelligence." This reaction is natural considering both the difficulty of writing intelligent systems and the past and present hype surrounding artificial intelligence (AI). At the AAAI national conference on AI in 1983 in Washington, D.C., expectations for AI-enhanced robots like R2D2 in the *Star Wars* movies ran rampant; these expectations have obviously not been met—yet.

One common criticism of many AI systems is the simple question, Where is the AI? Personally I prefer to refer to weak AI systems that simply use, for example, expert system rules, not as "AI systems," but as "intelligent systems," or as "distributed intelligent systems" if they are Internet or Intranet applications. Using this terminology, the field of AI is more research oriented because it addresses fundamental questions like the following:

- What is intelligence?
- What is recognition?
- Is what we call "intelligence" really recognition and categorization?
- Are symbol-processing systems really intelligent?

Products of AI research like heuristic search and expert system technology are best thought of as useful engineering tools for building intelligent-agent-based systems.

The material in this book is augmented with errata sheets and new information at my Web site:

`http://www.markwatson.com`

(home page also accessible via http://www.mkp.com/books_catalog/1-55860-420-0.asp)

Please visit my publisher's Web site for information on additional books on artificial intelligence and computer science:

`http://www.mkp.com`

Although there is much material in this book that can be applied directly to solving practical problems, this book also covers topics dealing with systems that help us to explore the characteristics of intelligence.

The software developed in this book is organized using the Java language package system, discussed in Appendix A. Appendix B contains a complete description of the material on the CD-ROM.

Many of you will want to peruse the software provided on the CD-ROM before spending time reading this book. To satisfy these eager readers, the following paragraphs describe the contents of the CD-ROM and quick-start directions for running prebuilt applets for the demonstration systems developed in this book.

The package structure of software on the CD-ROM

(classes are *italicized*)

mwa
mwa.agent (*Server* and *Client*)
mwa.ai
mwa.ai.neural (*Neural*, *NNdata*, and *NNfile*)
mwa.ai.genetic (*Genetic*)
mwa.ai.nlp (*Parser*, *ParseObject*)
mwa.data (*Alframe*, *Alframedata*)
mwa.gui (*GUI*, *GUIcanvas*)

The **agent** package contains client/server Java classes and utilities for encoding/ decoding data in messages. The **ai** package contains the AI-specific Java classes. The **data** package contains Java classes for frame data structures. The **gui** package contains a single framework for supporting a Java applet with optional graphics area, text input field, and scrolling text output field. The **gui** package is used throughout the book to make various test programs much shorter, allowing you to concentrate on the AI-related material.

The Java runtime environment uses an environment variable **CLASSPATH** to find compiled Java classes. The default **CLASSPATH** on your system (for Windows 95 or Windows NT) might look like

```
CLASSPATH=.;c:\ Java\classes
```

The default installation of the CD-ROM onto your hard disk puts all compiled files in package directories located in the directory **C:\JavaAI\class**. If you use this default, set your **CLASSPATH** environment variable to find the classes developed in this book in the **c:\JavaAI\class** directory:

```
CLASSPATH=.;c:\Java\classes;c:\JavaAI\class
```

This organization keeps the compiled files separate from the source code tree. In addition to Sun Microsystems reference Java compiler implementation, I also used Borland's, Symantec's, and Microsoft's Java integrated development environments for developing the example classes and programs in this book. Since Sun Microsystems Java development tools are available for free on the Internet, the CD-ROM is set up to compile with Sun's tools; every source directory has a **C.BAT** command file to compile the Java source files in that directory and to place them in the correct package directory in **\JavaAI\class**.

Many of the example programs in this book are distributed applications. In order to facilitate writing, testing, and modifying socket-based Java programs on a single computer, I default the host name to the IP address 127.0.0.1 (standard local host address) in the client/server Java classes in the **MWA\Agent** directory. If you are working on a Windows 95 PC, make sure that you have the TCP/IP extensions installed (this is done automatically if you install support for the Microsoft Network or the Windows 95 software provided by other Internet service providers) and that you have a file **\Windows\hosts** that contains the lines:

```
127.0.0.1 localhost
127.0.0.1 <your machine name>
```

For example, I call my machine "colossus" (after the D.F. Jones science fiction trilogy), so my **hosts** file looks like this:

```
127.0.0.1 localhost
127.0.0.1 colossus
```

Quick start: running the book project applets

Eventually, the reader will want to verify that his or her Java development environment is correctly configured by setting the **CLASSPATH** environment variable and re-compiling all of the Java class libraries and applets provided on the CD-ROM. Start by copying the contents of the CD-ROM to the **C:\JavaAI** directory:

```
xcopy m:\JavaAI c:\JavaAI /s
```

It is extremely important to make sure that long file names are preserved in this copy operation. Here I assume the **m:** refers to the CD-ROM drive (this may be **d:**, or **e:**, etc., on your system).

Assuming that your **CLASSPATH** environment variable contains **C:\JavaAI\class**, and that you have correctly installed any Java development environment that provides the **appletviewer** program, then you can run the example applets by

```
c:
cd \JavaAI
appletviewer testGUI.html
appletviewer testFrame.html
appletviewer History.html
```

Note that the **History** example runs as two separate client/server programs, so you will need TCP/IP installed on your computer to run this example.

If you are connected to the Internet, then try

```
appletviewer InfoAgent.html
appletviewer testURL.html
appletviewer testSendMail.html
```

All the prebuilt demos use the Java **appletviewer** program, which must be in your execution path.

Part I

Introduction to Artificial Intelligence

Introduction to
Artificial Intelligence

This chapter provides a brief history of artificial intelligence (AI) research and a short discussion of several interesting AI projects. This chapter is intended to excite you about AI; if you are already motivated to learn how to use Java for AI programming and for building intelligent distributed Internet and Intranet applications, you can skip directly to Chapters 2 and 3, which provide the user interface and distributed computing tool kits that are used for the programming examples in this book.

The history of AI research starts before the development of the first digital computers. The British computer scientist Alan Turing laid down a philosophical framework for AI in the era of analog computers. The science of AI draws on multiple disciplines: computer science, cognitive science, psychology, biophysics, systems theory, and neuroscience. The scope of AI research is best exemplified by problems that have yet to be fully solved:

- Machine translation of natural languages
- Medical diagnosis and possible treatment by medical expert systems
- Creative thought exemplified by the discovery of new and remarkable theorems in mathematics and novel theories in other hard sciences
- Automated help desk systems that answer customer questions without human intervention
- Machine vision exemplified by the recognition of arbitrary objects seen through a video camera

We will see that there are two major types of AI research: symbol-processing systems and neural networks. I am fairly impartial because I have developed commercial AI tool packages for both technologies (expert system tools for Xerox LISP machines and the Apple Macintosh and neural network modeling tools for Microsoft Windows). My philosophy: if it works, use it; if it is sufficiently interesting, study it.

1.1   History of artificial intelligence research

The engineering discipline of AI started with the advent of modern digital computers over 40 years ago. Early researchers, encouraged by the speed of performing repetitive programmed numerical calculations, were certain that soon computers could be built to mimic human intelligence. The evolving understanding of the huge difficulties in building true AI systems occurred at the same time that research in psychology and biology provided a clearer understanding of how human minds function.

Early work in AI largely dealt with efficiently searching for good solutions in large problem spaces. As the size of these problem spaces grew, new and more efficient search techniques were developed. Still, the so-called combinatorial explosion limited the application of brute-force search techniques. The next great advancement in the field of AI was the application of heuristic rules that were domain (or problem) dependent to discard large parts of problem spaces. Here we traded the possibility of occasionally overlooking good (or best!) solutions with the possibility of searching vastly larger problem spaces.

Much early AI research (with work on neural network simulations being a notable exception) involved the manipulation of symbols. These systems manipulated variables representing symbols without any real-world knowledge of what the symbols meant. For example, in the language Prolog, father-son relationships can be represented as

```
father(ken,mark).
father(ken,ron).
father(ron,anthony).
```

Here, a Prolog interpreter maintains relationships between symbols (i.e., **father**, **ken**, **mark**, **ron**, and **anthony**) without any knowledge that these are family relations and names. Unfortunately, it is too easy to watch the behavior of relatively simple symbol manipulation systems and supply our own meanings to the symbols, giving these systems more credit for intelligence than they deserve. For example, if we substitute symbols

```
a for father
b for ken
c for mark
d for ron
e for anthony
```

Then our Prolog code looks like this:

```
a(b,c).
a(b,d).
a(d,e).
```

Quite a difference to the human reader, but not to many symbol-based AI systems! To be fair, many knowledge-intensive natural language processing systems maintain and use detailed information for words. For example, the word "father" might be known to be both a noun and a verb, depending on sentence structure and meaning. In the natural language processing Java class libraries developed in this book, we will use especially detailed data structures for representing and processing verbs.

The quest for more efficient search algorithms (usually guided by problem-specific heuristics) and symbol-processing systems concentrated on the basic notion of what intelligence does rather than on how human brains work. Another major paradigm for AI is to directly model the low-level properties and behaviors of brain cells and, more importantly, the connections between brain cells. This neural network approach was considered quite distinct from AI at the time, but now, 30 years later, I feel more comfortable grouping neural approaches to modeling intelligence with the field of AI.

The Java neural network class libraries developed in this book support the most widely used type of neural networks: feed-forward backwards error propagation networks (known as *back-prop* or *delta rule* networks).

I became interested in neural networks in 1985 after reading a paper by David Walsh dealing with using neural networks to disambiguate different possible meanings of English sentences. (His example was "The astronomer married a star.") I participated in a DARPA advisory panel on neural networks in 1986 and 1987 (Panel 3: Simulation/Emulation Tools and Techniques) with Michael Cohen, Charles Elbaum, Knut Kongelbeck, Martin Fong, Robert Hecht-Nielsen, Paul Kolodzy, Mike Myers, Douglas Palmer, and Andrew Penz (chairman). This was a great experience since I was able to hear presentations from many neural network researchers.

At the first IEEE international neural network conference in 1987 I presented a paper on using neural networks to recognize phonemes (for speech recognition) and demonstrated my company's neural network product for Microsoft Windows: SAIC ANSim.

Neural networks are not programmed; rather, they learn to recognize input patterns provided in training data. The training process uses matched pairs of exemplars. An *exemplar* is a set of inputs for a neural network and a matching set of outputs. The external interface for all of the neural networks that we will use in this book is defined by

- the number of input neurons

- the number of output neurons
- a floating-point number in the range [-0.5,+0.5] for each input neuron
- a floating-point number in the range [-0.5,+0.5] for each output neuron

The software to simulate training and recall (or recognition) using neural networks is fairly simple. Usually the most difficult aspect of training neural networks is obtaining an effective set of training data. The Java neural network classes developed in this book also provide utilities for eliminating conflicting training exemplars and identifying regions of the neural network input space that need to be covered with additional training examples.

It is interesting to note that my earlier criticism of symbol-based systems also applies to neural networks. When we use neural networks in software systems, we associate some meaning to the floating-point value of each input or output neuron. For example, input neuron values might be associated with scaled sensor inputs, and output neuron values might be used for system control values. The mathematical model and software implementation of a neural network does not in any way "know" about these associations: the neural network simply recognizes patterns in data that it has "seen" before.

1.2   Machine learning

The science of machine learning deals with the development of algorithms that

- gain experience while operating in a specified environment
- reorganize their own internal state (perhaps both data and program) to make themselves more efficient in dealing with their environment
- have the ability to evaluate their own performance without any required external training stimulus

The study of AI includes both machine learning and the use of technologies like expert systems and neural networks that require large amounts of human effort to create sets of heuristic rules, training data, and so on. Machine learning systems are not covered directly in this book, although I would argue that the genetic-algorithm-based adaptive control systems developed in Chapter 9 demonstrate some aspects of machine learning systems.

1.3   Symbolic versus neural network approaches

The field of AI deals with difficult open-ended problems. It is not surprising that many different approaches to solving machine intelligence problems exist. It is perhaps not too great of a simplification to consider the two major viewpoints as supporting either symbolic or neural network solutions.

Both symbol-based expert systems and the technology of artificial neural networks have been used with great success in solving difficult practical problems. Still, it must be understood that the economically successful projects using AI have not been truly intelligent in a human sense. Expert systems are an effective way to encode (in a very labor-intensive activity) expert knowledge in narrow problem domains. Neural networks are effectively used for control systems and pattern recognition. It seems like the successful technologies that are developed in the science of AI are considered to be "just good engineering"—the frontier of AI research goals retreating before a wave of slow but steady progress. I have heard more than one person say, "Once it works, it isn't AI anymore."

While the ongoing debates between neural network and symbol-processing researchers is entertaining, I believe that the science of AI benefits from many different viewpoints and approaches; I am one of those people who enjoys talking most with people who have quite different viewpoints to my own. While in the end, it is results that count, "dead-end" research approaches are still important in the long run for shaping our ideas.

1.4   Problems with most artificial intelligence research

I divide the field of AI into two categories: practical engineering for solving problems and long-term research into both how humans think and what computational (data) structures and procedures will eventually yield flexible, general problem-solving AI systems. I think that it is important to differentiate both of these important categories.

On the near-term practical side, we live in a world of business and commerce; new technologies must pay their own way. It is important to derive maximum benefit from AI technologies that have proven to be useful for solving problems—for example, genetic algorithms (GAs) for optimization, expert systems for hand-encoding the knowledge and expertise of human experts in very narrow problem domains, and neural networks for pattern recognition and system control. These topics are fully covered later in this book.

Long-term research in AI is also extremely important. The problem is finding an appropriate business model for paying for long-term R&D. An excellent justification for investing in developing the technology to build flexible, autonomous AI systems is that autonomous systems are required to explore places where humans cannot go—for example, deep-space exploration, deep-sea exploration, and possibly very small-scale mechanical devices. Another justification for building the technology for flexible AI is the requirements for effective AI agents to collect information and work effectively on the Internet (Watson 1996b).

1.5　How we can do AI better

In the previous section, we discussed the need to support both near-term exploitation of practical AI technologies and long-term research. In this section I will give a brief overview of what I believe is a representative sample of the best AI research. If you are interested, you can get more information on these researchers and their projects by using your favorite World Wide Web search engine.

Douglas Hofstadter (1995) details his and many coworkers' research into flexible AI systems that build complex representations of problem states and manipulate these representations. This approach is quite different from manually designing a data structure for representing a problem state and simply playing with the data. In other words, these systems do not merely manipulate data; they also manipulate the format of the data. The careless observer will complain that the research of Hofstadter and his colleagues simply tries to solve trivial problems inefficiently. The truth, however, is these systems manipulate and "creatively" rearrange the format of information, possibly emulating the way that we, as human problem solvers, juggle information and ideas in our brains while we are thinking and solving problems.

Roger Schank and Chris Riesbeck (1981) argue for a semantics-based approach to natural language processing (NLP) in their development of conceptual dependency (CD) theory. We will use CD in Chapter 6 to design and implement Java classes for NLP. Schank and Riesbeck take a cognitive simulation approach to AI, rather than necessarily aiming for the best computational results. Real AI systems will be built on a foundation of understanding what people know and how they use this real-world knowledge to understand language and solve problems. Schank and Riesbeck use CD data structures to encode knowledge based on a relatively small number of semantic primitives; they stress meaning over syntax. We will see in Chapter 6 that information stored in CD data structures is relatively easy to use because different information (in this case, English sentences) with the same meaning is represented in an identical data structure using the same semantic primitives.

Pattie Maes and the Autonomous Agents Group at MIT work on a wide variety of projects exploring algorithms and prototype systems for implementing autonomous agents. *Agents* are here defined as complex (software) systems that inhabit dynamically changing environments. The fundamental problem is how agents use their past experience and sensor inputs from their environments to decide what current goals are, how to achieve these goals, and how to cooperate with other agents.

The ALIVE project at the Autonomous Agents Group explores the development of agents for controlling characters in an animated video environment. Agents are developed by combining many experts, each with knowledge of certain situations. I was inspired by this model when I developed a video game prototype system that involved driving a vehicle while competing with agent-driven vehicles. Each expert in my driving agent would offer goal and execution-of-goal advice. Each agent would also rate the relevance of its own advice. A simple control structure would choose to follow the advice of the expert with the highest relevance, taking care not to rapidly switch between experts during small fluctuations of relevance values.

Another area of research at the Autonomous Agents Group is interface agents for finding information for users. These agents have three goals:

1. They are proactive, or self-starting. They take the initiative in finding ways to help users.
2. From the user's actions, they learn how to adapt to help automate repetitive tasks.
3. They personalize themselves for individual users.

A World Wide Web search for the keywords "Maes Autonomous Agent MIT" will produce information on current research projects at the Autonomous Agents Group.

1.6 The big challenges

Although this is a book concerned with introducing several AI techniques for building intelligent Internet and Intranet applications through the design and implementation of Java classes, I would like to end the first part of this book by stating three difficult problems that I expect AI technologies to solve in the next decade or two (I am an optimist!). This is the eighth book that I have written. A large part of my motivation for writing books is the desire to present interesting (or fascinating!) technologies to readers with useful source code libraries so that they can make my ideas part of their own, and hopefully provide them with a quick start with some useful code. While you are busy, day in and day out, developing software systems to support yourself, keep an eye on the future. We will close this chapter with three challenging problems:

1.   Real NLP—backed up by some real-world knowledge
2.   Creativity and flexibility in AI systems
3.   Defining universal interfaces to be used by interacting AI-based agents

1.6.1   Real NLP—backed up by some real-world knowledge

The conceptual dependency (CD) style NLP parser that we will design and implement in Chapter 6 uses a practical technology. CD frames encode some real-world meaning for words that the parser can process. Still, there is an inherent inflexibility in CD data structures. They are carefully hand-encoded by humans in much the same spirit that human experts are required to encode rules for expert systems. Expert systems do not rewrite the format and content of their rules, and CD-based parsers do not create new CD frames to encode new words and concepts as they encounter them.

1.6.2   Creativity and flexibility in AI systems

Creativity and flexibility of AI systems can only be accomplished when these systems have the ability to autonomously create new data structures to represent their world (or the problems that they encounter and solve). NLP systems that can extend themselves by learning new words from context would meet my requirements for a creative, flexible AI system. I believe that these NLP systems will be built, but not for many decades; this is a very difficult but not, I think, an unsolvable problem.

Many AI systems use simulation models of aspects of the real world. A creative, flexible agent will have the capability to alter internal models to match real-world observations.

1.6.3   Defining universal interfaces to be used by interacting AI-based agents

Engineers have done an excellent job at developing standards for networked communication. The problem of developing universal interfaces for interacting AI-based agents is far more difficult because these interfaces will not only require knowledge of format, but also knowledge of how to define message formats for other agents. I think that a good analogy is the difference between HTML (hypertext markup language), which we all use daily when we read (and perhaps write) Web documents, and the SGML (standard graphics markup language) specification. SGML is a metalanguage; SGML documents can contain new types of tags and formatting information. The knowledge of how to interpret this formatting information is stored with the document. HTML, on the other hand, uses a fairly static syntax.

The ability of agents to negotiate changes in their interfaces with other agents requires knowledge of some (or perhaps all) of the following concepts:

- Task(s) that the agent performs
- Task(s) that other agents perform
- Ability to describe, using a universal notation, existing interfaces
- Ability to recognize and explain the requirements for changing an interface

I believe that the first two challenges (real NLP with real-world knowledge and flexibility to mutate the format of data structures to solve novel problems) must be met before we have a chance to build universal agent interfaces.

Part II

Software Libraries

Java User Interface Framework for Testing AI Programs **2**

In order to make the program examples in this book shorter and easier to read, we will design and develop a reusable graphic user interface (GUI) framework in this chapter for testing the AI Java classes developed in this book. This framework is implemented in the Java package **mwa.gui**. All Java packages developed in this book are contained in the "global" package **mwa** (Mark Watson Associates) in order to prevent name collision with other Java packages; it is easy to imagine several hundred different developers writing a package named **GUI**. See Appendix A for a discussion of Java packages. Test programs in this book will subclass (or extend) this class as required to test individual AI Java classes. The **GUI** class provides the following services or user interface components:

- Window
- Command buttons "Run" and "Reset"
- Scrolling display of text output
- One-line text input form
- Graphics pane including behaviors for line drawing, plotting gray-scale or color bar rectangles for showing numeric values, and text overlays

This chapter can be skipped by experienced Java programmers after reading the Booch class diagram in Figure 2.2. This chapter, with the short tutorial on Java programming in Appendix A, provides a brief introduction to Java programming and the Java abstract window tool kit (AWT).

2.1   Requirements for a Java framework for user interfaces

The major requirement for this package is to reduce the length and complexity of the test programs in the remaining part of this book. Figure 2.1 shows the components of the **GUI** class. Each component can be turned off if it is not required in an AI demonstration program.

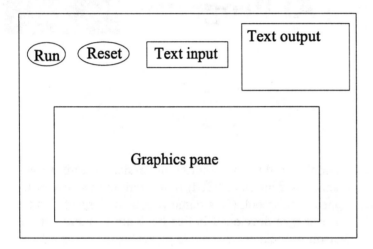

Figure 2.1   Graphical components of the **GUI** Java class

2.2   Implementation of a Java framework for user interfaces

Figure 2.2 shows Booch class diagrams for the GUI framework Java classes developed in this chapter and used throughout this book to significantly reduce the size of the test and example programs. These classes provide all of the user interface components that we need for every applet developed in later chapters.

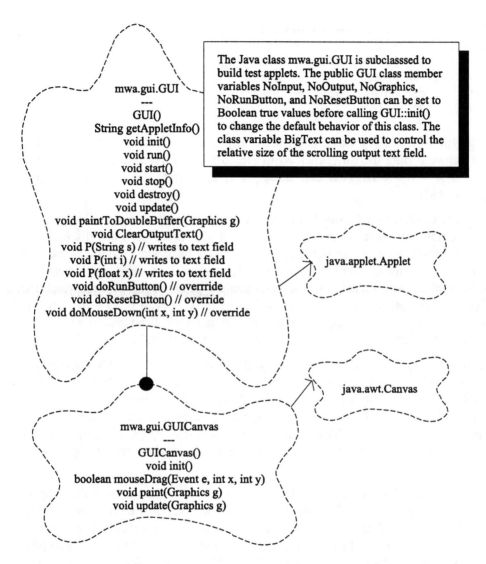

The Java class mwa.gui.GUI is subclasssed to build test applets. The public GUI class member variables NoInput, NoOutput, NoGraphics, NoRunButton, and NoResetButton can be set to Boolean true values before calling GUI::init() to change the default behavior of this class. The class variable BigText can be used to control the relative size of the scrolling output text field.

mwa.gui.GUI

GUI()
String getAppletInfo()
void init()
void run()
void start()
void stop()
void destroy()
void update()
void paintToDoubleBuffer(Graphics g)
void ClearOutputText()
void P(String s) // writes to text field
void P(int i) // writes to text field
void P(float x) // writes to text field
void doRunButton() // overrride
void doResetButton() // override
void doMouseDown(int x, int y) // override

java.applet.Applet

java.awt.Canvas

mwa.gui.GUICanvas

GUICanvas()
void init()
boolean mouseDrag(Event e, int x, int y)
void paint(Graphics g)
void update(Graphics g)

Figure 2.2   Booch class diagrams for **mwa.gui** package Java classes

The GUI framework will consist of two Java source files: **GUI.java** and **GUICanvas.java** as seen in Listings 2.1 and 2.2.

The class **mwa.gui.GUI** is defined in the file **..\MWA\GUI\GUI.java** shown in Listing 2.1. The class member method **init()** gets optional width and height parameters from either an enclosing HTML document or command line arguments. The **GUI** class contains six public variables that can be used to turn off selected **GUI** components:

```
public boolean NoInput       = false;
public boolean NoOutput      = false;
public boolean NoGraphics    = false;
public boolean NoRunButton   = false;
public boolean NoResetButton = false;
public int BigText        = 0;
```

When you use the **GUI** class, you can set any or all of these values to a Boolean true value before calling the **init()** method to turn off the corresponding user interface component. The variable **BigText** can be set to 1, 2, or 3 to get increasingly larger scrolling text fields.

The class **mwa.gui.GUI** extends the **Applet** class. Applets created using the **GUI** class are by default single-threaded. See Appendix A (Section A.6) for a discussion of single- and multithreaded applications. A class derived from class **GUI** can be multithreaded if it also implements the interface **Runnable**. If a class implements the interface **Runnable**, then it must define a **run()** method that is called by a thread created in the class's **init()** method, and create an instance of class **Thread** in its **init()** function. The neural network test programs and the neural network handwriting recognition programs all implement the class **Runnable** and use multiple threads.

We reduce applet graphics "flicker" by defining our own **update(Graphics g)** method. The **paint(Graphics g)** method does nothing in the base class **GUI**. The method **paintGridCell(...)** is a utility for painting colored cells in the optional graphics drawing pane. The method **paintToDoubleBuffer(Graphics g)** should be overridden in classes derived from the class **mwa.gui.GUI** in order to draw application-specific graphics in the optional graphics drawing pane. The method **repaint()** handles repainting the user interface surfaces.

Classes derived from **GUI** can redefine (or override) three methods that trap for user events: **doRunButton()**, **doResetButton()**, and **doMouseDown(int x, int y)**. If the input pane has not been disabled, then the method **String GetInputText()** retrieves the text that a user has typed into the text input pane. The method **ClearOuput()** clears all of the text from the text output pane. There are three utility methods for writing text to the output text pane: **void P(String s)**, **void P(int i)**, and **void P(float x)**.

The method **drawOnCanvas()** is not used directly by application programs, so it is declared **private**. The method **action(Event evt, Object obj)** is also not used directly by application programs. The method **action(Event evt, Object obj)** cannot be declared **private** because it is defined as **public** in the **GUI** base class **Applet**. However, the method **action(Event evt, Object obj)** is defined to be **final** since it should not be overidden in derived (or extended) classes.

Listing 2.1

```java
// GUI Java classes
//
// Copyright 1996, Mark Watson.  All rights reserved.

package mwa.gui;

import java.awt.*;
import java.applet.Applet;

public class GUI extends Applet {

    // Flags to disable standard GUI components:
    public boolean NoInput        = false;
    public boolean NoOutput       = false;
    public boolean NoGraphics     = false;
    public boolean NoRunButton    = false;
    public boolean NoResetButton = false;
    public int BigText            = 0;

    public String RunLabel   = new String("Run");
    public String ResetLabel = new String("Reset");

    public String InitialInput = "";

    Graphics background;  // used for double buffering
    Image im;
    int width = 640;
    int height = 480;

    protected Panel panel;
    TextField inputText;
    TextArea outputText;
    GUICanvas canvas;

    Color colors[];
    int NumColors = 16;

    public String getAppletInfo() {
        return "GUI classes by Mark Watson";
    }

    public void init() {
```

```java
String param = getParameter("width");
if (param != null) width = Integer.parseInt(param);

param = getParameter("height");
if (param != null) height = Integer.parseInt(param);

resize(width, height);

panel = new Panel();
panel.setLayout(new FlowLayout());
panel.resize(width - 10, height / 2);

if (NoRunButton == false)
   panel.add(new Button(RunLabel));
if (NoResetButton == false)
   panel.add(new Button(ResetLabel));

if (NoInput == false) {
   inputText = new TextField(InitialInput, 30);
   panel.add(new Label("Input:"));
   panel.add(inputText);
}
if (BigText==0) {
  if (NoOutput == false) {
    outputText = new TextArea("", 5, 35);
    panel.add(outputText);
  }
  add(panel);
}

if (BigText!=0) {
  add(panel);
  if (NoOutput == false) {
    if (BigText==1) {
       outputText = new TextArea("", 9, 45);
    } else if (BigText==2) {
       outputText = new TextArea("", 15, 60);
    } else {
       outputText = new TextArea("", 20, 70);
    }

    add(outputText);
  }
}
```

```
    if (NoGraphics == false) {
        canvas = new GUICanvas();
        canvas.parent = this;

        int c_width = width - 20;
        int c_height = (3 * height) / 2;
        canvas.resize(c_width, c_height);
        add(canvas);

        panel.setBackground(Color.darkGray);
        setBackground(Color.lightGray);

        colors = new Color[NumColors];
        for (int c=0; c<NumColors; c++) {
            float blue = 1.0f-(float)c/(float)NumColors;
            float red = (float)c / (float)NumColors;
            colors[c] = new Color(red, 0.0f, blue);
        }

        canvas.init();
    }
}

// reduce applet "flicker" by defining update():
public void update(Graphics g)
{
    if (NoGraphics == false)  paint(g);
}

public void paint(Graphics g) {
}

protected void paintGridCell(Graphics g, int x,
                             int y, int size,
                             float value, float min,
                             float max) {
    int index = (int)(((value-min)*(float)NumColors)/(max-min));
    if (index < 0) index = 0;
    else if (index > (NumColors - 1)) index=NumColors-1;
    g.setColor(colors[index]);
    g.fillRect(x, y, size, size);
    g.setColor(Color.black);
```

```java
        g.drawRect(x, y, size, size);
    }

    public void paintToDoubleBuffer(Graphics g) {
        System.out.println("entered GUI::paintToDoubleBuffer\n");
        paintGridCell(g, 20, 20, 30, 0.5f, 0.0f, 1.0f);
        System.out.println("leaving GUI::paintToDoubleBuffer\n");
    }

    public void repaint() {
        if (NoGraphics == false) {
            canvas.repaint();
            super.repaint();
        }
    }

    // subclasses should redefine these three functions:
    public void doRunButton()
    { System.out.print("Default GUI::doDoRunButton("); }
    public void doResetButton()
    {   System.out.print("Default GUI::doDoResetButton("); }
    public void doMouseDown(int x, int y) {
        System.out.print("Default GUI::doMouseDown(");
        System.out.print(x);
        System.out.print(", ");
        System.out.print(y);
        System.out.println("\n");
    }

    // Utility to get the input text field:
    public String GetInputText() {
        String s = inputText.getText();
        //P("input text:" + s + "\n");
        return s;
    }
    // Utility to set the input text field:
    public void SetInputText(String s) {
        inputText.setText(s);
    }
    // Utilities for output text field:
    public void ClearOutput() {
        outputText.replaceText("",0, 32000);
    }
    public void P(String s) {
```

```java
        outputText.appendText(s);
}
public void P(int i) {
        StringBuffer sb = new StringBuffer();
        sb.append(i);
        String s2 = new String(sb);
        outputText.appendText(s2);
}
public void P(float x) {
        StringBuffer sb = new StringBuffer();
        sb.append(x);
        String s2 = new String(sb);
        outputText.appendText(s2);
}

public boolean action(Event evt, Object obj) {
        System.out.println (evt.id);
        if (evt.target instanceof Button) {
            String label = (String)obj;
            if (label.equals(RunLabel)) {
                System.out.println("Run button pressed\n");
                doRunButton();
                repaint();
                if (canvas!=null) canvas.repaint();
                return true;
            }
            if (label.equals(ResetLabel)) {
                System.out.println("Reset button pressed\n");
                doResetButton();
                repaint();
                if (canvas!=null) canvas.repaint();
                return true;
            }
        }
        if (evt.id == 1001)  {
            if (NoInput == false) {
                // User hit a carriage return
                // so execute doRunButton():
                doRunButton();
                return true;
            }
        }
        return false;
}
```

```java
      private void drawOnCanvas() {
          if (canvas!=null) canvas.repaint();
      }
}


//////////////////////////////////////////////////
// Definition of the utility class GUICanvas that
// is used internally by the class GUI:

class GUICanvas extends Canvas {
    Graphics background;  // used for double buffering
    Image im;
    public GUI parent;
    public void init() {
        //System.out.println("entering GUICanvas::init\n");
        try {
                    Dimension d = size();
                    im = createImage(d.width, d.height);
                    background = im.getGraphics();
            } catch (Exception ex) {
                    background = null;
            }
    }
    public void paint(Graphics g) {
        //System.out.println("GUICanvas::paint()\n");
        if(background == null)  {  // Cannot use double buffering
            parent.paintToDoubleBuffer(g);
            System.out.println("No double buffer available");
        } else {
            // draw into the copy the
            // background (double buffering):
            parent.paintToDoubleBuffer(background);
            g.drawImage(im,0,0,this);
        }
    }
    // reduce applet "flicker" by defining update():
    public void update(Graphics g)
    {
            paint(g);
     }

    public boolean mouseDrag(Event evt, int x, int y) {
        // Call the containing apps' mouse handling function:
        parent.doMouseDown(x, y);
```

```
    return false;
  }


}
```

Listing 2.1 also shows the definition of utility class **GUIcanvas,** which is used for optional graphics output. The public member data **GUI parent** must be set before calling the **init()** method. The **init()** method attempts to create an offscreen drawing surface to support double buffering. If an offscreen drawing surface cannot be created, the application using the **GUIcanvas** object will still run, but the screen will flicker during graphics updates. In practice the attempt to create an offscreen drawing surface always succeeds. The method **paint(Graphics g)** uses the method **paintToDoubleBuffer(Graphics g)** to draw on itself. An application will create a class derived from **mwa.gui.GUI** that contains an application-specific **paintToDoubleBuffer(Graphics g)** method. The method **update(Graphics g)** is defined to reduce flicker during graphics updates. The **boolean mouseDrag(...)** method calls the parent GUI's **doMouseDown(...)** method to process mouse events inside the graphics pane.

The methods void **GUI.P(String s), void GUI.P(int i),** and **void GUI.P(float f)** are useful for writing formatted text to the output display field that is created automatically by the **GUI.init()** method (unless the variable **GUI.NoGraphics** is set to a Boolean true value before the **GUI.init()** method is called). As discussed in Appendix A, the Java **String** class overloads the + operator to convert all native Java types to instances of class **String.** In Java, instances of class **String** cannot be changed after they are created. The Java class **StringBuffer** is similar to the **String** class, except that instances of class **StringBuffer** can be dynamically modified. For example, the code

```
float pi=3.14159f;
P("PI = " + pi + "\n");
```

is functionally identical to the code

```
float pi=3.14159f;
StringBuffer sb = new StringBuffer("PI = ");
sb.append(pi).append("\n");
String str = new String(sb);
P(str);
```

It is obviously simpler (and makes it easier to read our code) if we take advantage of the built-in **String** concatenation operator +.

2.3   Example using the Java framework for user interfaces

Listing 2.2 shows a simple test program contained in file **..\MWA\GUI\testGUI.java** for the Java classes **GUI** and **GUIcanvas**. This example program forms a template for the sample applications in the rest of this book. Notice that this application is only about fifteen lines long. The time spent developing the **GUI** and **GUIcanvas** classes will allow the sample applications in this book to be short, containing mostly application-specific code. The class **testGUI** simply extends the class **GUI** in order to inherit all of the class **GUI**'s data and behavior. In this simple example, we turn off the input text field by setting the public member variable **NoInput** to a Boolean true value.

In Listing 2.2, the base class method **GUI.doRunButton()** is overridden to simply print out a message to the scrolling output text field using the method **GUI.P(String s)**. The sample application in Listing 2.2 creates, through default behavior of the **GUI** class, a "Reset" button, but does not override the base class **GUI.doResetButton()** method. Clicking the "Reset" button in the test application has no effect since the base class method **GUI.doResetButton()** does nothing.

Listing 2.2

```
// GUI Java classes
//
// Copyright 1996, Mark Watson.  All rights reserved.

package mwa.gui;

import java.awt.*;

public class testGUI extends GUI  {

  public void init() {
    NoInput = true;
    super.init();
  }
  public void paintToDoubleBuffer(Graphics g) {
    System.out.println("entered testGUI::paintToDoubleBuffer\n");
    paintGridCell(g, 20, 20, 110, 0.5f, 0.0f, 1.0f);
  }
  public void doRunButton() {
    P("OVERRIDDEN doRunButton()\n");
  }
}
```

Figure 2.3 shows the sample application shown in Listing 2.2.

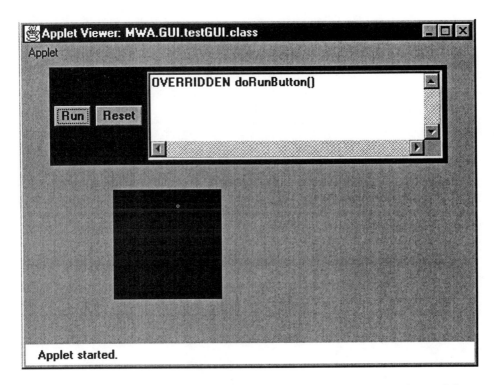

Figure 2.3   Sample fourteen-line **GUI** class test program shown in Listing 2.2.

Distributed AI 3

The Java language and class libraries provide excellent support for distributing applications as separate, cooperating programs over local and wide area networks. We will develop a framework for supporting distributed AI (DAI) based on a few simple Java classes to support client and server behavior, and a frame class **mwa.data.AIframe** for encoding and decoding arbitrary data in text streams to facilitate network transport. The remaining Java packages and classes developed in this book will be designed and implemented from the ground up to support building distributed systems by using the network-transportable **mwa.data.AIframe** class developed in this chapter.

This chapter provides low-level utility classes that are used in Chapter 7 to build Java classes for implementing software agents. This chapter can be skipped by experienced Java programmers who want to proceed directly to the development of AI Java classes starting in Chapter 4, after reviewing the public interfaces for the classes **mwa.data.AIframe**, **mwa.agent.Server**, and **mwa.agent.Client** in Figures 3.1, 3.3, and 3.4.

3.1 The importance of distributing intelligence in software systems

Classic AI demonstration systems have usually been written to execute on a single computer (and usually as a single process) and to solve problems in very specific problem domains. I believe that the next generation of intelligent systems will be the product of many people's efforts in different physical locations. In the future, the least expensive way to develop an AI application may be to integrate application-specific software agents from a variety of university, commercial, and internal software development sources. These knowledge sources will contain procedural code (perhaps in Java) and data.

Customers of these knowledge systems providers will be provided with simple interface agents that they can execute in their local computing environment to retrieve knowledge from the remote source. In this way customers can pay knowledge source providers a usage fee that can offset the development costs of knowledge bases. This business model will allow companies to invest the required resources to develop reusable AI components.

Information is certainly stored in a distributed fashion on the Internet. The ability to easily write distributed AI systems allows us to design system components that execute close to the source of their required data. Well-defined interfaces will allow us to build our systems using other developers' work as well as to share our work with other developers. I believe that a fair billing infrastructure will evolve for sharing royalties for revenue generated by systems that have components written or owned by many different people.

3.2   An abstract model for distributed AI

We will use a simple client/server architecture for supporting remote computation. In client/server architectures, a client program usually runs on a user's local computer. The client program communicates with a remote server program to retrieve data or to request other services. Clients and servers will communicate with guaranteed delivery data streams. In the next section, we will develop a useful set of classes to support flexible hierarchical data structures called *frames*. Our distributed applications can transport arbitrary complex nested data that is represented by frames.

3.3   Using hierarchical frame data

Most AI-specific languages provide a flexible way to manipulate complex data structures. LISP languages provide lists, and Prolog provides clauses. The Java language's support of garbage collection makes it fairly easy to deal with the types of complex data structures that we will use in this book. We will use frame data structures throughout this book for organizing data. A frame has one required attribute, a name that is a Java **String** object. Other optional data can consist of a reference to a parent frame and one or more "slots."

A slot consists of two associated data objects: a slot name and a value.

We will use a Java **String** to represent slot names. We will soon discuss the types of data that can be stored in the value part of a slot.

Any frame can have a "parent." If we want to retrieve a value for a specific slot name, we first look for that slot name in the current frame; if it does not exist and the slot has a parent, we look for the desired slot name in the parent. Actually, we continue this process recursively until either we find the desired slot name or we reach a frame with a null parent reference. There is a great deal of flexibility in the types of data that can be used for the value of a slot. In this book, we use three different types of slot values:

- A Java **String** object
- A Java **float** type
- A reference to another frame

Figure 3.1 shows the Booch class diagrams for Java classes **AIframe** and **AIframedata**. Note that an instance of class **AIframe** contains instances of class **AIframedata** in a private member variable of type **java.lang.Hashtable**.

Listing 3.1 shows the implementation of Java classes **mwa.data.AIframe** and **mwa.data.AIframedata**. The implementation of class **AIframe** is fairly simple because we use the behavior of the Java class **java.lang.Hashtable** to provide the storage and retrieval of named data items. The only difficult part of the implementation is the code to convert between an arbitrary **AIframe** object and a **String** object. This too would be a simple problem to solve if we did not have to support nested **AIframe** objects. I chose the exclamation mark character as an escape character for encoding **AIframe** objects as Java **String** objects, so it is important not to store any strings containing an exclamation mark in **AIframe** objects. As a simple example, consider the code that creates an **AIframe** instance named "test_frame" and inserts one new slot (slot name is "name" and the slot value is "Mark"):

```
AIframe frame1=new AIframe("test_frame");
frame1.put("name", new AIframedata("Mark"));
String s = frame1.toString();
System.out.println(s);
```

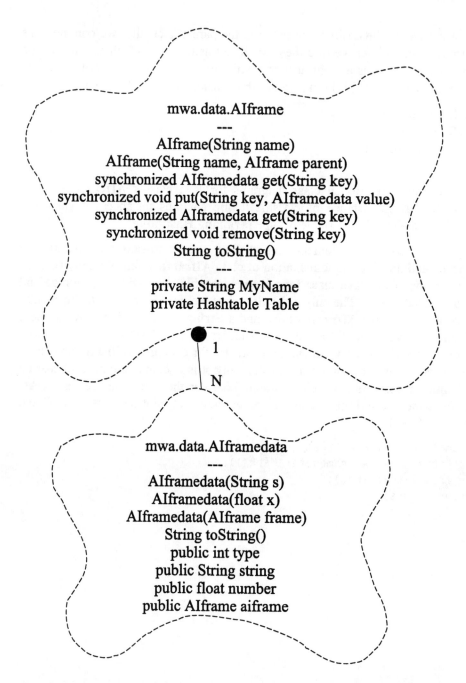

mwa.data.AIframe

AIframe(String name)
AIframe(String name, AIframe parent)
synchronized AIframedata get(String key)
synchronized void put(String key, AIframedata value)
synchronized AIframedata get(String key)
synchronized void remove(String key)
String toString()

---

private String MyName
private Hashtable Table

1

N

mwa.data.AIframedata

AIframedata(String s)
AIframedata(float x)
AIframedata(AIframe frame)
String toString()
public int type
public String string
public float number
public AIframe aiframe

Figure 3.1   Booch class diagrams for Java classes **AIframe** and **AIframedata**

The output would be

```
!!test_frame!1!name!!S!Mark!!0!
```

The "!1!" specifies that there is one slot/value combination in the **AIframe** object. The slot name is "name" with a data type **String** (specified with the "!!S!" string), and the slot value is "Mark". The string "!!N!" can be used to specify numeric slot values, and the string "!!F!" can be used to specify **AIframe** names.

There are two constructors for the class **mwa.data.AIframe**; one constructor has a single argument (the name of the frame), and the other constructor has two arguments (the name of the frame and a reference to a parent frame). Both constructors allow the name of a frame to be a string representation of an entire frame, which is a string starting with the characters "!!". Often, new instances of the class **AIframe** will be created using a string representation of a frame that is sent from a remote Java application using the client/server Java classes that are developed in Section 3.4.

The method **AIframe.get(String key)** returns the data for a slot in the frame object that is identified with the "key" name (or slot name). The method **AIframe.put(String key, AIframedata value)** is used to either add a new slot (with the slot name specified by the first **String** argument), or to change the data associated with an existing slot (or key value). The method **AIframe.remove(String key)** is used to remove a slot from a frame.

The two methods **AIframe.PP()** and **AIframe.PP(GUI myGUI)** are used to "pretty print" the contents of an instance of class **AIframe**. The method **PP()** prints to standard output; the method **PP(GUI myGUI)** prints to the scrolling output text field of an instance of class **GUI**.

Listing 3.1

```
// mwa.data.AIframe
// AIframe class. Copyright 1997 Mark Watson.

package mwa.data;

import java.io.*;
import java.net.*;
import java.util.*;
import mwa.gui.*;

public class AIframe {
  // support single inheritance with a single 'parent' pointer:
```

```
protected AIframe Parent = null;
public AIframe(String name, AIframe parent) {
  Helper(name, parent);
}
public AIframe(String name) {
  Helper(name, null);
}
protected void Helper(String name, AIframe parent) {
  if (name.startsWith("!!")) {
    // 'name' contains a complete AIframe
    // encoded into a String:
    String sb = new String(name);
    int index = 2;
    int next_bang = sb.indexOf('!',index);
    String frameName = sb.substring(2, next_bang);
    MyName = frameName;
    Table = new Hashtable(6, 0.99f);
    Parent = parent;
    index = next_bang+1;
    next_bang = sb.indexOf('!',index);
    String num_string = sb.substring(index, next_bang);
    int num_slots;
    if (num_string.length()<1) num_slots=0;
    else num_slots = (new Integer(num_string)).intValue();
    for (int i=0; i<num_slots; i++) {
      index = next_bang+1;
      next_bang = sb.indexOf('!',index);
      String slot_name = sb.substring(index, next_bang);
      // skip "!!" before AIframedata type:
      index = next_bang+2;
      AIframedata fd;
      int ch = sb.charAt(index);
      index += 2; // skip over "!!"
      next_bang = sb.indexOf('!',index);
      if (ch=='S') {
        fd = new AIframedata(sb.substring(index, next_bang));
      } else if (ch=='N') {
        Float f = new Float(sb.substring(index, next_bang));
        fd = new AIframedata(f.floatValue());
      } else { // has to be "F" == an AIframe object
        fd = new AIframedata("!!" +
                                sb.substring(index, next_bang));
      }
      Table.put(slot_name, fd);
```

```
        }
      } else {
        // Normal constructor: 'name' is name of frame:
        MyName = name;
        Table = new Hashtable(6, 0.99f);
        Parent = parent;
      }
  }
  public synchronized AIframedata get(String key) {
  AIframedata s = (AIframedata)Table.get(key);
  if (s==null && Parent!=null)
    s = Parent.get(key);
    return s;
  }
  public synchronized void put(String key,
                                  AIframedata value) {
    Table.put(key, value);
  }
  public synchronized void remove(String key) {
    Table.remove(key);
  }
  public String getName() { return MyName; }
  public String toString() {
    StringBuffer sb =
      new StringBuffer("!!" + MyName + "!"
                        + Table.size() + "!");
    for (Enumeration e = Table.keys() ;
         e.hasMoreElements() ;)
    {
      String s = e.nextElement().toString();
      sb.append(s).append("!");
      sb.append(Table.get(s)).append("!");
    }
    return new String(sb);
  }
  public void PP() {
    System.out.println("Data for AIframe: " + MyName);
    for (Enumeration e = Table.keys() ; e.hasMoreElements() ;) {
      String s = e.nextElement().toString();
      String sv = "" + Table.get(s);
      if (sv.endsWith("!")) {
        int index=sv.indexOf("!!!");
        int index2=sv.indexOf("!", index+4);
        String s2 = sv.substring(index+3, index2);
```

```
      } else {
        int index=sv.lastIndexOf("!");
        String s2 = sv.substring(index+1);
      }
    }
  }
  public void PP(GUI MyGUI) {
    MyGUI.P("Data for AIframe: " + MyName + "\n");
    for (Enumeration e = Table.keys();
         e.hasMoreElements() ;)
    {
      String s = e.nextElement().toString();
      String sv = "" + Table.get(s);
      if (sv.endsWith("!")) {
        int index=sv.indexOf("!!!");
        int index2=sv.indexOf("!", index+4);
        String s2 = sv.substring(index+3, index2);
        MyGUI.P("  Slot: " + s + ", Sub-frame name: " +
                 s2 + "\n");
      } else {
        int index=sv.lastIndexOf("!");
        String s2 = sv.substring(index+1);
        MyGUI.P("  Slot: " + s + ", Value: " + s2 + "\n");
      }
    }
  }

  private String MyName;
  private Hashtable Table;

};
```

Listing 3.2 shows the implementation of the class **mwa.data.AIframedata**. Instances of **AIframedata** are used to hold the data for individual "slots" in an instance of **AIframe**. An **AIframedata** object holds one of three types of data: a Java **String**, a floating-point number, or a reference to an **AIframe** object. This class has constructors for each of these three types of data. The public variable

```
public int AIframedata.type
```

takes on one of the following three values to indicate the type of data stored in an instance of class **AIframedata** (or "slot"):

```
final static public int STRING=1;
```

```
final static public int NUMBER=2;
final static public int AIFRAME=3;
```

Listing 3.2

```java
// mwa.data.AIframedata
//
// This class holds the "slot" data for instances
// of the class AIframe.

package mwa.data;

public class AIframedata {
  final static public int STRING=1;
  final static public int NUMBER=2;
  final static public int AIFRAME=3;
  public String string;
  public float number;
  public String aiframe;
  public int type;
  public AIframedata(String s) {
    if (s.startsWith("!!")) {
      // 'name' contains a complete AIframe encoded
      // into a String:
      aiframe = s.substring(2);
      type=AIFRAME;
    } else {
      string=s;
      type=STRING;
    }
  }
  public AIframedata(int x) {
    number=x;
    type=NUMBER;
  }
  public AIframedata(float x) {
    number=x;
    type=NUMBER;
  }

  public String toString() {
    String sb;
    switch (type) {
      case 1: sb=new String("!S!"+string);  break;
```

```
        case 2: sb=new String("!N!"+number);  break;
        case 3: sb=new String("!F!"+aiframe); break;
        default: sb=""; break;
      }
    return sb;
  }
}
```

Replacing the AIframe and AIframedata implementations

The Java language will probably be extended to provide better serialization of objects support in the future. If this happens, or if you have a preferred way to write **AIframe** objects to a **String** for network transport, the class implementations (but keep the class interface the same!) of **AIframe** and **AIframedata** can be replaced without requiring any software changes for the Java classes developed in the remainder of this book that use the **AIframe** and **AIframedata** classes.

Listing 3.3 shows a short test applet (derived from class **mwa.gui.GUI**) for testing the **AIframe** and **AIframedata** classes.

Listing 3.3

```
// Test AIframe and AIframedata classes
//
// Copyright 1996, Mark Watson.  All rights reserved.

package mwa.data;

import java.awt.*;
import java.util.*;

import mwa.gui.*;


public class testAIframe extends GUI {
    Graphics background;  // used for double buffering
    Image im;

    public String getAppletInfo() {
        return "Test the Frame stuff.  By Mark Watson";
    }
```

```java
public void init() {
  // Disable graphics and input areas of
  // standard GUI display:
  NoGraphics = true;
  NoResetButton=true;
  NoInput = true;
  BigText = 3;

  super.init();
  P("testFrame applet\n");
}

public void doRunButton() {
    P("entered doRunButton\n");
    AIframe frame1 = new AIframe("car1");
    P("created frame1\n");
    frame1.put("number of wheels", new AIframedata(4));
    frame1.put("color", new AIframedata("red"));
    frame1.put("type", new AIframedata("stingray"));
    AIframe sub_frame = new AIframe("driver");
    frame1.put("test_sub_frame",
               new AIframedata("!!" +
                               sub_frame.getName()));
    frame1.put("z_num_drivers", new AIframedata(1));
    frame1.put("slot_a", new AIframedata("a_value"));
    AIframe sub_frame2 = new AIframe("driver2");
    frame1.put("test_sub_frame2",
               new AIframedata("!!" +
                               sub_frame2.getName()));
    frame1.put("slot_b", new AIframedata("b_value"));
    frame1.put("slot_c", new AIframedata("c_value"));
    AIframe frame2 = new AIframe("car2", frame1);
    frame2.put("color", new AIframedata("blue"));
    P("created frame2\n");
    AIframedata s1=frame2.get("color");
    P("Color of car2 is " + s1.string + "\n");
    // now that we have created a reference to the first
    // frame, change a slot value to demonstrate that
    // two AIframe variables can reference the same frame:
    AIframe frame1A = frame1;
    frame1.put("number of wheels", new AIframedata(3));
    AIframedata s2=frame2.get("number of wheels");
    P("# of wheels for car2=" + s2.number + "\n");
    s2 = frame1A.get("number of wheels");
```

```
    P("# of wheels for car2 (frame1A)=" +
      s2.number + "\n");
    P("Dumping frame1 to a string:\n");
    String s = frame1.toString();
    P("frame1.toString        =" + s + "\n");
    AIframe restored_frame = new AIframe(s);
    s2 = restored_frame.get("number of wheels");
    P("# of wheels on frame from string=" +
      s2.number + "\n");
    s = restored_frame.toString();
    P("restored_frame.toString=" + s + "\n");
    P("leaving doRunButton\n");
    frame1.PP();
    frame1.PP(this);

    P("\n\nStarting toString() test:\n\n");
    String test1 = frame1.toString();
    AIframe ftest1 = new AIframe(test1);
    String test2 = ftest1.toString();
    P(test1 + "\n");
    P(test2 + "\n");
  }
}
```

Listing 3.4 shows the result of executing the method **frame1.toString()** in the example application in Listing 3.3. The variable **frame1** is an instance of the class **AIframe**. This resulting string contains no new line characters; the text in Listing 3.4 appears on three lines due to line wrap.

Listing 3.4

```
!!car1!9!slot_c!!S!c_value!slot_b!!S!b_value!slot_a!!S!a_value
!z_num_drivers!!N!1!type!!S!stingray
!number of wheels!!N!3!color!!S!red!test_sub_frame!
!F!!!driver!0!!test_sub_frame2!!F!!!driver2!0!!
```

Figure 3.2 shows the graphical structure of the **AIframe frame1** shown in Listing 3.4. Figure 3.2 also shows another **AIframe** object, **frame2**, which inherits the slot/values of **frame1** and overrides the value of the slot named "color" to the value "blue".

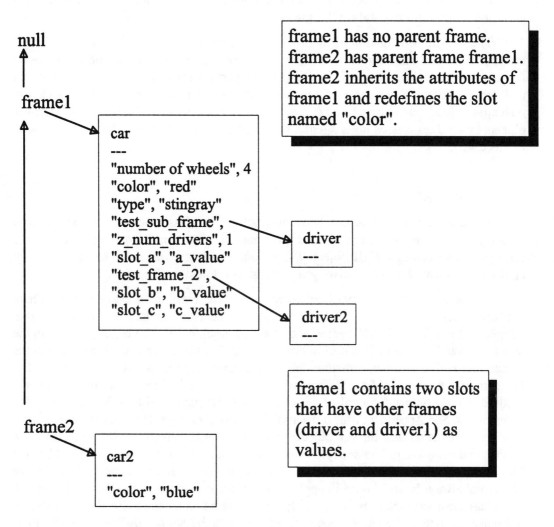

Figure 3.2   Graphical representation of example **Alframe** objects created by the program in Listing 3.3

3.4   Implementation of a Java package for distributed AI

The classes developed in this section are contained in the Java package named **mwa.agent**. There are two utility classes developed in this section: **mwa.agent.Server** and **mwa.agent.Client**.

In order to use structured listlike or frame data, the **Server** and **Client** classes support the transport of **mwa.data.AIframe** objects.

The first implementation of the Java client/server classes (not shown in this book) transported Java **String** objects. As I developed the example programs and Java classes for this book, I decided on standardizing the transport of **AIframe** objects between client and server applets. Since most of the non-neural network examples in this book use **AIframe** objects internally, it makes sense to directly support the transfer of **AIframe** objects by the Java classes **mwa.agent.Client** and **mwa.agent.Server** that are developed in this chapter.

3.4.1   mwa.agent.Server

As seen in Figure 3.3, there are two constructors for class **mwa.agent.Server**. Both constructors require an integer socket port number, and one constructor requires a reference to an **mwa.gui.GUI** object. The second constructor is useful when used in an applet that is created using the **mwa.gui** package developed in Chapter 2.

Listing 3.5 shows the Java implementation of the class **mwa.agent.Server**. There are three class constructors that take either no arguments, an integer port number, or an integer port number and a **GUI** reference. If the port number is zero or unspecified in the constructor call, then a default port number is used. If a **GUI** reference is supplied in the constructor call, then an informative debug printout of the server's actions is printed to the scrolling text field of the referenced **GUI** object. All three constructors use the method **Server_helper** to initialize a socket. The **run()** method listens for remote socket connections. See Appendix A for a discussion on using threads. If a remote client makes a socket connection to a **Server** object, an **mwa.agent.Connection** object is created to service that connection. The newly created **Connection** object uses the server's **AIframe DoWork(AIframe request)** method to process incoming service requests. The **Server** class must always be subclassed in applications in order to override the **DoWork** method. The class **mwa.agent.Server** is explicitly defined to be an abstract class because it does not make sense to create an instance of this class since the **Server.DoWork** method must be overridden for application-specific requirements.

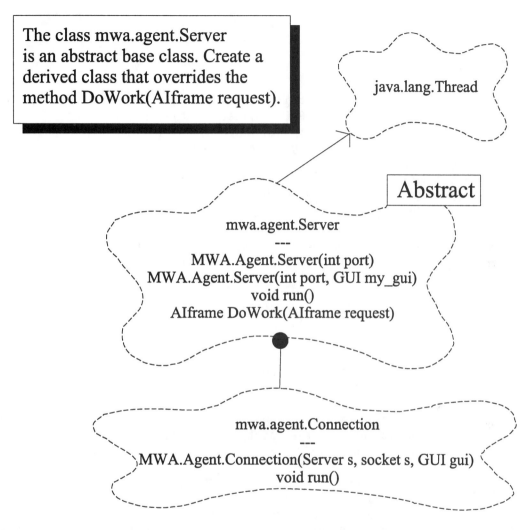

The class mwa.agent.Server
is an abstract base class. Create a
derived class that overrides the
method DoWork(AIframe request).

java.lang.Thread

Abstract

mwa.agent.Server

MWA.Agent.Server(int port)
MWA.Agent.Server(int port, GUI my_gui)
void run()
AIframe DoWork(AIframe request)

mwa.agent.Connection

MWA.Agent.Connection(Server s, socket s, GUI gui)
void run()

Figure 3.3   Booch class diagram for **mwa.agent.Server**. The complete package names
are added to the class names in the diagram to avoid any confusion with simi-
larly named classes in other packages that you might use.

Listing 3.5

```
// mwa.agent.Server.java
// Copyright 1996 Mark Watson

package mwa.agent;
```

```java
import java.io.*;
import java.net.*;
import mwa.gui.*;
import mwa.data.*;

abstract public class Server extends Thread {
    // Reference to an mwa.gui.GUI application object:
    GUI MyGUI = null;
    // input socket for listening for new clients:
    protected ServerSocket input_socket;
    // a default port number:
    public static final int PORT = 6001;
    protected int port;

    public void Error(Exception exception, String message) {
        System.err.println(message + " " +  exception);
    }
    public Server() {
        //System.out.println("Server()");
        //Server_helper(0, null);
    }
    public Server(int port) {
        System.out.println("Server(port)");
        Server_helper(port, null);
    }
    public Server(int port, GUI my_gui) {
        System.out.println("Server(port, my_gui)");
        Server_helper(port, my_gui);
    }
    protected void Server_helper(int port, GUI my_gui) {
        if (port == 0) port = PORT;
        if (my_gui!=null) MyGUI = my_gui;
        if (MyGUI!=null) MyGUI.P("in Server_helper()\n");
        this.port = port;
        try { input_socket = new ServerSocket(port); }
        catch (IOException exception) {
          Error(exception, "Error creating server socket");
        }
        if (MyGUI != null)
          MyGUI.P("Server is listening on port " + port + "\n");
        this.start();
    }
    public void run() {
        try {
```

```
        while(true) {
            Socket client_socket = input_socket.accept();
            if (MyGUI!=null) MyGUI.P("Opening socket...\n");
            Connection c =
                new Connection(this, client_socket, MyGUI);
            if (c==null) {
                System.out.println("Bad new Connection");
            }
        }
    }
    catch (IOException e) {
        Error(e, "Error waiting for connections");
    }
}

// public method to be redefined in derived classes:
public synchronized AIframe DoWork(AIframe request) {
  AIframe ret =new AIframe("Stub DoWork");
  ret.put("client_req", new AIframedata(request.toString()));
  return ret;
}
}

class Connection extends Thread {
    protected Socket my_socket;
    protected DataInputStream input_strm;
    protected PrintStream output_strm;
    protected Server MyServer;
    public GUI MyGUI=null;

    public Connection(Server server,
                      Socket client_socket,
                      GUI my_gui) {
      MyGUI = my_gui;
      MyServer = server;
      my_socket = client_socket;
      try {
        input_strm =
          new DataInputStream(my_socket.getInputStream());
        output_strm =
          new PrintStream(my_socket.getOutputStream());
      }
      catch (IOException io_exception) {
        try { my_socket.close(); } catch (IOException io_ex2)
```

```
        {   };
      System.err.println("Exception: getting socket streams " +
                         io_exception);
      if (MyGUI!=null)
        MyGUI.P("Exception: getting socket streams " +
                   io_exception);
      return;
    }
    this.start();
  }

  public void run() {
      String input_buf;
      try {
          while (true) {
              input_buf = input_strm.readLine();
              if (input_buf == null) break;
              // call the 'DoWork' function that should
              // be redefined in derived classes and return
              // string value to my_socket:
              if (MyGUI!=null) {
                  MyGUI.P("Connection::run(): request="
                          + input_buf + "\n");
              }
              // construct an AIframe from String:
              AIframe request = new AIframe(input_buf);
              AIframe frame = MyServer.DoWork(request);
              if (MyGUI!=null) {
                  MyGUI.P("Connection::run():" +
                          " return from DoWork: "
                          + frame.toString() + "\n");
              }
              output_strm.println(frame.toString());
          }
      }
      catch (IOException exception) { }
      finally {
          try {
           my_socket.close();
          }
          catch (IOException exception) { };
      }
  }
}
```

The class **mwa.agent.Connection** is also defined in Listing 3.5. This class is a utility class that is only used by the class **mwa.agent.Server**. You will not need to explicitly use the class **mwa.agent.Connection** in your programs. An instance of class **Connection** is automatically created in the method **mwa.agent.Server.run()** when a new socket connection with a remote client is established.

3.4.2   mwa.agent.Client

Figure 3.4 shows the Booch class diagram for the **mwa.agent.Client** class. This class is used to open a connection with an **mwa.agent.Server** object. Some client applications frequently open and close connections to remote servers by creating and destroying instances of class **mwa.agent.Client**. Other client applications my create a single instance of class **mwa.agent.Client** for multiple transactions with a remote server.

The Java class **mwa.agent.Client** has two constructors. The first constructor takes no arguments, and the host name defaults to the current machine that is executing the application using the **Client** class. The second constructor has two required arguments: **int port** and **String host**.

The first constructor is useful for software development in which both client and server applications are run on the development computer. The second constructor is used for building distributed applications. Either constructor makes a connection to a server application (using the **mwa.agent.Server** class) or fails, throwing an exception. See Appendix A for a discussion of exception handling in Java.

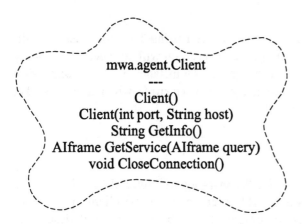

Figure 3.4   Booch class diagram for **mwa.agent.Client**

After a connection to a server is created, the following **Client** methods are used: **AIframe GetService(AIframe query)** and **void CloseConnection()**.

The **GetService(AIframe query)** method can be called repeatedly. When a server connection is no longer required, calling **CloseConnection()** closes the socket connection to the server application. After calling **CloseConnection()**, either make sure that the variable reference for the **Client** object goes out of scope or set it to null to garbage-collect the **Client** object. The implementation of class **mwa.agent.Client** is shown in Listing 3.6.

Listing 3.6

```
// mwa.agent.Client
// Copyright 1996 Mark Watson

package mwa.agent;

import java.io.*;
import java.net.*;
import mwa.data.*;

public class Client {
    // define a default host name that is the name
    // of the machine that this program is running on:
    public static final String HOST = "127.0.0.1";
    // define a default port number:
```

```java
public static final int PORT = 6001;

Socket socket;
DataInputStream input_strm;
PrintStream output_strm;

public Client(int port, String host)  {
    Client_Helper(port, host);
}

public Client()  {
    Client_Helper(PORT, HOST);
}

public void Client_Helper(int port, String host)  {
    socket = null;
    try {
        // Create a socket:
        socket = new Socket(host, port);
        // Create socket based streams:
        input_strm =
          new DataInputStream(socket.getInputStream());
        output_strm =
          new PrintStream(socket.getOutputStream());
    }
    catch (IOException exception) {
        System.err.println(exception);
    }
}
public String GetInfo() {
  return  "Connected to " + socket.getInetAddress() +
        ":" + socket.getPort();
}
public AIframe GetService(AIframe query) {
  // Send the service request to the server:
  output_strm.println(query.toString());
  // Get the response from the server:
  String response="";
  try { response = input_strm.readLine(); }
  catch (IOException exception) {
     System.err.println("Client::GetService(): error reading "
                      + "response from server");
  };
  return new AIframe(response);
```

```
   }

   public void CloseConnection() {
     try { if (socket != null) { socket.close(); } }
         catch (IOException exception) { };
     socket=null;
   }
   public void finalize() {
       if (socket!=null)  CloseConnection();
   }
}
```

3.4.3 Test programs

There are two distinct test programs developed in this section, one to test the
mwa.agent.Client class and one to test the **mwa.agent.Server** class. Both test programs
use the **mwa.gui.GUI** class to build a simple test application.

mwa.agent.Server test program

The class **testServer**, which is used to test the class **mwa.agent.Server**, extends the class
mwa.gui.GUI. All user interface components of the **GUI** class except for an output
scrolling text field are disabled for the program. Listing 3.7 shows the implementation
of the **testServer** class. The method **testServer.init()** creates an instance of class
MyServer. The class **MyServer**, which is derived from class **mwa.agent.Server**, is
defined at the end of Listing 3.7 and is described immediately after it.

Listing 3.7

```
// Test server classes
//
// Copyright 1996, Mark Watson.  All rights reserved.

package mwa.agent;

import java.awt.*;
import java.util.*;

import mwa.gui.GUI;
import mwa.data.*;

public class testServer extends GUI {
```

```
MyServer server;
Graphics background;  // used for double buffering
Image im;


public String getAppletInfo() {
    return "Test the agent stuff.  By Mark Watson";
}

public void init() {
  // Disable all standard GUI display
  // components except output:
  NoGraphics    = true;
  NoInput       = true;
  NoRunButton   = true;
  NoResetButton = true;

  super.init();
  P("testServer applet");

  server = new MyServer(0, this);  // use default port
}

}


class MyServer extends Server {
    // Derived class constructors just need to call
    // the appropriate super class constructor:
    public MyServer(int port) { super(port); }
    public MyServer(int port, GUI my_gui) {
        super(port, my_gui);
    }
    // public method redefined from parent class:
    public AIframe DoWork(AIframe request) {
      AIframe ret =new AIframe("My DoWork");
      ret.put("client_request",
              new AIframedata(request.toString()));
      return ret;
    }
}
```

The **testServer** class shown in Listing 3.7 uses the class **MyServer** (also defined in Listing 3.7), which is derived from the class **mwa.agent.Server**. The **Server** class is always subclassed in order to define an application-specific **DoWork** method. Since the

Server class is explicitly declared abstract, it is illegal (i.e., a compiler error is generated) if you attempt to create an instance of the **Server** class. The returned value (an **AIframe** object) from the **DoWork** method is passed through the socket connection back to the application containing the **mwa.agent.Client** object that made the service request.

mwa.agent.Client test program

The class **testClient**, which is used to test the class **mwa.agent.Client**, is shown in Listing 3.8. This class is derived from the **mwa.gui.GUI** class and creates a "Run" command button, an input text field, and a large scrolling output text field. When the "Run" button is clicked, the contents of the input text field is placed in a slot in a new **mwa.data.AIframe** object, which is sent to a server at IP address 127.0.0.1 using the default port number of the **mwa.agent.Client** class. The response from the **Server** object in the separate **testServer** application is converted from an **mwa.data.AIframe** to a Java **String** and printed in the output text field.

Listing 3.8

```
// Test client classes
//
// Copyright 1996, Mark Watson.  All rights reserved.

package mwa.agent;

import java.awt.*;
import java.util.*;

import mwa.gui.GUI;
import mwa.data.*;

public class testClient extends GUI {
    mwa.agent.Client client;

    public String getAppletInfo() {
        return "Test the agent stuff.  By Mark Watson";
    }

    public void init() {
      // Disable graphics and input areas of
      // standard GUI display:
```

```
   NoGraphics = true;
   NoResetButton=true;
   BigText=1;

   super.init();
   P("testClient applet\n");
}

public void doRunButton() {
   client = new Client();
   String r = client.GetInfo();
   P(r + "\n");
   AIframe frame=new AIframe("testframe");
   frame.put("name", new AIframedata(GetInputText()));
   AIframe response = client.GetService(frame);
   if (response!=null) {
      String res = response.toString();
      P("Response from server:" + res + "\n");
   } else  {
      P("No response from server\n");
   }
   client.CloseConnection();
   client = null;
}
public void doResetButton() {
}
}
```

The HTML code shown in Listing 3.9 is used for testing both the **Client** and **Server** classes. Listing 3.9 shows a good technique for testing cooperating Java applications: a single HTML file can simultaneously start more than one Java applet.

Listing 3.9

```
<title>Test client/server agent classes</title>
<hr>
<applet code=mwa.agent.testServer.class width=300 height=120>
</applet>
<applet code=mwa.agent.testClient.class width=640 height=120>
</applet>
<hr>
```

Figure 3.5 shows a screen shot with both **testClient** and **testServer** applets running. The top application window in Figure 3.5 shows an instance of the class **testServer** running. An instance of class **MyServer** has started, listening for connections on port 6001.

The bottom application window in Figure 3.5 shows an instance of class **testClient** running. The text "test input" has been typed into the input text field, and the "Run" button has been clicked. The method **testClient.doRunButton()** has created an instance of class **mwa.agent.Client**, passed the input text to the server, received an **mwa.data.AIframe** object back from the server, and then called the method **Client.CloseConnection()** to close the socket connection with the server application.

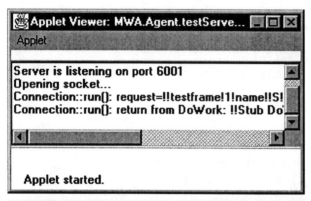

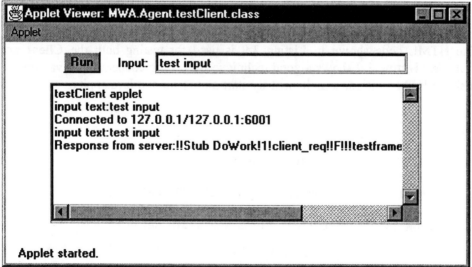

Figure 3.5   **testServer** and **testClient** applications

Neural Networks **4**

Neural networks have been successfully used for a wide variety of practical applications including pattern recognition and adaptive controllers. In this chapter we will discuss the theory, implementation, and use of the most widely used type of network, the backwards error propagation (often called back-prop or delta rule) network. These neural networks use supervised learning: the network is trained with data representing both the input and desired output values of a network. Although hardware implementations of neural networks exist, most applications of neural network technology use simulated neural networks like those created using the Java classes developed in this chapter. Throughout this chapter the phrase "neural network" implies the specific case of a backwards error propagation network.

4.1   How neural networks work

Each neuron in a neural network has a numeric value representing an activation energy. For the Java classes developed in this chapter, we will always scale this activation energy to the range [-0.5, +0.5]. We will use networks with three sets of neurons, or *layers*: input, hidden, and output. These three-layer neural networks are capable of solving most pattern recognition and control problems. Occasionally four-layer networks containing two hidden layers are required to solve some recognition problems (Watson 1995; Watson 1991).

Figure 4.1 shows a simple neural network. Since there are three input and two hidden neurons, we require a total of 3 * 2 = 6 connection weights to totally connect the input and hidden neuron layers. Since there are two hidden layer neurons and two output layer neurons, we require 2 * 2 = 4 connection weights to totally connect the hidden and output neuron layers. The activation energy of hidden neuron 1 is calculated by summing the terms

(input neuron 1 activation) * (weight connecting input neuron 1 to hidden neuron 1) +

(input neuron 2 activation) * (weight connecting input neuron 2 to hidden neuron 1) +

(input neuron 3 activation) * (weight connecting input neuron 3 to hidden neuron 1)

This sum of terms is then passed as an argument to the **Sigmoid** method to calculate the activation energy for hidden neuron 1. The activation energies for hidden neuron 2, output neuron 1, and output neuron 2 are calculated in a similar way.

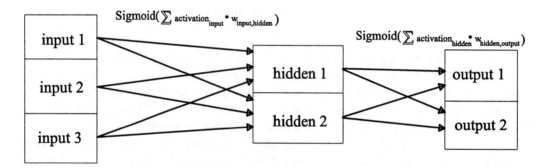

Figure 4.1   A simple backwards error propagation neural network with three input neurons, two hidden neurons, and two output neurons. Each input neuron is connected with a connection weight to each hidden neuron, and each hidden neuron is connected with each output neuron.

This neural network uses supervised learning. We train the network by initially assigning small random connection weight values to the network and then repetitively applying the following learning algorithm to each set of training data containing input neuron values and corresponding output values:

1. Copy the input values to the activation energy values of the input neurons.
2. Calculate the activation energy for the hidden layer neurons by using the sum of products of input neuron activation values and input-to-hidden-layer connection weights and by applying the **Sigmoid** method.
3. Calculate the activation energy for the output layer neurons by using the sum of products of hidden neuron activation values and hidden-to-output-layer connection weights and by applying the **Sigmoid** method.

4. For each output neuron, calculate the error, or difference between the desired output activation value and the forward propagated activation value.

5. Use the error in the output activation energy values to calculate small changes to the hidden-to-output weights to slowly reduce the error.

6. Estimate the activation error for the hidden neurons.

7. Use the estimated errors for the hidden neurons to calculate small changes to the input-to-hidden weights to slowly reduce the error.

As we will see when we design and implement Java neural network classes, it is fairly simple to simulate neural networks. The difficulty in applying neural networks to practical problems is collecting the training data cases. In Chapter 12 we will use genetic algorithms to fine-tune the training data for neural networks.

Figure 4.2 shows a plot of both the **Sigmoid** method and the derivative of the **Sigmoid** method. In Listing 4.1 the **Sigmoid** function is implemented in method **mwa.ai.neural.Sigmoid** and the derivative of the **Sigmoid** function is implemented in method **mwa.ai.neural.SigmoidP**.

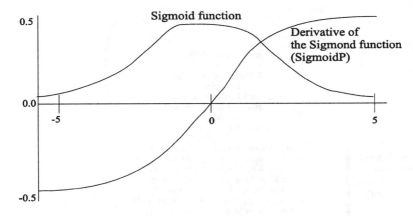

Figure 4.2   **Sigmoid** and derivative of **Sigmoid** (**SigmoidP**) functions

4.2   Design of Java neural network classes

Figure 4.3 shows the Booch class diagram for the Java neural network class **mwa.ai.neural.Neural** and the class **mwa.ai.neural.NNfile** that are developed in this chapter. The class **mwa.ai.neural.NNfile** will be used in Chapter 11 to save and load neural networks to and from disk files in Java classes that automatically improve neural network training data.

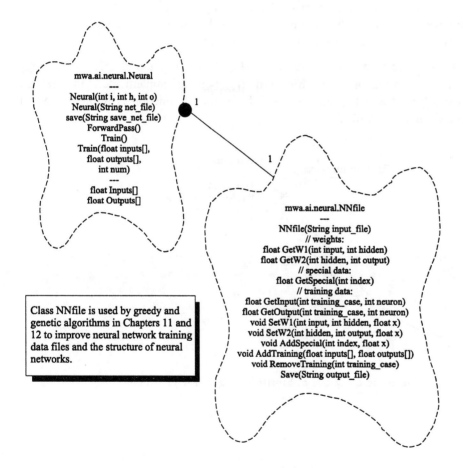

Figure 4.3   Booch class diagram for neural network classes. The implementation of class **Neural** is shown in Listing 4.3; the implementation of class **NNfile** is shown in Listing 4.7.

As we see in Figure 4.3, the class **Neural** has two constructors:

- **Neural(int i, int h, int o)**. Use the **Train(float inputs[], float outputs[], int num)** method for this network.
- **Neural(String net_file)**. Use the **Train()** method for this network.

The first constructor is used to create a new neural network object by specifying how many neurons will be in the input, hidden, and output layers. A network created with this form of the constructor can be trained by calling the method **Train(float inputs[], float outputs[], int num)**, passing training data as arguments to the **Train** method. This constructor/**Train** method combination is useful for demonstrating neural networks on Web pages because the training data can be fetched from an HTML document (see the example in Listing 4.4 in Section 4.3).

The second form of the constructor is useful for real applications (rather than Web-page-based demonstrations). An input network description file defines the size of a network, and optionally training data and/or saved weights from a previously trained network. This network description file is read from an instance of class **mwa.ai.neural.NNfile** (which is defined in Listing 4.7). Listing 4.1 shows a very simple network description file that contains training data as written by an instance of class **NNfile**.

Listing 4.1

```
#  Neural network data written by NNfile
3  # number of neuron layers
3  # neurons in layer 0
3  # neurons in layer 1
3  # neurons in layer 2
0  # weight flag
0  # special data flag
3  # number of training cases in file

# Training data:
-0.4 0.4 0.4    0.4 -0.4 0.4
0.4 -0.4 0.4    0.4 0.4 -0.4
0.4 0.4 -0.4    -0.4 0.4 0.4
```

The network file shown in Listing 4.1 specifies that a neural network will be constructed with three input, three hidden, and three output neurons (useful applications will use many more neurons). There are three training cases listed; each training case specifies the value for each input neuron and the desired output value for each output neuron.

Each separate training example appears on a separate line (these files are free format). In this example, the first three numbers are input neuron values, and the last three are desired output neuron activation values.

Listing 4.2 shows the results of creating a neural network with the input network description file seen in Listing 4.1, training the network with the training data contained in Listing 4.1, and using the **mwa.ai.neural.NNfile.Save()** method to save the trained network to a new file.

Listing 4.2

```
#  Neural network data written by NNfile

3  # number of neuron layers
3  # neurons in layer 0
3  # neurons in layer 1
3  # neurons in layer 2
1  # weight flag
0  # special data flag
3  # number of training cases in file

# Input layer to hidden layer weights:
0.0112542 -0.0432932 -0.00623174
-0.04761 -0.0225022 -0.0375257
0.0359218 -0.012686 0.038833

# Hidden layer to output layer weights:
0.0278448 0.026646 0.0411143
-0.0158825 -0.00881048 0.0295604
-0.00206302 0.0208291 0.0424572

# Training data:
-0.4 0.4 0.4    0.4 -0.4 0.4
0.4 -0.4 0.4    0.4 0.4 -0.4
0.4 0.4 -0.4    -0.4 0.4 0.4
```

4.3   Implementation of a neural network package in Java

Listing 4.3 (file **Neural.java**) shows the implementation of a back-prop neural network. The constructor **Neural()** creates a new neural network with no neurons, which is not very useful. The constructors for creating neural networks in your applications are **Neural(String filename)** and **Neural(int i, int h, int o)**. Network description files written with method **mwa.ai.neural.NNfile.Save** can be used later to construct a pre-trained neural network with the constructor **Neural(String filename)**. The utility method **randomizeWeights()** is used to initialize all weights in a neural network to small random values before training the network. The method **ForwardPass()** is used for two purposes:

- In methods **Train()** and **Train(float inputs[], output[], int num)**, for calculating the activation values for hidden and output layer neurons
- In applications using pretrained neural networks, for calculating output neuron activation values from a set of input values

The methods **Train()** and **Train(float inputs[], output[], int num)** are used for modifying the connection weights in neural networks to minimize the output errors for a specific set of training data. The method **Sigmoid**, seen in Figure 4.2, is used for two purposes:

- To force neuron activation values to the range [-0.5, +0.5].
- Since the **Sigmoid** function is differentiable, the steepest descent learning algorithm is guaranteed to at least find local minima. In practice, the **Sigmoid** function is sometimes replaced with a table lookup or a linear increasing function with a threshold cutoff at +0.5.

The **SigmoidP** function, also seen in Figure 4.2, is the derivative of the **Sigmoid** function. The **SigmoidP** function is used to apply corrections to connection weights that are scaled to how much a given weight contributed to the error of output layer neurons.

Listing 4.3

```
// Neural Network Java classes
//
// Copyright 1996, Mark Watson.  All rights reserved.

package mwa.ai.neural;

import java.awt.*;
import java.applet.Applet;
import java.lang.*;
import java.util.*;

import mwa.gui.GUI;
import mwa.data.*;

class Neural extends Object {
```

```java
// For debug output:
GUI MyGUI = null;

protected int NumInputs;
protected int NumHidden;
protected int NumOutputs;

protected int NumTraining;
protected int WeightsFlag;
protected int SpecialFlag;

public float Inputs[];
protected float Hidden[];
public float Outputs[];

protected float W1[][];
protected float W2[][];

protected float output_errors[];
protected float hidden_errors[];

protected float InputTraining[];
protected float OutputTraining[];

// mask of training examples to ignore (true -> ignore):
public boolean IgnoreTraining[] = null;
// mask of input neurons to ignore:
public boolean IgnoreInput[] = null;

Neural() {
 NumInputs = NumHidden = NumOutputs = 0;
}
public NNfile NeuralFile=null;

Neural(String file_name) {
  NeuralFile = new NNfile(file_name);
  NumInputs = NeuralFile.NumInput;
  NumHidden = NeuralFile.NumHidden;
  NumOutputs = NeuralFile.NumOutput;
  NumTraining= NeuralFile.NumTraining;
  WeightsFlag= NeuralFile.WeightFlag;
  SpecialFlag= NeuralFile.SpecialFlag;
```

```java
    Inputs = new float[NumInputs];
    Hidden = new float[NumHidden];
    Outputs = new float[NumOutputs];
    W1 = new float[NumInputs][NumHidden];
    W2 = new float[NumHidden][NumOutputs];
    // Retrieve the weight values from the NNfile object:
    if (WeightsFlag!=0) {
      for (int i=0; i<NumInputs; i++) {
        for (int h=0; h<NumHidden; h++) {
          W1[i][h] = NeuralFile.GetW1(i, h);
        }
      }
      for (int h=0; h<NumHidden; h++) {
        for (int o=0; o<NumOutputs; o++) {
          W2[h][o] = NeuralFile.GetW2(h, o);
        }
      }
    } else {
      randomizeWeights();
    }

    output_errors = new float[NumOutputs];
    hidden_errors = new float[NumHidden];

    // Get the training cases (if any) from the training file:

}

public void LoadTrainingCases() {
  NumTraining = NeuralFile.NumTraining;
  if (NumTraining > 0) {
     InputTraining  = new float[NumTraining * NumInputs];
     OutputTraining = new float[NumTraining * NumOutputs];
  }
  int ic=0, oc=0;

  for (int k=0; k<NumTraining; k++) {
     for (int i=0; i<NumInputs; i++)
        InputTraining[ic++] = NeuralFile.GetInput(k, i);
     for (int o=0; o<NumOutputs; o++)
        OutputTraining[oc++] = NeuralFile.GetOutput(k, o);
  }
}
```

```
Neural(int i, int h, int o) {
  System.out.println("In BackProp constructor");
  Inputs = new float[i];
  Hidden = new float[h];
  Outputs = new float[o];
  W1 = new float[i][h];
  W2 = new float[h][o];
  NumInputs = i;
  NumHidden = h;
  NumOutputs = o;
  output_errors = new float[NumOutputs];
  hidden_errors = new float[NumHidden];

  // Randomize weights here:
  randomizeWeights();
}

void Save(String output_file) {
  if (NeuralFile==null) {
    System.out.println("Error: no NeuralFile " +
                       "object in Neural::Save");
  } else {
    for (int i=0; i<NumInputs; i++) {
      for (int h=0; h<NumHidden; h++) {
        NeuralFile.SetW1(i, h, W1[i][h]);
      }
    }
    for (int h=0; h<NumHidden; h++) {
      for (int o=0; o<NumOutputs; o++) {
        NeuralFile.SetW2(h, o, W2[h][o]);
      }
    }
    NeuralFile.Save(output_file);
  }
}

public void randomizeWeights() {
 // Randomize weights here:
  for (int ii=0; ii<NumInputs; ii++)
    for (int hh=0; hh<NumHidden; hh++)
      W1[ii][hh] =
          0.1f * (float)Math.random() - 0.05f;
  for (int hh=0; hh<NumHidden; hh++)
    for (int oo=0; oo<NumOutputs; oo++)
```

```java
                W2[hh][oo] =
                    0.1f * (float)Math.random() - 0.05f;
    }

    public void ForwardPass() {
        int i, h, o;
        for (h=0; h<NumHidden; h++) {
          Hidden[h] = 0.0f;
        }
        for (i=0; i<NumInputs; i++) {
            for (h=0; h<NumHidden; h++) {
                Hidden[h] +=
                    Inputs[i] * W1[i][h];
            }
        }
        for (o=0; o<NumOutputs; o++)
          Outputs[o] = 0.0f;
        for (h=0; h<NumHidden; h++) {
            for (o=0; o<NumOutputs; o++) {
                Outputs[o] +=
                    Sigmoid(Hidden[h]) * W2[h][o];
            }
        }
        for (o=0; o<NumOutputs; o++)
          Outputs[o] = Sigmoid(Outputs[o]);
    }

    public float Train() {
        return Train(InputTraining, OutputTraining, NumTraining);
    }

    public float Train(float ins[],
                       float outs[],
                       int num_cases) {
      int i, h, o;
      int in_count=0, out_count=0;
      float error = 0.0f;
      for (int example=0; example<num_cases; example++) {
        if (IgnoreTraining != null)
          if (IgnoreTraining[example]) continue;
        // zero out error arrays:
        for (h=0; h<NumHidden; h++)
          hidden_errors[h] = 0.0f;
        for (o=0; o<NumOutputs; o++)
```

```
      output_errors[o] = 0.0f;
// copy the input values:
for (i=0; i<NumInputs; i++) {
   Inputs[i] = ins[in_count++];
}


if (IgnoreInput != null) {
  for (int ii=0; ii<NumInputs; ii++) {
     if (IgnoreInput[ii]) {
        for (int hh=0; hh<NumHidden; hh++) {
           W1[ii][hh] = 0;
        }
     }
  }
}


// perform a forward pass through the network:

ForwardPass();

if (MyGUI != null)  MyGUI.repaint();
for (o=0; o<NumOutputs; o++)  {
    output_errors[o] =
      (outs[out_count++] -
      Outputs[o])
      *SigmoidP(Outputs[o]);
}
for (h=0; h<NumHidden; h++) {
  hidden_errors[h] = 0.0f;
  for (o=0; o<NumOutputs; o++) {
     hidden_errors[h] +=
        output_errors[o]*W2[h][o];
  }
}
for (h=0; h<NumHidden; h++) {
   hidden_errors[h] =
     hidden_errors[h]*SigmoidP(Hidden[h]);
}
// update the hidden to output weights:
for (o=0; o<NumOutputs; o++) {
  for (h=0; h<NumHidden; h++) {
     W2[h][o] +=
        0.5 * output_errors[o] * Hidden[h];
  }
```

```
    }
    // update the input to hidden weights:
    for (h=0; h<NumHidden; h++) {
        for (i=0; i<NumInputs; i++) {
            W1[i][h] +=
                0.5 * hidden_errors[h] * Inputs[i];
        }
    }
    for (o=0; o<NumOutputs; o++)
        error += Math.abs(output_errors[o]);
    }
    return error;
}

protected float Sigmoid(float x) {
    return
    (float)((1.0f/(1.0f+Math.exp((double)(-x))))-0.5f);
}

protected float SigmoidP(float x) {
    double z = Sigmoid(x) + 0.5f;
    return (float)(z * (1.0f - z));
}

}
```

Listing 4.4 (file **testNeural.java**) shows a test program for the neural network class that also uses the Java classes in the files **GUI.java** and **GUICanvas.java** in the package **mwa.gui**. Listing 4.5 shows the HTML file for initializing this applet. Note that method **init()** in Listing 4.4 reads the following values from the HTML file:

- Applet window width
- Applet window height
- Number of input neurons
- Number of hidden neurons
- Number of output neurons
- Training data

These values are also given default values in method **init()** so that the applet will work even if some of the values are left unspecified. Clicking the applet's "Run" button executes the method **doRunButton()**, which sets the flag variable **active** to a nonzero value. The method **run()** checks the **active** flag variable; if it is nonzero, the method **train()** is called. Method **train()** calls the **Neural** network class method **Train()** up to

140 times to train the test neural network. Figure 4.4 shows this applet after the **Neural** class method **Train()** has been called 140 times.

The class **testNeural** is derived from the class **mwa.gui.GUI**, but it also implements the **Runnable** interface. Any class implementing the **Runnable** interface must define a method **run()**, create an instance of class **Thread**, and call the method **Thread.start()** to initiate the thread. A running thread repeatedly calls the **run()** method. See Appendix A for a discussion of using threads.

Listing 4.4

```
// NeuralNet Java classes
//
// Copyright 1996, Mark Watson.  All rights reserved.

package mwa.ai.neural;

import java.awt.*;
import java.util.*;

import mwa.gui.*;

public class testNeural extends GUI implements Runnable {

    //String param;

    int active = 0;   // if 1, then train network

    // Neural network parameters:
    int NumInputs  = 3;
    int NumOutputs = 3;
    int NumHidden  = 3;

    Neural network;

    float Errors[];
    int NumErrors = 0;
    int width = 340;
    int height = 200;

    // For training:
    private float outs[];
    private float ins[];
    private float error = -9999.9f;
```

```java
private String param; // hides super class param.

public String getAppletInfo() {
    return "Neural Network Simulator by Mark Watson";
}

private Thread workThread = null;

public void init() {

    NoInput = true;   // we do not need an input text field

    param = getParameter("NumHidden");
    if (param != null) NumHidden = Integer.parseInt(param);

    param = getParameter("NumInputs");
    if (param != null) NumInputs = Integer.parseInt(param);

    param = getParameter("NumOutputs");
    if (param != null) NumOutputs = Integer.parseInt(param);

    network = new Neural(NumInputs, NumHidden, NumOutputs);
    network.MyGUI = this;

    // For testing the Ignore training data option:
    //network.Ignore = new boolean[100];
    //for (int i=0; i<100; i++) network.Ignore[i] = false;
    //network.Ignore[1] = true;

    Errors = new float[512];
    NumErrors = 0;
    outs = new float[20];
    ins  = new float[20];
    StringTokenizer st;
    param = getParameter("inputs");
    if (param != null)
       st = new StringTokenizer(param);
    else
       st = new StringTokenizer("-5 -5 5 5 -5 -5 -5 5 -5");
    int j;
    for(j=0;j<9;j++) {
       ins[j] = 0.08f *
         (float)(Integer.parseInt(st.nextToken()));
    }
```

```
      param = getParameter("outputs");
      if (param != null)
         st = new StringTokenizer(param);
      else
         st = new StringTokenizer("5 -5 -5 -5 5 -5 -5 -5 5");
      for(j=0;j<9;j++) {
            outs[j] =   0.08f *
                          (float)(Integer.parseInt(st.nextToken()));
       }
       super.init();
       network.MyGUI = this;


      if (workThread==null) {
      workThread = new Thread(this);
      workThread.start();
       }
 }

 public void train() {
   if (NumErrors < 140) {
     Errors[NumErrors++] = error = network.Train(ins, outs, 3);
     P("Output error=");
     P(error);
     P("\n");
     repaint();
   } else {
     active = 0;
   }
 }

 private void paintNeuronLayer(Graphics g, int x, int y,
                                 String title, float values[],
                                 int num) {
     for (int i=0; i<num; i++) {
         paintGridCell(g, x+60 + i*12, y, 10, values[i],
                       -0.5f, 0.5f);
     }
     g.drawString(title, x, y+10);
 }

 private void paintWeights(Graphics g, int x, int y, String title,
                             float values[][], int num1, int num2) {
     for (int i=0; i<num1; i++) {
```

```java
            for (int j=0; j<num2; j++)  {
                paintGridCell(g, x+60 + i*12, y + j * 12, 10,
                                values[i][j], -1.5f, 1.5f);
            }
        }
        g.drawString(title, x, y+10);
    }

    public void paintToDoubleBuffer(Graphics g) {
        // Draw the input/hidden/output neuron layers:
        paintNeuronLayer(g, 170, 10, "Inputs:",
                        network.Inputs, network.NumInputs);
        paintNeuronLayer(g, 170, 80, "Hidden:",
                        network.Hidden, network.NumHidden);
        paintNeuronLayer(g, 170, 140, "Outputs:",
                        network.Outputs, network.NumOutputs);
        paintWeights(g, 170, 30, "Weights 1:",
                    network.W1, network.NumInputs,
                    network.NumHidden);
        paintWeights(g, 170, 100, "Weights 2:", network.W2,
                            network.NumHidden, network.NumOutputs);
        // Draw a plot of error summed over output neurons:
        g.drawString("Cumulative error summed over output neurons",
                        10, height - 10);
        if (NumErrors < 2)  return;
        int x1= 0, x2;
        int y1 = height - (int)(50.0f * Errors[0]), y2;
        setForeground(Color.red);
        g.setColor(getForeground());
        for (int i=1; i<NumErrors-1; i++) {
            x2 = 2*i;
            y2 = height - (int)(50.0f * Errors[i]);
            g.drawLine(x1, y1, x2, y2);
            x1 = x2;
            y1 = y2;
        }
    }
    public void run() {
        System.out.println("Entering testNeural::run()");
        System.out.println("..after super.run()");
        while (true)  {
            if (active == 1)  train();
        }
    }
```

```
public void doRunButton() {
    active = 1;
 }
public void doResetButton() {
    active = 0;
    ClearOutput();
    network = new Neural(NumInputs, NumHidden, NumOutputs);
    network.MyGUI = this;
    NumErrors = 0;
  }
}
```

The HTML file shown in Listing 4.5 can be used to test this Java class. The following arguments are defined in the HTML file:

- inputs = -5 -5 5 5 -5 -5 -5 5 -5
- outputs = 5 -5 -5 -5 5 -5 -5 -5 5

These values represent scaled input and target output neuron activation values. These values are scaled, in the method **testNeural.init()**, by a factor of 0.1 to produce activation values in the correct range [-0.5, 0.5].

Listing 4.5

```
<title>Test neural stuff</title>
<hr>
<applet code=mwa.ai.neural.testNeural.class
        width=480 height=300
        inputs="-5 -5 5 5 -5 -5 -5 5 -5"
        outputs="5 -5 -5 -5 5 -5 -5 -5 5">
</applet>
<hr>
```

Figure 4.4 shows a screen shot of the neural network application in Listing 4.4 executing.

Listing 4.6 shows another neural network test applet. This applet uses the Java class **NNfile** that is shown in Listing 4.7 to initialize a neural network from a disk file. We will see that the class **NNfile** provides behavior for both loading and saving neural networks. The classes **NNfile** and **Neural** are both used in the projects in Chapters 11 and 12. The **Neural(String net_file)** constructor is used to create a network from the data file seen in Listing 4.1. This test applet is simpler than the test applet seen in Listing 4.4 because the neural network size parameters and training data are simply obtained from a neural network data file. This applet is otherwise similar to the applet seen in Listing 4.4, except the method **train()** only calls the **Neural** class method **Train()** a maximum of 20 times. The method **save(String output_file)** is called when the "Reset" button is clicked to save the trained network to the file **test2.dat**.

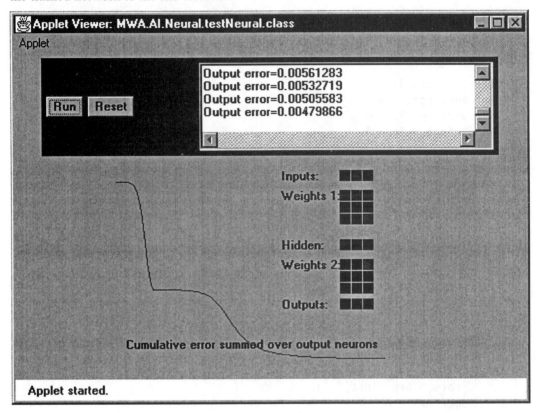

Figure 4.4   Applet shown in Listing 4.4 has called the method **Train(float input[ ], float outputs[ ], int num)** 140 times. Each time **Train** is called, it returns the summed cumulative output error, which is plotted in the applet window. This error is also printed in the scrolling text field in the applet.

Listing 4.6

```
// NeuralNet Java classes
//
// Copyright 1996, Mark Watson.  All rights reserved.

package mwa.ai.neural;
```

```java
import java.awt.*;

import mwa.gui.GUI;
import mwa.data.*;

public class testNeuralFile extends GUI {

    Neural network;

    float Errors[];
    int NumErrors = 0;
    int width = 380;
    int height = 260;

    // For training:
    private float outs[];
    private float ins[];
    private float error = -9999.9f;

    public String getAppletInfo() {
        return "Neural Network Simulator by Mark Watson";
    }

    public void init() {

        NoInput = true;  // we do not need an input text field
        //ResetLabel = new String("Save file");

        Errors = new float[512];
        NumErrors = 0;

        super.init();

        network = new Neural("test.dat");
        network.MyGUI = this;
    }

    private void paintNeuronLayer(Graphics g, int x, int y,
                                  String title, float values[],
                                  int num) {
        for (int i=0; i<num; i++) {
            paintGridCell(g, x+60 + i*12, y, 10, values[i],
                          -0.5f, 0.5f);
```

```java
        }
        g.drawString(title, x, y+10);
    }



    private void paintWeights(Graphics g, int x,
                              int y, String title,
                              float values[][],
                              int num1, int num2) {
        for (int i=0; i<num1; i++) {
            for (int j=0; j<num2; j++) {
                paintGridCell(g, x+60 + i*12,
                              y + j * 12, 10,
                              values[i][j],
                              -1.5f, 1.5f);
            }
        }
        g.drawString(title, x, y+10);
    }

    public void paintToDoubleBuffer(Graphics g) {
        // Draw the input/hidden/output neuron layers:
        paintNeuronLayer(g, 170, 10, "Inputs:",
                         network.Inputs, network.NumInputs);
        paintNeuronLayer(g, 170, 80, "Hidden:",
                         network.Hidden, network.NumHidden);
        paintNeuronLayer(g, 170, 140, "Outputs:",
                         network.Outputs, network.NumOutputs);
        paintWeights(g, 170, 30, "Weights 1:",
                     network.W1, network.NumInputs,
                     network.NumHidden);
        paintWeights(g, 170, 100, "Weights 2:", network.W2,
                     network.NumHidden, network.NumOutputs);
        // Draw a plot of error summed over output neurons:
        g.drawString("Cumulative error summed over " +
                     "output neurons",
                     10, height - 10);
        if (NumErrors < 2)  return;
        int x1= 0, x2;
        int y1 = height - (int)(100.0f * Errors[0]), y2;
        setForeground(Color.red);
        g.setColor(getForeground());
```

```
        for (int i=1; i<NumErrors-1; i++) {
            x2 = 2*i;
            y2 = height - (int)(100.0f * Errors[i]);
            g.drawLine(x1, y1, x2, y2);
            x1 = x2;
            y1 = y2;
        }
    }
    public void doRunButton() {
        for (int i=0; i<30; i++) {
            Errors[NumErrors++] = error = network.Train();
            P("Output error=" + error + "\n");
            repaint();
        }
    }

    public void doResetButton() {
        ClearOutput();
        P("Weights saved to file test2.dat\n");
        network.NeuralFile.AddSpecial(1001.0f);
        network.NeuralFile.AddSpecial(1002.0f);
        network.NeuralFile.AddSpecial(1003.0f);
        network.NeuralFile.AddSpecial(1004.0f);
        network.NeuralFile.RemoveTraining(2);
        network.NeuralFile.AddSpecial(1005.0f);
        network.NeuralFile.AddSpecial(1006.0f);
        network.Save("test2.dat");
    }
}
```

Figure 4.5 shows the results of running the applet seen in Listing 4.6.

Listing 4.7 (file **..\MWA\AI\Neural\NNfile.java**) shows the implementation of the class **NNfile** that is used by both the class **NNgreedy** in Chapter 11 and by the class **GenNeural** in Chapter 12. The constructor for class **NNfile** requires a **String** argument specifying a file name for a neural network specification file. The constructor opens an input stream and passes this input stream to the method **ReadFile(InputStream inp)** to read all values in a file into an array of **float** values. These specification files always contain information on the size of the neural network, and optionally specify values for previously trained weights, application-specific data, and training data.

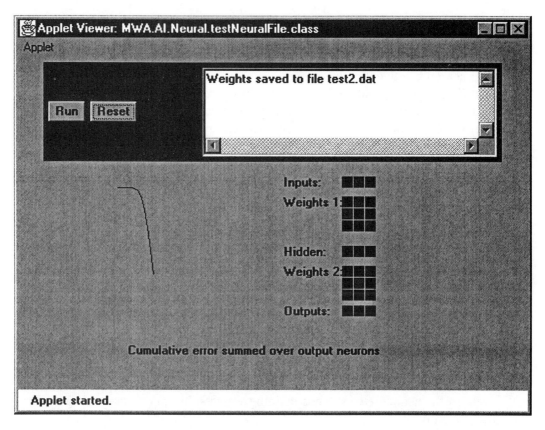

Figure 4.5   After running the applet seen in Listing 4.6. The method **Train()** was called 20 times when the "Run" button was clicked. The button "Reset" was clicked, saving the complete network file to **test2.dat**, which is seen in Listing 4.2.

The method **ParseData()** is used internally by class **NNfile** to use the **float** values in the input neural network description file to specify the size of the neural network and to determine which of the following optional data is stored in the description file: previously trained weights, application-specific data, or training cases.

The class **NNfile** provides several access methods for fetching and changing neural network data:

- **float GetW1(int i, int h)** fetches the value of one specified weight connecting input layer neuron **i** with hidden layer neuron **h**.
- **float GetW2(int h, int o)** fetches the value of one specified weight connecting hidden layer neuron **h** with output layer neuron **o**.

- **void SetW1(int i, int h, float x)** sets the values of the weight connecting input layer neuron **i** with hidden layer neuron **h**.
- **void SetW2(int h, int o, float x)** sets the values of the weight connecting hidden layer neuron **h** with output layer neuron **o**.
- **float GetSpecial(int index)** fetches application-specific data at index.
- **void AddSpecial(float x)** adds application-specific data.
- **float GetInput(int training_case, int neuron_index)** fetches the specified input neuron value for the training case specified by the index **training_case**.
- **float GetOutput(int training_case, int neuron_index)** fetches the specified target output neuron value for the training case specified by the index **training_case**.

The method **RemoveTrainingData(int index)** deletes the specified training case. The method **AddTraining(float inputs[], float outputs[])** adds an additional training case.

The method **ReadFile(InputStream inp)** is used internally by class **NNfile** to read all floating-point values in a file into a large array of type **float**. Comments are any characters starting with a # character to the end of a line; comments are skipped.

The method **Save(String save_file_name)** is used to write a modified neural network description file. Usually this method is used after performing one or more of the following actions:

- Training the neural network, thus defining weights that can be used in an application program
- Adding application-specific data
- Adding training cases
- Deleting training cases

The Java class **mwa.ai.neural.NNfile** is used to save and load neural networks to and from disk files. A neural network file is ASCII data containing this information:

- Number of layers (currently this is always three)
- Number of neurons in the input layer
- Number of neurons in the hidden layer
- Number of neurons in the output layer
- A flag indicating if previously calculated weights are stored in the file
- A flag indicating if any special application-specific data is stored in the file (a nonzero value indicates the number of special data values in the file)
- Number of training cases in the file
- Input-layer-to-hidden-layer weights (optional)
- Hidden-layer-to-output-layer weights (optional)

- Application-specific data (optional)
- Training data (optional)

Listing 4.7

```
// NNfile class: parses neural network input files
// storing network parameters and optional training
// data in memory.

package mwa.ai.neural;

import java.io.*;
import java.net.URL;
import java.util.*;
//import java.lang.*;

class FileFormatException extends Exception {
  public FileFormatException(String str) {
    super(str);
  }
}

public class NNfile {
  public int NumLayers;
  public int NumNeuronsPerLayer[];
  public int NumInput, NumHidden, NumOutput, NumTraining;
  public int WeightFlag;
  public int SpecialFlag;
  public int BaseIndex, TopIndex;
  private float data[];

  public NNfile() {
    NumLayers=NumInput=NumHidden=NumOutput=0;
  }

  public NNfile(String input_file) {
    data = new float[40000];
    TopIndex = 0;
    FileInputStream is = null;
    try {
      is = new FileInputStream(input_file);
    } catch (Exception E) {
        System.out.println("cannot open file " +
```

```
                              input_file);
       }
       try {
          if (is != null)  ReadFile(is);  is.close();
       } catch (Exception E) {
           System.out.println("cannot process file");
       }
       System.out.println("Done with ReadFile, " +
                          "calling ParseData...");
       ParseData();
       OutputStream f = null;
       System.out.println("Done with ParseData(), " +
                          "write output...");
    }

    void ParseData() {
       int k = 0;
       NumLayers = (int)data[k++];
       NumNeuronsPerLayer = new int[NumLayers];
       for (int i=0; i<NumLayers; i++)
          NumNeuronsPerLayer[i]=(int)data[k++];
       NumInput    = NumNeuronsPerLayer[0];
       NumHidden   = NumNeuronsPerLayer[1];
       NumOutput   = NumNeuronsPerLayer[2];
       WeightFlag  = (int)data[k++];
       if (WeightFlag==0) {
          // Make room in data array for any
          // weights added in later:
          int NumW = NumInput*NumHidden + NumHidden*NumOutput;
          for (int i=TopIndex; i>6; i--)  {
             data[i+NumW] = data[i];
          }
          TopIndex += NumW;
       }
       SpecialFlag = (int)data[k++];
       NumTraining = (int)data[k++];
       BaseIndex = k;
    }

    // To get weights:
    public float GetW1(int input, int hidden) {
       if (WeightFlag==0) return 0.0f;
       return data[BaseIndex +
                  input * NumHidden + hidden];
```

```java
    }
    public float GetW2(int hidden, int output) {
        if (WeightFlag==0) return 0.0f;
        return data[BaseIndex +
                    NumInput * NumHidden +
                    hidden * NumOutput + output];
    }

    // To set weights:
    public void SetW1(int input, int hidden, float x) {
        WeightFlag=1; // set this so save() will save weights
        data[BaseIndex +
            input * NumHidden + hidden] = x;
    }
    public void SetW2(int hidden, int output, float x) {
        WeightFlag=1; // set this so save() will save weights
        data[BaseIndex +
            NumInput * NumHidden +
            hidden * NumOutput + output] = x;
    }

    // To get any application specific data:
    public float GetSpecial(int i) {
        if (SpecialFlag==0) return 0.0f;
        return data[BaseIndex +
                    NumInput*NumHidden +
                    NumHidden*NumOutput
                    + i];
    }

    // To add application specific data:
    public void AddSpecial(float x) {
        // Make room in data array for a
        // new special data value:
        int index = BaseIndex + NumInput*NumHidden +
                    NumHidden*NumOutput + SpecialFlag;
        for (int i=TopIndex-1; i>=index; i--)  {
            data[i+1] = data[i];
        }
        TopIndex++;

        data[index] = x;
        SpecialFlag++;
    }
```

```
// To get training cases:
public float GetInput(int training_case,
                      int neuron_index) {
    return data[BaseIndex +
                NumInput*NumHidden +
                NumHidden*NumOutput +
                SpecialFlag +
                training_case*(NumInput + NumOutput) +
                neuron_index];
}

public float GetOutput(int training_case,
                       int neuron_index) {
    return data[BaseIndex +
                NumInput*NumHidden +
                NumHidden*NumOutput +
                SpecialFlag +
                training_case*(NumInput + NumOutput) +
                NumInput +
                neuron_index];
}

public void RemoveTraining(int num) {
    if (num < 0 || num >= NumTraining) {
        System.out.println("Error in RemoveTraining(" +
                           num + ")");
        return;
    }
    int index = BaseIndex +
                NumInput*NumHidden +
                NumHidden*NumOutput +
                SpecialFlag +
                num * (NumInput + NumOutput);
    for (int i=index;
         i<=TopIndex - NumInput - NumOutput;
         i++) {
      data[i] = data[i + NumInput + NumOutput];
    }
    TopIndex -= NumInput + NumOutput;
    NumTraining--;
}

public void AddTraining(float inputs[],
```

```java
                              float outputs[]) {
    for (int i=0; i<NumInput; i++)
       data[TopIndex++] = inputs[i];
    for (int o=0; o<NumOutput; o++)
       data[TopIndex++] = outputs[o];
    NumTraining++;
  }

  void ReadFile(InputStream inp)
          throws IOException, FileFormatException {
    System.out.println("Entered ReadFile");
    StreamTokenizer st = new StreamTokenizer(inp);
    st.commentChar('#');
    st.eolIsSignificant(false);
    st.parseNumbers();
    System.out.println("Before while" );
    process:
    while (true) {
      switch(st.nextToken()) {
        case StreamTokenizer.TT_EOL:
          System.out.println("EOF found");
        break process;
        case StreamTokenizer.TT_NUMBER:
          float x = (float)st.nval;
          data[TopIndex++] = x;
        break;
        default:
          System.out.println("Token (default):" + st.sval);
        break process;
      }
    }
    System.out.println("Done with while loop");
    inp.close();
    if (st.ttype!=StreamTokenizer.TT_EOF)
      throw new FileFormatException(st.toString());
  }

  public void Save(String save_file_name) {
    try {
      FileOutputStream f =
        new FileOutputStream(save_file_name);
      PrintStream ps = new PrintStream(f);
      ps.println("#  Neural network data " +
                 "written by NNfile\n");
```

```
ps.println(NumLayers + "  # number of neuron layers");
for (int i=0; i<NumLayers; i++) {
   ps.println(NumNeuronsPerLayer[i] +
                " # neurons in layer " + i);
}
// always write out weights:
ps.println("1  # weight flag");
ps.println(SpecialFlag + "  # special data flag");
ps.println(NumTraining +
            "  # number of training cases in file");

ps.println("\n# Input layer to hidden " +
            "layer weights:\n");
for (int i=0; i<NumInput; i++) {
  for (int h=0; h<NumHidden; h++) {
    ps.print(GetW1(i, h) + " ");
  }
  ps.print("\n");
}
ps.println("\n# Hidden layer to output " +
            "layer weights:\n");
for (int h=0; h<NumHidden; h++) {
  for (int o=0; o<NumOutput; o++) {
    ps.print(GetW2(h, o) + " ");
  }
  ps.print("\n");
}
if (SpecialFlag > 0) {
  ps.println("\n# Special network data:\n");
  for (int i=0; i<SpecialFlag; i++) {
    ps.println(GetSpecial(i) + " ");
  }
  ps.println("\n");
}
ps.println("\n# Training data:\n");
for (int i=0; i<NumTraining; i++) {
   for (int j=0; j<NumInput; j++) {
      ps.print(GetInput(i,j) + " ");
   }
   ps.print("    ");
   for (int j=0; j<NumOutput; j++) {
      ps.print(GetOutput(i,j) + " ");
   }
   ps.println("");
```

```
      }
      System.out.println("Done writing to output file.");
      ps.close();
      f.close();
    } catch (Exception E) {
        System.out.println("cannot process the file " +
                            save_file_name);
    }
  }
  public static void main(String argv[]) {
    NNfile test = new NNfile("test.dat");
  }
}
```

Listing 4.8 shows an input file without weights or application-specific data. Listing 4.9 shows the results of training the network defined from the file shown in Listing 4.8 and saving the network to a new file.

Listing 4.8

```
#  Neural network data written by NNfile

3  # number of neuron layers
3  # neurons in layer 0
3  # neurons in layer 1
3  # neurons in layer 2
0  # weight flag
0  # special data flag
3  # number of training cases in file


# Training data originally in file:

-0.4 0.4 0.4    0.4 -0.4 0.4
0.4 -0.4 0.4    0.4 0.4 -0.4
0.4 0.4 -0.4    -0.4 0.4 0.4
```

Listing 4.9 is similar to Listing 4.8 except that weights have been added for a network that has been trained with the training data shown at the bottom of Listings 4.8 and 4.9.

Listing 4.9

```
#   Neural network data written by NNfile

3  # number of neuron layers
3  # neurons in layer 0
3  # neurons in layer 1
3  # neurons in layer 2
1  # weight flag
0  # special data flag
3  # number of training cases in file

# Input layer to hidden layer weights:

0.199731 -1.38554 -2.13924
-2.15951 0.269235 1.3038
1.9978 1.26893 0.811149

# Hidden layer to output layer weights:

4.59512 0.501738 -5.2624
2.60325 -3.12619 0.524894
1.7996 -4.95945 3.00359

# Training data originally in file:

-0.4 0.4 0.4    0.4 -0.4 0.4
0.4 -0.4 0.4    0.4 0.4 -0.4
0.4 0.4 -0.4    -0.4 0.4 0.4
```

Both Listings 4.8 and 4.9 show a simple neural network description file containing

- A neural network with three input, three hidden, and three output neurons
- Training data with three input and output patterns

4.4   Preprocessing neural network training data

One of the difficulties in using neural networks is preparing training data. Frequently training data needs to be hand-tuned by removing conflicting training cases. After 10 years of manually editing training cases, I decided to partially automate this process. The Java classes developed in Chapter 11 will form a tool kit for preprocessing neural network training data. It is very important to eliminate conflicting training cases that prevent the training process from completing (i.e., when the cumulative error at the output neurons approaches zero).

The training data used in this chapter was simple: a set of input and output test patterns in which the data in each input sample was simply copied to the corresponding output sample, and rotated one position to the right. In Chapters 11 and 12, we will use neural networks to recognize handwritten characters, and it will be important to properly preprocess the training data required to teach neural networks to recognize the characters represented in the training data.

Genetic Algorithms   5

Genetic algorithms are an efficient way to search large data spaces using principles from population biology. The search space is defined by the representation chosen for a *chromosome*. The information stored in chromosomes is represented by *genes*. In simulating genetic algorithms with the Java classes developed in this chapter, a gene is represented as one bit of information (or a single true/false value). In manipulating the genes in a chromosome, we use the term *locus* for representing the index of any specific gene in the chromosome; for example, if we have 50 genes in a chromosome, then the locus (index) of the genes runs from 0 to 49. In simulating genetic algorithms, we deal with a set of chromosomes, called the *population*, that all contain the same number of genes.

In formatting a genetic algorithm solution to a problem, we need a numerical *fitness function*, which takes a single argument, a chromosome, and returns a numeric fitness value. Larger fitness values indicate chromosomes that represent better solutions. A chromosome represents a single point in a problem's search space.

A *mutation* in a chromosome is a random "flipping" of a single true/false value representing a gene. For example, consider a chromosome with five genes:

```
true true false false false
```

If we have a random mutation at locus two (the third gene since we use zero-based addressing), then the resulting chromosome is

```
true true true false false
```

The *crossover* operation is used to swap genes between two chromosomes. For example, consider the following two five-gene chromosomes:

```
true true true | false false
false true true | true true
```

If we perform a crossover operation after locus two (this position is indicated with |), the chromosomes swap genetic material and end up looking like this:

```
true true true true false
false true true false false
```

5.1   An example of how genetic algorithms work

Genetic algorithms are very efficient tools for searching large spaces if we can formulate appropriate fitness functions for ranking the chromosomes in genetic populations in order of how well they represent solutions to the problems that we are trying to solve. We must also take some care in formulating the search space. We will often be searching spaces defined by non-Boolean (e.g., floating-point) data.

As a simple example, we might have a complicated function of three independent floating-point variables $F(x, y, z)$. We might want to find what is approximately the largest value of F for x, y, z in the range [0.0, 10.0]. Function F might have hundreds of terms involving transcendental functions and high-order polynomials in x, y, z. Here we are given the fitness function F to solve the problem. Assuming a generalized library for simulating genetic algorithms (like the one implemented in Section 5.2), we can find a good solution to this problem by designing a chromosome to cover the search space.

First, we must make a decision concerning how much precision we require in our answer. That is, do we want seven digits of accuracy in each of the x, y, z values of our answer (remember that we are searching for a single point in space represented by a value for $x, y,$ and z), or will three digits be enough? For this example, assume that a few digits of accuracy for each of the x, y, z coordinates is sufficient: we will store each coordinate in 10 bits (or 10 genes). Each of the three coordinates can take on an integer value from 0 to 1023. These integer values can be scaled by multiplying them by approximately 0.009775. With this quantization, our search space contains 1024 raised to the third power (which equals 1,073,741,824 points, slightly over one billion points).

In designing the format of the chromosome used to solve this problem, we require three parts to the chromosome for representing the x, y, z coordinates, each with 10 bits (or genes). The chromosome to solve this problem contains 30 genes (or bits). If the function F was fairly simple, we could simply perform an exhaustive search by evaluating this function 1,073,741,824 times looking for the largest value. For complex functions F, it is much more efficient to accept a good solution (although perhaps not the best solution) that we can calculate orders of magnitude faster using a genetic algorithm rather than using an exhaustive search.

We need to iterate over the following steps in order to find a good solution to this problem. Each iteration is called a *generation*:

- Apply mutations to a few chromosomes.
- Sort the chromosomes by fitness.
- Discard the least-fit chromosomes, replacing them with crossovers from randomly selected fit chromosomes. Do not modify the best-of-generation chromosome.

In Chapter 9, we will use a genetic algorithm to adjust in real time the parameters for controlling sprite objects in an arcade game. The control parameters will continually evolve during a game to adapt to a player's strategy or mode of play.

5.2 Implementation of a genetic algorithm package in Java

The description in the previous section of how to formulate a search problem as a simulation of a genetic algorithm also served as a preliminary requirements specification for the genetic algorithm Java classes that we will implement in this section. Further requirements for this library are the following:

- Base class for genetic algorithms that hides the details of performing mutation and crossover operations on chromosomes, and for sorting and selecting chromosomes based on fitness
- Mechanism for extending this base class to provide a problem-specific fitness function
- Control mechanism for producing many generations of chromosomes

There will be two expensive operations, in general, in simulating genetic algorithms: applying the fitness function many times and sorting the population by fitness after each generation.

Figure 5.1 shows the Booch class diagram for the Java class **mwa.ai.genetic.Genetic**.

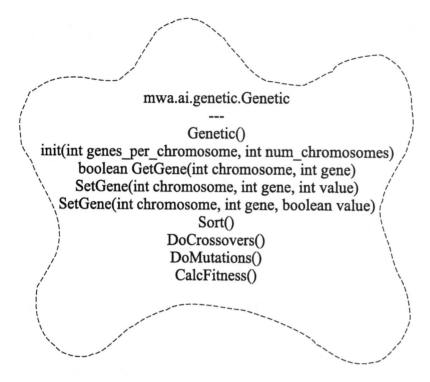

mwa.ai.genetic.Genetic

Genetic()
init(int genes_per_chromosome, int num_chromosomes)
boolean GetGene(int chromosome, int gene)
SetGene(int chromosome, int gene, int value)
SetGene(int chromosome, int gene, boolean value)
Sort()
DoCrossovers()
DoMutations()
CalcFitness()

Figure 5.1   Booch class diagram for class **Genetic**

Listing 5.1 shows the implementation of the class **mwa.ai.genetic.Genetic**. The class constructor **Genetic( )** sets the number of chromosomes and the chromosome size to zero. The method **init(int genes_per_chromosome, int num_chromosomes)** defines the population by specifying the size of each chromosome (the number of genes per chromosome) and the number of chromosomes. Individual chromosomes are stored as instances of the class **java.util.BitSet**. The **BitSet** class provides a compact representation for storing the Boolean values that represent individual genes in our implementation of genetic algorithms. The method **boolean GetGene(int chromosome, int gene)** fetches the value of a gene from a specified chromosome in the population. The methods **Set-Gene(int chromosome, int gene, int value)** and **SetGene(int chromosome, int gene, boolean value)** are access methods used to access private class data (i.e., the **Genes[]** array of **BitSet** objects). The method **Sort( )** reorders the chromosome so that the most-fit chromosomes are located at the beginning of the array (i.e., at index 0, 1, etc.). The method **DoCrossovers( )** discards the least-fit chromosomes, replacing them with crossovers from the most-fit chromosomes in the population. The method **DoMutations( )** selects a single gene from one chromosome in the population and "flips" its value. The method **void CalcFitness( )** should be overridden in extended (derived) classes to reassign the fitness value of each chromosome based on a problem-specific   fitness function. Listing 5.2 contains an example of a problem-specific fitness function.

Listing 5.1

```
// Genetic Algorithm Java classes
//
// Copyright 1996, Mark Watson.  All rights reserved.

package mwa.ai.genetic;

import java.util.*;

public class Genetic extends Object {

    protected int NumGenes;  // number of genes per chromosome
    protected int NumChrom;  // number of chromosomes
    protected BitSet Genes[];
    protected float Fitness[];

    public Genetic() {
        System.out.println("In dummy Genetic constructor");
        NumGenes = NumChrom = 0;
    }

    public void init(int g, int c) {
        System.out.println("In Genetic::init(...)");
        Genes = new BitSet[c];
        for (int i=0; i<c; i++) {
           Genes[i] = new BitSet(g);
           for (int j=0; j<g; j++) {
               if (Math.random() < 0.5) Genes[i].set(j);
           }
        }
        NumChrom = c;
        NumGenes = g;
        Fitness = new float[c];
        for (int f=0; f<c; f++)          Fitness[f] = -999;
        Sort();
     }
    public boolean GetGene(int chromosome, int gene) {
        return Genes[chromosome].get(gene);
     }
```

```java
public void SetGene(int chromosome, int gene, int value) {
    if (value == 0)  Genes[chromosome].clear(gene);
    else             Genes[chromosome].set(gene);
}
public void SetGene(int chromosome, int gene, boolean value) {
    if (value)  Genes[chromosome].set(gene);
    else        Genes[chromosome].clear(gene);
}
public void Sort() {
   BitSet btemp;
   for (int c=0; c<NumChrom; c++) {
       for (int d=(NumChrom - 2); d>=c; d--) {
           if (Fitness[d] < Fitness[d+1]) {
               btemp = Genes[d];
               float x = Fitness[d];
               Genes[d] = Genes[d+1];
               Fitness[d] = Fitness[d+1];
               Genes[d+1] = btemp;
               Fitness[d+1] = x;
           }
       }
   }
}
public void DoCrossovers()  {
  for (int m=0; m<NumChrom/2; m++) {
      CopyGene(m + NumChrom/2, m);
  }

  // copy the 2 best genes so that their
  // genetic material is replicated frequently:
  for (int i=0; i<NumGenes; i++) {
    SetGene(NumChrom - 1, i, GetGene(0, i));
    SetGene(NumChrom - 2, i, GetGene(0, i));
    SetGene(NumChrom - 3, i, GetGene(0, i));
    SetGene(NumChrom - 4, i, GetGene(1, i));
    SetGene(NumChrom - 5, i, GetGene(1, i));
  }

  int num = NumChrom / 4;
  for (int i=0; i<num; i++) {
    int c1 = 2 + (int)((NumChrom - 2) * Math.random() * 0.99);
    int c2 = 2 + (int)((NumChrom - 2) * Math.random() * 0.99);
    if (c1 != c2) {
        int locus = 2 + (int)((NumGenes - 3) * Math.random());
```

```java
            for (int g=0; g<locus; g++) {
                boolean temp = GetGene(c1, i);
                SetGene(c1, i, GetGene(c2, i));
                SetGene(c2, i, temp);
            }
        }
    }
}
// 'to' and 'from' are 'sorted' indices:
private void CopyGene(int to, int from) {
    for (int i=0; i<NumGenes; i++)
        if (GetGene(from, i))  SetGene(to, i, 1);
        else                   SetGene(to, i, 0);
}
public void DoMutations() {
    int c = 2 + (int)((NumChrom - 2) * Math.random() * 0.95);
    int g = (int)(NumGenes * Math.random() * 0.95);
    if (GetGene(c, g))  SetGene(c, g, 0);
    else                SetGene(c, g, 1);
}
// Override the following function in subclasses:
public void CalcFitness() {
}
}
```

Listing 5.2 shows a test applet for the **mwa.ai.genetic.Genetic** class. A new class **MyGenetic** extends the class **Genetic** shown in Listing 5.1. The method **CalcFitness( )** has been overridden to sort chromosomes based on the number of "true" valued genes. A **main( )** method processes 50 generations.

Listing 5.2

```java
// File: textGenetic.java
// This file contains a text-mode test program
// for class Genetic.

package mwa.ai.genetic;


public class testGenetic {

    static public void main(String args[]) {
```

```
        MyGenetic G = new MyGenetic();
        G.init(30,15);  // 30 genes/chrom.   15 chrom in pop.
        for (int i=0; i<51; i++) {
            G.CalcFitness();
            G.Sort();
            if ((i%5)==0) {
                System.out.println("Generation " + i);
                G.Print();
            }
            G.DoCrossovers();
            G.DoMutations();
        }
    }
}


class MyGenetic extends Genetic {
    MyGenetic() {
        System.out.println("Entered MyGenetic::MyGenetic()\n");
    }
    public void init(int g, int c) {
        super.init(g, c);
    }
    public void CalcFitness() {
        for (int i=0; i<NumChrom; i++) {
            float fitness = 0.0f;
            for (int j=0; j<NumGenes; j++)  {
                if (GetGene(i, j)) fitness += 1.0f;
            }
            Fitness[i] = fitness;
        }
    }
    public void Print() {
        for (int i=0; i<2; i++) {
            System.out.print("Fitness for chromosome ");
            System.out.print(i);
            System.out.print(" is ");
            System.out.println(Fitness[i]);
        }
    }
}
```

Listing 5.3 shows the result of running the sample applet shown in Listing 5.2. The population contains 15 chromosomes. Each chromosome contains 30 genes. The fitness function maximizes the number of genes with a Boolean true value.

Listing 5.3

```
In dummy Genetic constructor
Entered MyGenetic::MyGenetic()

In Genetic::init(...)
Generation 0
Fitness for chromosome 0 is 18
Fitness for chromosome 12 is 17
Fitness for chromosome 2 is 16
Fitness for chromosome 3 is 16
Generation 5
Fitness for chromosome 0 is 18
Fitness for chromosome 7 is 18
Fitness for chromosome 10 is 18
Fitness for chromosome 11 is 18
Generation 10
Fitness for chromosome 1 is 20
Fitness for chromosome 10 is 20
Fitness for chromosome 11 is 20
Fitness for chromosome 6 is 20
Generation 15
Fitness for chromosome 13 is 21
Fitness for chromosome 11 is 21
Fitness for chromosome 1 is 20
Fitness for chromosome 10 is 20
Generation 20
Fitness for chromosome 5 is 22
Fitness for chromosome 13 is 21
Fitness for chromosome 11 is 21
Fitness for chromosome 9 is 21
Generation 25
Fitness for chromosome 2 is 23
Fitness for chromosome 10 is 23
Fitness for chromosome 5 is 22
Fitness for chromosome 1 is 22
Generation 30
Fitness for chromosome 2 is 23
Fitness for chromosome 10 is 23
Fitness for chromosome 6 is 23
Fitness for chromosome 7 is 23
Generation 35
```

```
Fitness for chromosome 2 is 23
Fitness for chromosome 10 is 23
Fitness for chromosome 7 is 23
Fitness for chromosome 13 is 23
Generation 40
Fitness for chromosome 8 is 24
Fitness for chromosome 0 is 24
Fitness for chromosome 9 is 24
Fitness for chromosome 11 is 24
Generation 45
Fitness for chromosome 8 is 24
Fitness for chromosome 0 is 24
Fitness for chromosome 9 is 24
Fitness for chromosome 11 is 24
Generation 50
Fitness for chromosome 4 is 26
Fitness for chromosome 5 is 25
Fitness for chromosome 2 is 25
Fitness for chromosome 6 is 25
```

The fitness values printed in Listing 5.3 represent the number of genes in each chromosome with a "true" Boolean value. This simple problem is adequate to test the **Genetic** class. We will use the **Genetic** class in Chapter 9 for an adaptive real-time control application, and in Chapter 12 to optimize training data for neural networks.

Natural Language Processing 6

Understanding natural language certainly requires both knowledge of a human language and the ability to apply rules of grammar for that language. Most natural language processing (NLP) systems work by matching patterns with little or no knowledge of what processed text really means. The Java classes developed in this chapter are a compromise; they use both conceptual dependency theory (Schank and Riesbeck 1981) and some real-world knowledge. These Java classes are practical to use as components of larger systems.

6.1 Types of natural language processing systems

The simplest NLP systems are often constructed using finite-state transition networks (FSTNs). Finite-state transition networks can be used to recognize sentences but are not adequate to build useful NLP systems. Recursive transition networks (RTNs) extend the idea of using finite-state machines by adding the ability to use multiple named FSTNs that can call each other, just as methods in Java programs can call each other. Augmented transition networks (ATNs) add the ability to add extra transition tests and register variables to RTNs. ATN systems were widely used in the 1970s and early 1980s as a "programming language" for building NLP systems. William Woods wrote a well-known NLP system using ATNs that competently parsed English language questions regarding moon rocks and formulated replies.

Using ATNs is similar to using a conventional programming language. A major drawback of ATN-based NLP systems is that ATNs recognize patterns in text using a depth-first search. An improvement on ATN parsers are *chart parsers*, which perform a breadth-first search. NLP research in the last decade has emphasized the addition of real-world knowledge to NLP systems.

6.2 Conceptual dependency theory

The NLP Java classes that I develop in this chapter are loosely based on the work of Roger Schank, Christopher Riesbeck, and their students. I give them credit for inspiring my parser, while I take responsibility for the limitations of my system. Conceptual dependency (CD) uses a small number of semantic primitives to represent concepts. We will use four semantic primitives in the parser developed in Section 6.3:

- **atrans**: transfer of possession
- **ptrans**: physically move some object from one place to another
- **propel**: apply a force to set in motion
- **mtrans**: transfer of information

Consider the sentences "Mark gave a book to Carol" and "Carol received a book from Mark." The semantic meaning of these sentences is identical: "Mark transferred possession of a book from Mark to Carol." Ideally, any NLP system that we develop should capture the meaning of these two sentences and produce the same output for either sentence. ATN-based NLP parsers would produce very different results for these two example sentences; for example, a typical ATN-based parser would find that the subject would be "Mark" in the first sentence and the subject would be "Carol" in the second sentence. As we will see, CD-based parsers have the ability to produce output based on underlying meaning rather than word choice and sentence structure.

The drawback to CD-based parsers is the complexity of the lexicon. In ATN and chart parsers, individual words in a lexicon might be simply tagged with possible parts of speech; for example, the word "run" might be tagged as a verb ("I run to work") and a noun ("I built a dog run"). CD-based parsers use lexicons with complex entries for each word. Verbs are represented by frame data structures with slot/value pairs for

- actor—the person or entity performing an action
- action—action represented by a CD primitive
- recipient—specifies who is affected by an action
- location—where the action takes place
- object—optional object involved in the action
- time—optional time that the action occurred
- tense—verb tense: past, present, or future

The parser that is implemented in Section 6.3 produces the following frame data structure when processing either of the two sample sentences:

- actor: Mark
- action: **atrans**
- recipient: Carol
- object: book
- tense: past

We will use CD frame data structures to specify a verb in the lexicon. When a CD-based parser processes a verb, it copies the frame data structure representing the verb and attempts to use the remaining words in the sentence to fill in as many of the undefined variables as possible in the frame. Variables appear in slot values as a question mark, or a variable name starting with a question mark. See Section 6.6 for examples showing the use of matching variables in frames.

6.3 Design of a semantic-based natural language processing system

The requirements for the Java NLP **mwa.ai.nlp.Parser** class implemented in the next section are the following:

- Built-in support for a small number of frequently used words and concepts
- Ability to extend the functionality of the **mwa.ai.nlp.Parser** class by extending it with new subclasses that add knowledge of additional words and concepts
- "Network readiness" to support building distributed systems

Figure 6.1 shows the Booch class diagram for the Java NLP classes. The class **mwa.ai.nlp.ParseObject** is derived from the class **mwa.data.AIframe**. The class **mwa.ai.nlp.ParseObject** is used to contain the results of processing one sentence. An instance of the class **mwa.ai.nlp.Parser** contains an array of instances of class **mwa.ai.nlp.ParseObject** for processing multiple sentences. Knowledge of words in the parsing lexicon is hard-coded into the implementation of the class **mwa.ai.nlp.Parser**, which contains a small lexicon for test purposes. The class **mwa.ai.nlp.Parser** will be extended by writing derived classes that add specific additional words to lexicons tailored for specific applications. The class **mwa.ai.nlp.Parser** will be extended in Chapter 13 to support a program for answering questions dealing with ancient and medieval history.

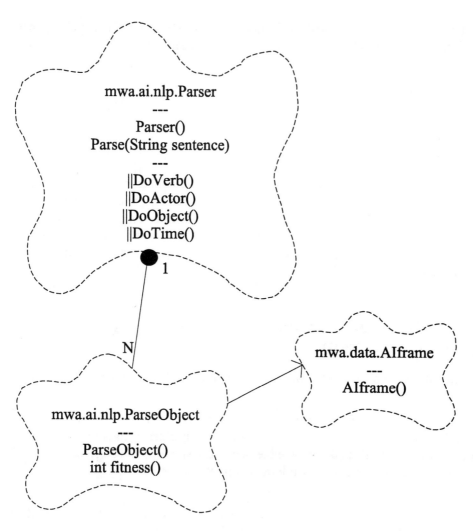

Figure 6.1   Booch class diagram for Java NLP classes

6.4   Implementation of a Java package for natural language processing

Listing 6.1 shows the implementation of the Java class **mwa.ai.nlp.Parser**. The class **mwa.ai.nlp.Parser** defines a static constant **MAX_CDS**, which is the maximum number of parsed sentences that a **Parse** object can hold. This constant value is set to sixteen. The test programs in this chapter only parse one sentence for each instance of class **mwa.ai.nlp.Parser**. The ability to handle many input sentences is provided so that the

mwa.ai.nlp.Parser class can be extended to handle discourse processing (see Section 6.6). Each parsed sentence is stored in an instance of **mwa.ai.nlp.ParseObject** (a class derived from **mwa.data.AIframe**), which is implemented in Listing 6.2.

The **mwa.ai.nlp.Parser** class constructor takes no arguments and simply initializes an array of **ParseObject[NUM_CDS]**. This array is public so that applications using an instance of any class derived from class **mwa.ai.nlp.Parser** can access the data for each processed sentence. Sentences can be parsed by calling the method **mwa.ai.nlp.Parser.Parse(String sentence)** after the constructor is called. Method **mwa.ai.nlp.Parser.Parse(String sentence)** calls the following four utility methods: **DoVerb( )**, **DoActor( )**, **DoObject( )**, and **DoTime( )**.

The class **mwa.ai.nlp.Parser** has a small built-in lexicon (which is encoded in these four utility methods) for testing purposes. We will see later that the parser's lexicon is extended by subclassing **Parser**, redefining these four utility methods. In derived (extended) classes, the **DoVerb, DoActor, DoObject**, and **DoTime** methods in class **Parser** should call the methods with the same names in the superclass in addition to any additional processing that they do (to use also the lexicon encoded in the base class). Each of these four utility methods can redefine the values of any slots in the **ParseObject** (derived from class **mwa.data.AIframe**) object used to hold the results of the parsing operation on the current sentence being processed.

The simple lexicon that is built into the class **mwa.ai.nlp.Parser** includes support for the verbs *give, gave, receive*, and *received*; the nouns *book* and *ball*; and the adjective *yesterday*.

Listing 6.1

```
// Conceptual Dependency Natural Language Processing Java classes
//
// Copyright 1996, Mark Watson.  All rights reserved.

package mwa.ai.nlp;

import java.util.*;
import java.io.*;

import mwa.gui.GUI;
import mwa.data.*;

public class Parser {

  // For debug output:
  GUI MyGUI = null;
```

```java
// Handle up to 16 sentences:
static final int MAX_CDS=16;
public ParseObject sentences[];
public int num_sentences;

String Words[] = null;
int NumWords;

public Parser() {
  sentences = new ParseObject[MAX_CDS];
  for (int i=0; i<MAX_CDS; i++) {
      sentences[i] = new ParseObject();
  }
  // sentence count is incremented when a new
  // test CD form is created:
  num_sentences = 0;
  Words = new String[20];
}

public void Parse(String sentence) {

  try {
    GetWords(sentence);
  } catch (Exception E) {
      System.out.println("Cannot process:" + sentence);
  }
  for (int i=0; i<NumWords; i++) {
      System.out.println("Word[" + i + "]=" + Words[i]);
      if (MyGUI!=null) {
          MyGUI.P("Word[" + i + "]=" + Words[i] + "\n");
      }
  }
  DoVerb();
  DoActor();
  DoObject();
  DoTime();

  num_sentences++;
}
protected void DoVerb() {
  for (int i=0; i<NumWords; i++) {
      if (Words[i].equals("give")) {
          sentences[num_sentences].put("tense",
                             new AIframedata("present"));
```

```java
        sentences[num_sentences].put("action",
                                new AIframedata("atrans"));
      if (MyGUI!=null) {
        MyGUI.P("Action: " + "atrans\n");
      }
      if (i>0) {
          if (Words[i-1].equals("will")) {
              sentences[num_sentences].put("tense",
                                new AIframedata("future"));
            if (MyGUI!=null) {
              MyGUI.P("  (future tense)\n");
            }
          }
      }
    }
    if (Words[i].equals("gave")) {
      sentences[num_sentences].put("tense",
                                new AIframedata("past"));
      sentences[num_sentences].put("action",
                                new AIframedata("atrans"));
      if (MyGUI!=null) {
        MyGUI.P("Action: " + "atrans (past tense)\n");
      }
    }
    if (Words[i].equals("received")) {
      sentences[num_sentences].put("tense",
                                new AIframedata("past"));
      sentences[num_sentences].put("action",
                                new AIframedata("atrans"));
      sentences[num_sentences].ReverseVerb=1;
      if (MyGUI!=null) {
        MyGUI.P("Action: " + "atrans (past tense) " +
                "(verb reversed)\n");
      }
    }
    if (Words[i].equals("receive")) {
      sentences[num_sentences].put("tense",
                                new AIframedata("present"));
      sentences[num_sentences].put("action",
                                new AIframedata("atrans"));
      if (i>0) {
          if (Words[i-1].equals("will")) {
              sentences[num_sentences].put("tense",
                                new AIframedata("future"));
```

```java
            }
          }
        }
      }
    }
    protected void DoActor() {
      // First fill in actor:
      if (sentences[num_sentences].ReverseVerb==0) {
        for (int i=0; i<NumWords; i++) {
          System.out.println("  processing " + Words[i]);
          if (ProperName(Words[i])) {
            AIframedata fd =
                sentences[num_sentences].get("actor");
            if (fd.string.equals("?")) {
              sentences[num_sentences].put("actor",
                                new AIframedata(Words[i]));
              if (MyGUI!=null) {
                MyGUI.P("Actor: " + Words[i] + "\n");
              }
              break;
            }
          }
        }
      } else {
        for (int i=NumWords-1; i>=0; i--) {
          System.out.println("  processing " + Words[i]);
          if (ProperName(Words[i])) {
            AIframedata fd =
                sentences[num_sentences].get("actor");
            if (fd.string.equals("?")) {
              sentences[num_sentences].put("actor",
                                new AIframedata(Words[i]));
              if (MyGUI!=null) {
                MyGUI.P("Actor: " + Words[i] + "\n");
              }
              break;
            }
          }
        }
      }
      // Then fill in recipient:
      if (sentences[num_sentences].ReverseVerb==1) {
        for (int i=0; i<NumWords; i++) {
          System.out.println("  processing " + Words[i]);
```

```java
      if (ProperName(Words[i])) {
        AIframedata fd =
              sentences[num_sentences].get("recipient");
        if (fd.string.equals("?")) {
          sentences[num_sentences].put("recipient",
                            new AIframedata(Words[i]));
          if (MyGUI!=null) {
            MyGUI.P("Recipient: " + Words[i] + "\n");
          }
          break;
        }
      }
    }
  } else {
    for (int i=NumWords-1; i>=0; i--) {
      System.out.println("  processing " + Words[i]);
      if (ProperName(Words[i])) {
        AIframedata fd =
          sentences[num_sentences].get("recipient");
        if (fd.string.equals("?")) {
          sentences[num_sentences].put("recipient",
                            new AIframedata(Words[i]));
          if (MyGUI!=null) {
            MyGUI.P("Recipient: " + Words[i] + "\n");
          }
          break;
        }
      }
    }
  }
}
static String objects[] = {"book", "ball"};
static int num_objects=2;
protected void DoObject() {
  for (int i=0; i<NumWords; i++) {
    if (InList(Words[i], objects, num_objects)) {
      AIframedata fd =
          sentences[num_sentences].get("object");
      if (fd.string.equals("?")) {
        sentences[num_sentences].put("object",
                            new AIframedata(Words[i]));
        if (MyGUI!=null) {
          MyGUI.P("Object: " + Words[i] + "\n");
        }
```

```java
                break;
          }
       }
    }
  }
  protected void DoTime() {
    for (int i=0; i<NumWords; i++) {
      if (Words[i].equals("yesterday")) {
        AIframedata fd =
            sentences[num_sentences].get("time");
         if (fd.string.equals("?")) {
            sentences[num_sentences].put("time",
                            new AIframedata(-24.0f));
            if (MyGUI!=null) {
               MyGUI.P("Time: -24.0\n");
            }
            break;
         }
      }
    }
  }

  protected boolean InList(String s, String lst[], int num) {
    for (int i=0; i<num; i++) {
        if (s.equals(lst[i])) return true;
    }
    return false;
  }


  protected void GetWords(String sentence)
             throws IOException, StreamFormatException {
    StringTokenizer st;
    st = new StringTokenizer(sentence);
    NumWords=0;
    // Fill in the Word array:
    process:
    while (st.hasMoreTokens()) {
      System.out.println("Top of while loop");
          Words[NumWords]=new String(st.nextToken());
          NumWords++;
    }
    System.out.println("Done with while loop");
    if (NumWords==0)
      throw new StreamFormatException(st.toString());
```

```
    }
    protected boolean ProperName(String name) {
      boolean ret = false;
      if (name.equals("Mark"))  ret = true;
      if (name.equals("Carol")) ret = true;
      if (ret) {
          if (MyGUI!=null) {
              MyGUI.P("   proper name: " + name + "\n");
          }
      }
      return ret;
    }

};


class StreamFormatException extends Exception {
  public StreamFormatException(String str) {
    super(str);
  }
}
```

The utility class **StreamFormatException** is defined at the end of Listing 6.1. See Appendix A for a discussion of Java exception handling.

Listing 6.2 shows the implementation of Java class **mwa.ai.nlp.ParseObject**, which is derived from (or extended from) the class **mwa.data.AIframe**. The class constructor calls the superclass constructor to create a new **AIframe** object named **CDframe<instance count>** (i.e., the first instance is named **CDframe0**, the second **CDframe1**, etc.). It is important to remember that an **mwa.ai.nlp.ParseObject** is a type (subclass) of **mwa.data.AIframe**. The **mwa.ai.nlp.ParseObject** constructor adds the following slots to itself:

- actor
- action
- recipient
- location
- object
- time
- tense

The method **fitness( )** returns an integer count of the number of slots that have been assigned a value.

Listing 6.2

```
// Conceptual Dependency Natural Language Processing Java classes
//
// Copyright 1996, Mark Watson.  All rights reserved.

package mwa.ai.nlp;

import mwa.data.*;

public class ParseObject extends mwa.data.AIframe {

 static public int instanceCount=0;
   ParseObject() {
    super("CDframe" + instanceCount++);
    put("actor", new AIframedata("?"));
    put("action", new AIframedata("?"));
    put("recipient", new AIframedata("?"));
    put("location", new AIframedata("?"));
    put("object", new AIframedata("?"));
    put("time", new AIframedata("?"));
    put("tense", new AIframedata("?"));
    ReverseVerb=0; // assume actor before verb in sentence
  }
  int fitness() {
    int ret_value=0;
    if (goodValue("actor")) ret_value++;
    if (goodValue("action")) ret_value++;
    if (goodValue("location")) ret_value++;
    if (goodValue("object")) ret_value++;
    if (goodValue("time")) ret_value++;
    return ret_value;
  }

  boolean goodValue(String key) {
    AIframedata fdata = get(key);
    if (fdata.type==AIframedata.STRING) {
        if (fdata.string != "?") {
            return true;
        }
    }
    return false;
```

```
    }
  public int ReverseVerb;
}
```

Listing 6.3 shows the implementation of a short Java applet to test the NLP parsing classes. The class **mwa.gui.GUI** is extended to define the class **mwa.ai.nlp.testNLP**. An instance of class **mwa.ai.nlp.Parser** is created in the **init( )** method. This instance of class **mwa.ai.nlp.Parser** can be used repetitively by typing sentences into the input text file and clicking the "Run" button to execute the **doRunButton( )** method of class **Parser**. Since the **Parser** object was constructed with a reference to the applet's instance of class **testNLP** (derived from **GUI**), the **Parser** object is able to write the results of the parsing operation directly into this applet's scrolling output text field.

Listing 6.3

```
// Test NLP Java classes
//
// Copyright 1996, Mark Watson.  All rights reserved.

package mwa.ai.nlp;

import java.awt.*;

import mwa.gui.GUI;

public class testNLP extends GUI {

    mwa.ai.nlp.Parser MyParser;

    public String getAppletInfo() {
        return "NLP demo by Mark Watson";
    }

    public void init() {
        NoGraphics=true;
        BigText=1;
        NoResetButton=true;
        super.init();

        MyParser = new mwa.ai.nlp.Parser();
        MyParser.MyGUI = this;
        MyParser.MyGUI.SetInputText(
```

```
                "Mark gave Carol a book yesterday");
    }

    public void paintToDoubleBuffer(Graphics g) {
        g.drawString("NLP demo", 10, 10);
        setForeground(Color.red);
        g.setColor(getForeground());
        g.drawLine(10, 10, 100, 150);
    }

    public void doRunButton() {
        MyParser.Parse(GetInputText());
    }
    public void doResetButton() {
        ClearOutput();
    }
}
```

Figures 6.2 and 6.3 show the sample program in Listing 6.3. Figure 6.2 shows the results of parsing the sentence "Mark gave Carol a book yesterday." Figure 6.3 shows the results of parsing the sentence "Yesterday Carol received a book from Mark." The results of the parse are identical in Figures 6.2 and 6.3.

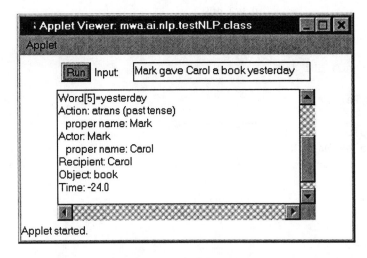

Figure 6.2   Test program for the class **mwa.ai.nlp.NLP**. The sentence "Mark gave Carol a book yesterday" is parsed.

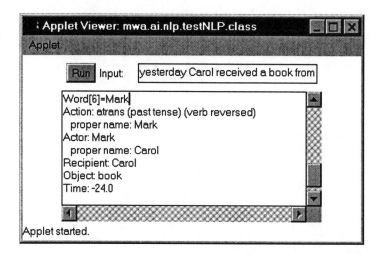

Figure 6.3   Test program for the class **mwa.ai.nlp.NLP**. The sentence "Yesterday Carol received a book from Mark" is parsed.

6.5 Extending the vocabulary of the Java-based natural language parser

The Java NLP classes implemented in Section 6.3 and tested in Section 6.4 contain a small built-in lexicon. We will extend the class **mwa.ai.nlp.Parser** in this section to demonstrate how to add additional words and capability to the lexicon. The Java class **Parser** should be extended to support specific topics of conversation or types of text material.

Listing 6.4 contains a small test program similar to that seen in Listing 6.3 except the references to the class **Parser** have been changed to the new class **testParser**, which is defined at the end of Listing 6.4. The base class methods **DoVerb( )** and **DoObject( )** have been redefined.

Both of these redefined methods call the methods with the same name to support the lexicon entries encoded in the base class versions of **DoVerb** and **DoObject**. The following new verbs are added to the lexicon supported by the new test class **testParser** that is derived from **mwa.ai.nlp.Parser**: *move*, *moved*, *drive*, and *drove*. The following nouns have been added to the lexicon: *car*, *money*, and *ball*.

Listing 6.4

```
// NLP Java classes: test program and new subclass of Parser
```

```
//
// Copyright 1996, Mark Watson.  All rights reserved.

package mwa.ai.nlp;

import mwa.gui.GUI;
import mwa.data.*;

public class testNLP2 extends GUI {

    // use subclass defined at end of this file
    testParser MyParser;

    public String getAppletInfo() {
        return "NLP demo by Mark Watson";
    }

    public void init() {
       NoGraphics=true;
       BigText=1;
       NoResetButton=true;
       super.init();

       MyParser = new testParser();
       MyParser.MyGUI = this;
       MyParser.MyGUI.SetInputText(
           "Mark gave Carol a book yesterday");
    }

    public void doRunButton() {
        MyParser.Parse(GetInputText());
    }
    public void doResetButton() {
        ClearOutput();
    }
}

//
//      Extend the base class mwa.ai.nlp.Parser to
//      add a few new verbs and object names:
//

class testParser extends Parser {
  protected void DoVerb() {
```

```java
super.DoVerb();  // FIRST CALL SUPERCLASS FUNCTION
    for (int i=0; i<NumWords; i++) {
        if (Words[i].equals("move") ||
            Words[i].equals("drive"))
        {
            sentences[num_sentences].put("tense",
                                new AIframedata("present"));
            sentences[num_sentences].put("action",
                                new AIframedata("ptrans"));
            if (MyGUI!=null) {
                MyGUI.P("Action: " + "ptrans\n");
            }
            if (i>0) {
                if (Words[i-1].equals("will")) {
                    sentences[num_sentences].put("tense",
                                new AIframedata("future"));
                    if (MyGUI!=null) {
                        MyGUI.P("  (future tense)\n");
                    }
                }
            }
        }
        if (Words[i].equals("moved") ||
            Words[i].equals("drove"))
        {
            sentences[num_sentences].put("tense",
                                new AIframedata("past"));
            sentences[num_sentences].put("action",
                                new AIframedata("ptrans"));
            if (MyGUI!=null) {
                MyGUI.P("Action: " + "ptrans (past tense)\n");
            }
        }
    }
}

static String objects[] = {"car", "money", "ball"};
static int num_objects=3;
protected void DoObject() {
    super.DoObject();  // FIRST CALL SUPERCLASS FUNCTION
    for (int i=0; i<NumWords; i++) {
        if (InList(Words[i], objects, num_objects)) {
            AIframedata fd =
                sentences[num_sentences].get("object");
```

```
    if (fd.string.equals("?")) {
        sentences[num_sentences].put("object",
                                new AIframedata(Words[i]));
        if (MyGUI!=null) {
            MyGUI.P("Object: " + Words[i] + "\n");
        }
        break;
    }
  }
 }
}
}
```

6.6   Scripts

A script is a sequence of CD frames that represents a scenario. Scripts form a basis for both understanding discourse (i.e., a sequence of sentences) and help fill in "default" or real-world information. For example, consider the following two sentences: "Mark went to the store" and "He bought a book."

A script that might help process this text might look like the following (variables start with a question mark):

```
Script: purchase_at_store

    Frame 1:    actor: ?shopper
                action: ptrans
                object: ?shopper
                location: store
    Frame 2:    actor: ?shopper
                action: atrans
                object: money
                recipient: store_owner
                location: store
    Frame 3:    actor: store_owner
                action: atrans
                object: ?purchased_object
                recipient: ?shopper
                location: store
```

These three frames represent a sequence of three common actions in the process of going to the store. In English, these three frames mean the following:

- A shopper moves himself to the location of the store.

- The shopper transfers the possession of money from himself to the store owner.
- The store owner transfers possession of some purchased object from himself to the shopper.

Often we leave out information in our discourse that people listening to us fill in based on shared common experiences.

In matching the two input sentences to the three frames in the script, the following variables are assigned values:

- ?shopper = Mark
- ?purchased_object = book

It is not unreasonable to expect a CD-based discourse processor to match the two input sentences (after parsing to CD frames) to this script (out of perhaps hundreds of available scripts) and to answer questions about the two input sentences like

- What did Mark give to the store owner?
- Where did the store owner give Mark a book?
- Where did Mark go to buy a book?
- What did Mark buy at the store?

Discourse processing is a difficult problem. It requires a CD-based lexicon with word entries appropriate for the topic(s) of discourse and a set of scripts that cover the expected situations discussed. It is left as a difficult exercise to build a discourse processing system, but the Java parser developed in Section 6.3 supports parsing a sequence of sentences. Instances of the class **mwa.data.AIframe** can be used to store scripts.

AI Agents 7

Software agents automate tasks that otherwise we would have to do ourselves. What distinguishes software agents from other utility software programs is both the ability to perform in distributed computing environments and the ability to supply some domain knowledge to automating tasks for users.

There are two types of Java classes for building agents that we will discuss in this chapter: classes for distributed cooperating agents and for data collection agents that run on a local machine and automate fetching information from public services like the World Wide Web and electronic mail. This chapter deals with Intranet and Internet utility libraries rather than AI techniques and specific implementations of agents. Several of the programs developed in the third part of this book will add "intelligent" behavior to the Java class libraries developed in this chapter for providing communication infrastructure. In Chapter 13, we will use the utilities developed in this chapter to build a distributed natural language query system. In Chapter 14, we will use other utilities developed in this chapter to build a customized Internet search agent.

There is an industry standard methodology for sharing data objects in distributed systems. The Object Management Group (OMG) is a nonprofit consortium created in 1989. The OMG promotes the theory and practice of object technology in distributed computing environments. The Object Management Architecture (OMA) is a high-level plan for building distributed environments. The most important component of the OMA is the Object Request Broker (ORB). An ORB manages all communication between components of a distributed system. Most importantly, ORBs allow different programs in large distributed systems to run on different types of computers. There are several public domain and commercial Java-compatible ORBs. If you are interested, you can search the World Wide Web using the keywords "ORB Java."

There are several publicly available tools for handling object storage and remote procedure calls in the Java language. We will implement a simple set of tools for object management for the purpose of discussion and to support the project applications developed in Chapters 13 and 14. Most of the class libraries and test program examples in this chapter are useful for implementing data collection agents that run on a local machine and access remote data.

Distributed agents are cooperating programs that can execute on any computers connected on a network. The current Java language definition does not allow passing data with Java applets across a network. Furthermore, because of security concerns, we will not assume that agent-based applets can write data to local disk files. We will develop Java classes that provide an ORB-like server and client interfaces to store objects that are accessible by any Java application. Our simple ORB will maintain the following data for each active object:

- Unique object name
- Single instance of an **mwa.data.AIFrame** object to store an object's state

It is important to note that an ORB provides for transport and sharing of arbitrary objects; the **mwa.agent.AIframeServer** class that we develop in this chapter is limited to storing and to allowing the sharing of **mwa.data.AIframe** objects. An ORB also allows methods to execute on remote data objects. The example classes developed in this chapter do not support remote method calling. Sun Microsystems is currently writing a specification for remote method invocation (RMI); if you are interested, you can search the World Wide Web using the keywords "Java RMI."

7.1   AI agents: current and future capabilities

A hundred years ago most people thought the idea of traveling quickly around the world by flying to be an impossible fantasy. It is dangerous to bet against technology. Still, building artificially intelligent systems is much more difficult than engineering a new type of vehicle because human thought and intelligence cannot be understood and measured like physical objects obeying Newtonian physics. Creative thought is not a simple statistical process that can be understood like applying thermodynamics to model the large-scale behavior of hot gasses. Sciences like psychology, biophysics, computer science, cybernetics, and complexity theory allow us to use different points of view to start to understand how it might be possible to build artificial intelligence that is capable of creative thought. Will there be artificially intelligent agents that help us with almost every aspect of our lives, adapting to our own personalities and requirements? I think that there will be truly intelligent artificial agents in the distant future.

What is possible with the technology of today? I believe that there are at least three factors that will make it economically possible to build agents that help us in day-to-day business, technical, entertainment, and even social activities (e.g., by helping us find other people who share our interests):

- Rapid growth of and access to the Internet
- Inability to find useful information using conventional keyword searching of text on the Internet
- A basic shift from an energy-dominated economy to information-dominated economies

Technology does not usually develop without a need, and there is certainly a need for more intelligent agents to help us cope with huge quantities of raw information (Negroponte 1995). The organization of knowledge is often more valuable than the information itself.

I think that some of the technologies that will be successfully applied to the construction of agents in the next few years are the following (Watson 1996b):

- Natural language processing experts that have lexicons built specifically to support individual areas of interest (e.g., expert agents for processing text dealing with music, films, or mechanical engineering)
- Higher network bandwidth to provide cheaper access to raw information
- Universal software interfaces to use knowledge components developed by other people

I hope that the material in this chapter and the example application in Chapter 14 will provide you with a good start building custom agents to automate personal information processing systems. The libraries developed in this chapter provide infrastructure support for sharing data objects between distributed agents and for accessing remote data sources on the Internet.

7.2 Requirements for distributed AI agents

Distributed agents need to be able to easily access shared data objects. There are two models for supporting this: decentralized storage of objects and a central object server. It is easier to use a centralized object server, and that is what we will implement in this chapter. The shared data objects will be of type **mwa.data.AIframe** and have two required attributes:

- Name—All **mwa.data.AIframe** objects have a name.

- Type—Any frame processed by the object server must have a slot named "Type" with a value that is an **mwa.data.AIframedata** string object.

Any reference to "frame" in this chapter is understood to reference an instance of the class **mwa.data.AIframe**. An object server provides six basic services to remote client programs that communicate with the object server with the class **mwa.agent.Client** developed in Chapter 3:

- Add a new frame to the object storage
- Return a list of all frame types currently in object storage
- Return a list of all frame names of a specified frame type
- Return the data for a frame with a specified name
- Update the data for a frame with a specified name
- Print a report listing all stored objects

7.3   Implementation of a Java library to support distributed AI agents

The class **mwa.agent.Server** will be used to support network access to an object server. The new Java class **mwa.agent.AIframeServer** will extend the class **mwa.agent.Server**, adding data and behavior for storing and maintaining frames in memory. Figure 7.1 shows the Booch class diagram for the **mwa.agent.AIframeServer** class.

Listing 7.1 shows the implementation of the **AIframeServer** class. The method **DoWork( )** has been extended from the **Server** base class to process service requests based on the value of the slot named "service." An instance of the **AIframeServer** class is almost identical to the behavior of the base class **Server**, except for this extra functionality in the **DoWork( )** method. The **DoWork( )** method must be synchronized because multiple **Connection** objects can be created if multiple requests are being processed by an object server.

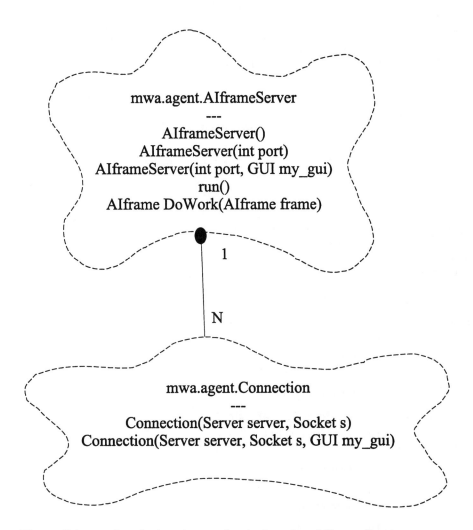

Figure 7.1   Booch class diagram for the Java class **AIframeServer**

Listing 7.1

```
// mwa.agent.AIframeServer.java
// Copyright 1996, Mark Watson.

package mwa.agent;

import java.io.*;
import java.net.*;
import mwa.gui.GUI;
```

```
import mwa.data.*;

// An AIframeServer instance adds the following services to the
// base class mwa.agent.Server:
//
//    1. return a list of all frame types
//    2. return a list of all names of a specified frame type
//    3. return a frame with a specified name
//    4. update the value of a frame with a specified name
//    5. add a new frame to object storage
//    6. print out all objects

public class AIframeServer extends Server {

    final static int MAXOBJS=200;
    public int NumObjects;
    public AIframe MyObjects[];
    public AIframeServer() {
        System.out.println("AIframeServer()");
        super.Server_helper(0, null);
        NumObjects=0;
        MyObjects=new AIframe[MAXOBJS];
    }
    public AIframeServer(int port) {
        System.out.println("AIframeServer(port)");
        super.Server_helper(port, null);
        NumObjects=0;
        MyObjects=new AIframe[MAXOBJS];
    }
    public AIframeServer(int port, GUI my_gui) {
        System.out.println("AIframeServer(port, my_gui)");
        super.Server_helper(port, my_gui);
        NumObjects=0;
        MyObjects=new AIframe[MAXOBJS];
    }
    public void run() {
        try {
            while(true) {
                Socket client_socket = listen_socket.accept();
                if (MyGUI!=null) MyGUI.P("Opening socket...\n");
                Connection c =
                    new Connection(this, client_socket, MyGUI);
            }
        }
```

```
            catch (IOException e) {
                Error(e, "Error waiting for connections");
            }
    }


    // public method defined in base class.  Here we
    // redefine DoWork to provide six new AIframeServer services:
    public synchronized AIframe DoWork(AIframe request) {
      AIframe ret =new AIframe("return_values");
      AIframedata s1=request.get("service");
      if (s1==null) {
        System.out.println("No service slot in request frame");
        if (MyGUI!=null)
              MyGUI.P("No service slot in request frame\n");
        return null;
      }
      String service=s1.string;
      if (service.equals("get_types")) {
        int count=0;
        for (int i=0; i<NumObjects; i++) {
            AIframedata fd=MyObjects[i].get("type");
            if (fd!=null) {
                if (fd.type==AIframedata.STRING) {
                    ret.put("s"+count,
                            new AIframedata(fd.string));
                    count++;
                }
            }
        }
      }
      if (service.equals("get_names")) {
        AIframedata fdtype=request.get("type");
        if (fdtype!=null) {
            if (fdtype.type==AIframedata.STRING) {
                int count=0;
                for (int i=0; i<NumObjects; i++) {
                    AIframedata fd=MyObjects[i].get("type");
                    if (fd!=null) {
                        if (fd.type==AIframedata.STRING) {
                            if (fd.string.equals(fdtype.string)) {
                                ret.put("s"+count,
                                  new AIframedata(MyObjects[i].getName()));
                                count++;
                            }
```

```
                        }
                    }
                }
            }
        }
    }
    if (service.equals("fetch")) {
        AIframedata s2=request.get("name");
        if (s2==null) {
            System.out.println("No name slot in request frame");
            if (MyGUI!=null)
                MyGUI.P("No name slot in request frame\n");
            return null;
        }
        if (s2.type==AIframedata.STRING) {
            String name=s2.string;
            ret=null;
            for (int i=0; i<NumObjects; i++) {
                if (MyObjects[i].getName().equals(name)) {
                    ret=MyObjects[i];
                }
            }
        }
    }
    if (service.equals("update")) {
        AIframedata s2=request.get("name");
        if (s2==null) {
            System.out.println(
                    "No name slot in update request frame");
            if (MyGUI!=null)
                MyGUI.P("No name slot in update request frame\n");
            return null;
        }
        if (s2.type==AIframedata.STRING) {
            String name=s2.string;
            ret=null;
            for (int i=0; i<NumObjects; i++) {
                if (MyObjects[i].getName().equals(name)) {
                    request.remove("service");
                    MyObjects[NumObjects++]=request;
                    ret.put("status", new AIframedata("OK"));
                }
            }
        }
    }
```

```
        }
    if (service.equals("add")) {
        if (NumObjects < (MAXOBJS-2)) {
            request.remove("service");
            MyObjects[NumObjects++]=request;
            ret.put("status", new AIframedata("OK"));
        }
    }
    if (service.equals("print")) {
        for (int i=0; i<NumObjects; i++) {
            if (MyGUI==null)
                MyObjects[i].PP();
            else
                MyObjects[i].PP(MyGUI);
        }
    }
    return ret;
    }
}
```

The **mwa.agent.AIframeServer** class is very simple because it does not support saving objects to disk and maintaining the data for objects distributed across more than one object server.

7.4   Testing the library for distributed agents

Listing 7.2 shows a test program for the **mwa.agent.AIframeServer** class. The class **testAIframeServer** is derived from the class **mwa.gui.GUI** and only has one new statement,

```
new AIframeServer(0, this);   // use default port
```

which creates an instance of the **AIframeServer** class. An instance of this class uses the inherited behavior of the **GUI** base class to create an applet that contains an output text field. A reference to the **testAIframeServer** (the **this** variable) is passed as the second (optional) argument of the **AIframeServer** constructor so that the instance of class **AIframeServer** can write diagnostic output to this application's scrolling text field.

Listing 7.2

```
// Test server classes
//
// Copyright 1996, Mark Watson.  All rights reserved.

package mwa.agent;

import java.awt.*;
import java.util.*;

import mwa.gui.*;


public class testAIframeServer extends GUI {

    AIframeServer server;

    public String getAppletInfo() {
        return "Test the agent stuff.  By Mark Watson";
    }

    public void init() {
      // Disable all standard GUI display components except output:
      NoGraphics     = true;
      NoInput        = true;
      NoRunButton    = true;
      NoResetButton = true;
      BigText=1;

      super.init();
      P("testServer applet\n");

      server = new AIframeServer(0, this);  // use default port
    }

}
```

Listing 7.3 shows a test program for a client to test the **mwa.agent.AIframeServer** class. This test client program is derived from the class **mwa.gui.GUI** and uses the **mwa.agent.Client** class to pass messages (instances of class **mwa.data.AIframe**) to an instance of class **AIframeServer**. The **testAIframeServer** method **DoRunButton( )** creates a new **Client** object and uses it to pass two newly created **AIframe** instances to an instance of class **AIframeServer** for storage.

Listing 7.3

```
// Test client classes
//
// Copyright 1996, Mark Watson.  All rights reserved.

package mwa.agent;

import java.awt.*;
import java.util.*;

import mwa.gui.*;
import mwa.data.*;

// Note: we can use the mwa.agent.Client class to
// test the mwa.agent.AIframeServer class (no separate
// ObjectClient class is required).

public class testObjectClient extends GUI {

    public String getAppletInfo() {
        return "Test the agent stuff.  By Mark Watson";
    }

    public void init() {
      // Disable graphics and input areas of standard GUI display:
      NoGraphics = true;
      NoResetButton=true;
      BigText=1;

      super.init();
      P("testObjectClient applet\n");
    }

    public void doRunButton() {
       Client client = new Client();
       String r = client.GetInfo();
       P(r + "\n");

       // send a new frame to the AIframeServer:
```

```
      AIframe frame=new AIframe("testframe1");
      frame.put("service", new AIframedata("add"));
      frame.put("type", new AIframedata("test_type"));
      frame.put("data", new AIframedata(GetInputText()));
      AIframe response = client.GetService(frame);
      if (response!=null) {
         String res = response.toString();
         P("Response from server:" + res + "\n");
      } else {
         P("No response from server\n");
      }

      // send a second frame to the AIframeServer:
      frame=new AIframe("testframe2");
      frame.put("service", new AIframedata("add"));
      frame.put("type", new AIframedata("test_type"));
      frame.put("zipcode", new AIframedata(92071));
      response = client.GetService(frame);
      if (response!=null) {
         String res = response.toString();
         P("Response from server:" + res + "\n");
      } else {
         P("No response from server\n");
      }

      client.CloseConnection();
      client = null;
   }
}
```

Figure 7.2 shows both the test client and test **mwa.agent.AIframeServer** applications. The top application window in Figure 7.2 shows the **testAIframeServer** application after processing two work requests from the client test program seen running in the bottom application window in Figure 7.2.

7.5   Requirements for World Wide Web data collection agents

The Java package **java.net** provides built-in support for fetching World Wide Web documents. There are two utility classes that can be used: **java.net.URL** and **java.net.URLConnection**. The class **java.net.URL** fetches the raw text associated with an HTML document. The **java.net.URLConnection** class fetches both the raw text of an

HTML document and status information (i.e., content type, content length, modification date, and content encoding) of the fetched HTML document (Flanagan 1996).

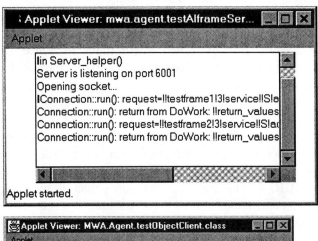

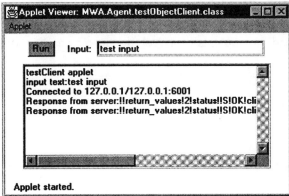

Figure 7.2   Testing the **AlframeServer** class

The requirements for the class **mwa.agent.URLdata** are

- Encapsulate the use of the URL class to return a string containing the contents of an HTML-formatted document.
- Catch any runtime errors and simply return a null string if any errors occur.

7.6   Implementation of a Java library for World Wide Web data collection agents

The implementation of the class **mwa.agent.URLdata** is fairly simple because we use the **java.net.URL** and **java.net.URLConnection** classes. Figure 7.3 shows the Booch class diagram for the **mwa.agent.URLdata** class. The **java.net.URL** class encapsulates a reference to a uniform resource locator (for example, a complete reference to **http://domain.com/example.html** or a reference to a local file like **file:://temp.dat**). The class **java.net.URL** has four constructors that provide options for specifying combinations of protocol, host, port number, and the remote file name. All examples in this book use the **java.net.URL** constructor that requires a single **String** argument that is interpreted as a complete URL (e.g., **http://users.aol.com/MarkWatson**). The class **java.net.URLConnection** is used to open a socket connection to a remote (or local) World Wide Web HTTP server (e.g., a Web server) to retrieve a document with a specified URL address. The **java.net.URLConnection** class has more than 40 methods for accessing relevant data for a connection to a Web document. The class **mwa.agent.URLdata** uses the class constructor and a single method, **getInputStream()**, of the class **java.net.URLConnection**. The input stream from an instance of **java.net.URLConnection** is used to read the contents of a Web document one line at a time.

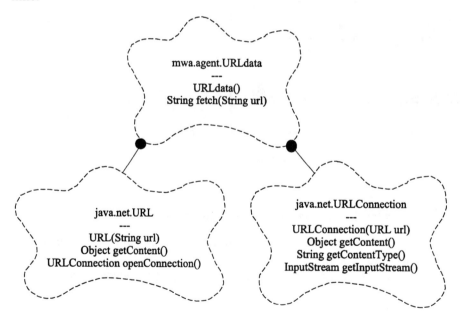

Figure 7.3   Booch class diagram for **mwa.agent.URLdata**

Listing 7.4 shows the implementation of the Java class **mwa.agent.URLdata**. The implementation of class **mwa.agent.URLdata** is simple because we use the behavior of the built-in classes **URL** and **URLConnection**. The only complexity in the method **String fetch(String url)** is the use of two try/catch statements to detect illegal URL addresses and any IO errors. All behavior of this class belongs in the **fetch** method; the constructor does not perform any work.

Listing 7.4

```
// mwa.agent.URLdata
//
// Encapsulates the use of the java.net.URL class
//
// Copyright 1996, Mark Watson.
//

package mwa.agent;

import java.net.*;
import java.io.*;

public class URLdata {
    public URLdata() {
    }
    String fetch(String url) {
        URL a_url;
        try {
            a_url = new URL(url);
        }
        catch (MalformedURLException e) {
            System.out.println("Unable to fetch " +
                            url + "(MalformedURLException)");
            return new String("no document");
        }
        try {
            System.out.println("after URL a_url = new URL(url);");
            URLConnection uc = a_url.openConnection();
            StringBuffer sb = new StringBuffer();
            DataInputStream dis =
                new DataInputStream(uc.getInputStream());
            while (true) {
                String s = dis.readLine();
```

```
            if (s == null) break;
            sb.append(s + "\n");
        }
        return new String(sb);
    }
    catch (IOException e) {
        System.out.println("Unable to fetch " +
                            url + "(IOexception)");
        return new String("no document");
    }
  }
}
```

Catching runtime exceptions is buried in the behavior of the **fetch** method. This has the benefit of not requiring wrapping calls to **fetch** in a try/catch statement; if any errors occur, a diagnostic message is written to standard output and the **fetch** method returns an empty string. A good alternative to this design is writing method **fetch** to throw an exception if there is a runtime error.

7.7   Testing the library for World Wide Web data collection agents

Listing 7.5 shows a test program for testing the **mwa.agent.URLdata** class. The class **mwa.agent.testURLdata** is derived from the class **mwa.gui.GUI**, which provides most of the class data and behavior. The method **doRunButton( )** has been overridden to use any text in the applet's text input field as a URL address, which is passed to an instance of **mwa.agent.URLdata**, using the **fetch** method. The string output of method **fetch** is copied to the applet's scrolling text output field.

In Listing 7.5, the following line of code sets the initial string in the input text field:

```
SetInputText("http://127.0.0.7/index.htm");
```

I am assuming that you have a local Web server running on your PC. If you do not have a local Web server for testing, then you can alternatively specify a URL that is a local file—for example,

```
SetInputText("file:///C:/MWA/MyWWW/index.htm");
```

This works on a PC running Windows 95 or Windows NT. Notice that forward slashes are allowed in URLs on PCs, even though the normal directory-delimiting character is a backslash character. If you are running on a UNIX system, then use a UNIX-style file name (i.e., no **C**:).

Listing 7.5

```
// Test URLdata class
//
// Copyright 1996, Mark Watson.

package mwa.agent;

import mwa.gui.GUI;

public class testURLdata extends GUI {

    public String getAppletInfo() {
        return "Test the URLdata stuff.  By Mark Watson";
    }

    public void init() {
      // Disable graphics and input areas of standard GUI display:
      NoGraphics = true;
      NoResetButton=true;
      BigText=1;

      super.init();
      P("testURLdata applet\n");
      //SetInputText("http://users.aol.com/MarkWatson/index.htm");
      SetInputText("http://127.0.0.7/index.htm");
    }

    public void doRunButton() {
      URLdata ud = new URLdata();
      // fetch the input filed text and treat as a URL address:
      String s = ud.fetch(GetInputText());
      P(s + "\n");
    }
}
```

Figure 7.4 shows the program in Listing 7.5 referencing the author's home page at URL **http://www.markwatson.com/index.html** on the World Wide Web.

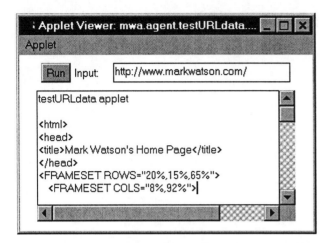

Figure 7.4   Testing the **URLdata** class by fetching the home page from my World Wide
                      Web site at **www.markwatson.com**

7.8   Requirements for sending electronic mail

The Simple Mail Transfer Protocol (SMTP) is used to send electronic mail to a remote
POP (Post Office Protocol) electronic mail server. The commands for the POP protocols
are four-letter ASCII commands. The following subset of SMTP commands are used in
the Java libraries developed in Section 7.11 (Jamsa and Cope 1995):

- **HELO**—identifies the sender to the receiver
- **MAIL**—initializes a connection to the remote E-mail server
- **RCPT**—identifies the E-mail address of the recipient of the E-mail message
- **DATA**—defines the data for the body of the E-mail address

It is reasonable to assign persistent software agents their own E-mail addresses so
that they can communicate with each other and humans via normal electronic mail. In
order to make it simple to send E-mail from inside any Java program (that is not running
in a Web browser), the class constructor of **mwa.agent.SendMail** should totally encapsulate the behavior of interfacing with a remote POP server over Intranets or the Internet.
The following information is required for sending electronic mail via a POP server:

- Host name where the POP server is running
- Domain name where the Java program sending E-mail is running
- IP address of the machine running the Java program that is sending E-mail
- Complete E-mail address of the message recipient
- String containing the body of the E-mail text

7.9 Implementation of a Java library for sending electronic mail

Figure 7.5 shows the Booch class diagram for the class **SendMail.**

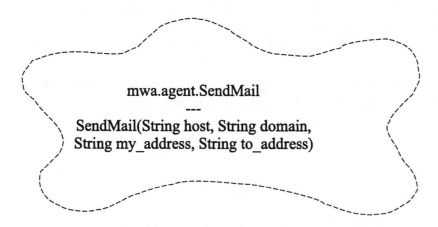

mwa.agent.SendMail

SendMail(String host, String domain,
String my_address, String to_address)

Figure 7.5   Booch class diagram for **SendMail**

Listing 7.6 shows the implementation of the class **mwa.agent.SendMail**, and Listing 7.7 shows the implementation of the class **mwa.agent.GetMail**. The **GetMail** and **SendMail** classes were written by Harm Verbeek. The class constructor for **SendMail** requires five arguments: Java **String** values for the mail host name, domain name, the user's or software agent's E-mail address, the recipient's address, and the data for the body of the E-mail message. POP mail servers treat a message text line that consists of a single period character as a flag indicating the end of the message data.

The class **java.net.Socket** is used to open a socket connection to the remote mail host using the standard socket port number 25. An instance of **java.io.DataInputStream** is opened to buffer and makes available data sent from the remote POP server. The **DataInputStream** class allows programs to read primitive Java types in a portable way from different types of computers on a network (i.e., allows programs to work in heterogeneous computer networks). The class **java.io.PrintStream** is used for writing formatted data back over the socket connection to the remote POP server. For the following examples, I will use the data for my remote POP server and account (I use the PacBell Internet Services):

- Mailhost = **pacbell.net**
- My address = **mwa@pacbell.net**

- POP domain name = **pacbell.net**
- Address that I am mailing to = **mwa@netcom.com**

A string containing a login prompt and the domain name, **HELO pacbell.net,** is sent to the POP server. The constructor for the **SendMail** class informs the POP server that an E-mail message is going to be sent by sending the string **MAIL FROM:<mwa@pacbell.net>** to the remote POP server. The string **RCPT TO:<mwa@netcom.com>** is sent to the POP server to specify the recipient of the E-mail message. The string **DATA** is sent to the POP server to indicate that the message text will be sent.

Finally, the message data is sent, ending with the string **\r\n.\r\n** to terminate the message text. The socket connection to the remote server is then closed.

Listing 7.6

```
/**
 * Copyright (c)1996 Harm Verbeek, All Rights Reserved.
 *
 * Description: Send E-mail (using SMTP) from within Java applet,
 *              won't work with applets in WWW-browser
 *              (security violation !!!).
 *
 * Usage Notes: Java 2.0 Beta
 *
 * Date       : 01/23/96
 *
 *
 * Permission to use, copy, modify, and distribute this software
 * and its documentation for NON-COMMERCIAL or COMMERCIAL purposes and
 * without fee is hereby granted.
 *
 * (API modifications by Mark Watson)
 **/

package mwa.agent;

import java.io.*;
import java.net.*;
import java.lang.*;
import java.applet.*;
```

```java
public class SendMail
{
  static Socket          socket;
  static InputStream     in;
  static OutputStream    out;
  static DataInputStream din;
  static PrintStream     prout;


  public SendMail(String mailhost, String domain, String my_address,
                  String to_address, String data)
  {
    int            SMTPport =  25;
    String         incoming = new String();

    String         MailHost = mailhost;

    String         HELO     = "HELO " + domain;
    String         MAILFROM = "MAIL FROM:<" + my_address + ">";
    String         RCPTTO   = "RCPT TO:<" + to_address + ">";
    String         DATA     = "DATA";

    /* you must terminate your message string with
       "\r\n.\r\n" to indicate end of message.
    */
    String         Msg      = data + "\r\n.\r\n";

    /* mailhost returns either "220" or "250"
       to indicate everything went OK
    */
    String         OKCmd    = "220|250";


/* connect to the mail server */
    System.out.println("Connecting to " + MailHost + "...");
    System.out.flush();

    try {
      socket = new Socket(MailHost, SMTPport);
    } catch (IOException e) {
      System.out.println("Error opening socket.");
      return;
    }
```

```java
    try {
      in    = socket.getInputStream();
      din   = new DataInputStream(in);

      out   = socket.getOutputStream();
      prout = new PrintStream(out);
    }
    catch (IOException e) {
      System.out.println("Error opening inputstream.");
      return;
    }

/* OK, we're connected, let's be friendly and say hello to the mail
server... */
    prout.println(HELO);
    prout.flush();
    System.out.println("Sent: " + HELO);

    try {
      incoming = din.readLine();
    }
    catch (IOException e) {
      System.out.println("Error reading from socket.");
      return;
    }
    System.out.println("Received: " + incoming);

  /* let server know YOU wanna send mail... */
    prout.println(MAILFROM);
    prout.flush();
    System.out.println("Sent: " + MAILFROM);

    try {
      incoming = din.readLine();
    }
    catch (IOException e) {
      System.out.println("Error reading from socket.");
      return;
    }
    System.out.println("Received: " + incoming);

/* let server know WHOM you're gonna send mail to... */
    prout.println(RCPTTO);
    prout.flush();
```

```
      System.out.println("Sent: " + RCPTTO);

      try {
        incoming = din.readLine();
      }
      catch (IOException e) {
        System.out.println("Error reading from socket.");
        return;
      }
      System.out.println("Received: " + incoming);


/* let server know you're now gonna send the message contents... */
      prout.println(DATA);
      prout.flush();
      System.out.println("Sent: " + DATA);

      try {
        incoming = din.readLine();
      }
      catch (IOException e) {
        System.out.println("Error reading from socket.");
        return;
      }
      System.out.println("Received: " + incoming);

/* finally, send the message... */
      prout.println(Msg);
      prout.flush();
      System.out.println("Sent: " + Msg);

      try {
        incoming = din.readLine();
      }
      catch (IOException e) {
        System.out.println("Error reading from socket.");
        return;
      }
      System.out.println("Received: " + incoming);

/* we're done, disconnect from server */
    System.out.print("Disconnecting...");
     try {
       socket.close();
```

```
    }
    catch (IOException e) {
      System.out.println("Error closing socket.");
    }

    System.out.println("done.");
  }

}
```

Test programs for both sending and receiving electronic mail are listed in Section
7.12. I would like to thank Harm Verbeek for writing (most of) the code in Listing 7.6
and making it freely available on the Internet.

7.10 Requirements for receiving electronic mail

Electronic mail servers support the POP interface standard for querying the status of
pending electronic mail and fetching mail if desired. There are two incompatible standards: POP2 and POP3; we will use the POP3 protocol. The commands for the POP
protocols are four-letter ASCII commands. The following subset of POP3 commands are
used in the Java libraries developed in Section 7.9 (Jamsa and Cope 1995):

* **USER**—for specifying a user login name
* **PASS**—for specifying a login password
* **STAT**—the server returns the number of messages available
* **RETR**—retrieves a specified message number
* **DELE**—marks a specified message number to be deleted
* **QUIT**—for closing a TCP/IP connection

The POP interface standard is used by the **mwa.agent.GetMail** Java class. In order
to make it simple to receive E-mail from inside any Java program (that is not running in a
Web browser), the class constructor of **mwa.agent.GetMail** should totally encapsulate
the behavior of interfacing with a remote POP server over Intranets or the Internet and
for fetching all pending E-mail messages. Public class data provides access to both the
number of E-mail messages that were fetched and an array of strings (one string per
message using new line characters). The following information is required for fetching
electronic mail from a POP server:

* Host name of computer running the POP server
* User name of the Java agent (or the human who owns the agent)
* Password of the Java agent (or the human who owns the agent)

After constructing an instance of class **mwa.agent.GetMail**, a Java program can fetch the individual E-mail messages from public class data.

7.11 Implementation of a Java library for receiving electronic mail

Figure 7.6 shows the Booch class diagram for **mwa.agent.GetMail**. After constructing an instance of class **mwa.agent.GetMail**, a program can retrieve the strings containing any E-mail messages that were fetched from a remote or local POP server.

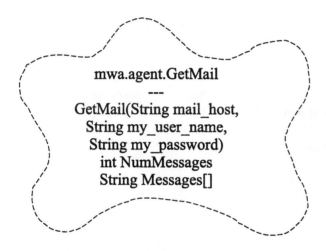

mwa.agent.GetMail

GetMail(String mail_host,
String my_user_name,
String my_password)
int NumMessages
String Messages[]

Figure 7.6   Booch class diagram for **GetMail**

Listing 7.7 contains the implementation of the **mwa.agent.GetMail** class written by Harm Verbeek. The method **getNumberofMessagesfromString** parses a string returned from a remote POP server to determine how many, if any, pending E-mail messages are available. The **GetMail** class constructor opens a connection on socket 110 to a remote POP server, sends the user name and password, and waits for acknowledgment. The class constructor attempts to read each available E-mail message; successfully read messages are stored in the public **String** array **Messages**. The socket connection is always closed before the class constructor method returns. The following strings are sent to the author's POP server to retrieve E-mail messages:

- **USER mwa@pacbell.net**
- **PASS <my password>**
- **STAT**

The POP server will return the number of E-mail messages available to be read. The POP server then sends all of the available E-mail messages, placing the characters **\r\n.\r\n** after each individual E-mail message.

Listing 7.7

```
/**
 * Copyright (c)1996 Harm Verbeek, All Rights Reserved.
 *
 * Description: Retrieve E-mail (using POP) from within Java applet,
 *              won't work with applets in WWW-browser
 *              (security violation !!!).
 *
 * Usage Notes: Java 2.0 Beta
 *
 * Date        : 01/23/96
 *
 *
 * Permission to use, copy, modify, and distribute this software
 * and its documentation for NON-COMMERCIAL or COMMERCIAL purposes and
 * without fee is hereby granted.
 *
 * (API modifications by Mark Watson)
**/

package mwa.agent;

import java.io.*;
import java.net.*;
import java.lang.*;
import java.applet.*;


public class GetMail
{
    static Socket           socket;
    static InputStream      in;
    static OutputStream     out;
    static DataInputStream din;
    static PrintStream      prout;

    public StringBuffer Messages[];
    public int NumMessages;
```

```java
static int getNumberofMessagesfromString(String m)
{
  int i,j;
  String s;

  i = m.indexOf(" mes");
  s = m.substring(4, i);

  i = s.lastIndexOf(" ");
  s = s.substring(i+1);

  i = Integer.parseInt(s);

  return i;
}


public GetMail(String mailhost, String my_user_name,
             String my_password)
{
  int           POPport  = 110;
  String        incoming = new String();

  String        MailHost = mailhost;
  String        user     = my_user_name;
  String        password = my_password;
  String        USER     = "USER " + user;
  String        PASSWORD = "PASS " + password;
  String        STAT     = "STAT";
  String        RETR     = "RETR ";
  String        DELE     = "DELE ";
  String        QUIT     = "QUIT";

  /* send this command to the server if you
     want to keep connected while you're busy
     doing something else
  */
  String        DONTQUIT = "NOOP";

  /* mailhost returns string that starts with
     "+OK" to indicate everything went OK.
  */
  String        OK       = "+OK";
```

```
    /* mailhost returns string that starts with
       "-ERR" to indicate something went wrong.
    */
    String          Err       = "-ERR";


/* connect to the mail server */
    System.out.println("Connecting to " + MailHost + "...");
    System.out.flush();

    try {
      socket = new Socket(MailHost, POPport);
    } catch (IOException e) {
      System.out.println("Error opening socket.");
      return;
    }

    try {
      in    = socket.getInputStream();
      din   = new DataInputStream(in);

      out   = socket.getOutputStream();
      prout = new PrintStream(out);
    }
    catch (IOException e) {
      System.out.println("Error opening inputstream.");
      return;
    }

  /* let server know who's calling... */
    prout.println(USER);
    prout.flush();
    System.out.println("Sent: " + USER);

    try {
      incoming = din.readLine();
    }
    catch (IOException e) {
      System.out.println("Error reading from socket.");
      return;
    }
    System.out.println("Received: " + incoming);

/* give server your password... */
```

```
    prout.println(PASSWORD);
    prout.flush();
    System.out.println("Sent: " + PASSWORD);

    try {
      incoming = din.readLine();
    }
    catch (IOException e) {
      System.out.println("Error reading from socket.");
      return;
    }
    System.out.println("Received: " + incoming);


/* ask server if there's mail for you... */
    prout.println(STAT);
    prout.flush();
    System.out.println("Sent: " + STAT);

    try {
      incoming = din.readLine();
    }
    catch (IOException e) {
      System.out.println("Error reading from socket.");
      return;
    }
    System.out.println("Received: " + incoming);

    int n = getNumberofMessagesfromString(incoming);

    NumMessages = n;

/* retrieve mail... */
    if (n>0) {

      Messages = new StringBuffer[NumMessages+1];

      for (int i=1; i<=n; i++) {
        Messages[i-1] = new StringBuffer();
        prout.println(RETR + i);
        prout.flush();
        System.out.println("Sent: " + RETR + i);

        try {
```

```
        incoming = din.readLine();

        while (!incoming.equals(".")) {
          System.out.println("Received: " + incoming);
          Messages[i-1].append(incoming);
          Messages[i-1].append("\n");
          incoming = din.readLine();
        }
      }
      catch (IOException e) {
        System.out.println("Error reading from socket.");
        return;
      }

      /* delete retrieved mail from server... */
      prout.println(DELE + i);
      prout.flush();
      System.out.println("Sent: " + DELE + i);

      try {
        incoming = din.readLine();
      }
      catch (IOException e) {
        System.out.println("Error reading from socket.");
        return;
      }
      System.out.println("Received: " + incoming);
    }
  }

/* ready, let's quit... */
  prout.println(QUIT);
  prout.flush();
  System.out.println("Sent: " + QUIT);

  try {
    incoming = din.readLine();
  }
  catch (IOException e) {
    System.out.println("Error reading from socket.");
    return;
  }
  System.out.println("Received: " + incoming);
```

```
/* we're done, disconnect from server */
   System.out.print("Disconnecting...");
    try {
      socket.close();
    }
    catch (IOException e) {
      System.out.println("Error closing socket.");
    }

    System.out.println("done.");
  }

}
```

Test programs for both sending and receiving electronic mail are listed in Section 7.12. I would like to thank Harm Verbeek for writing (most of) the code in Listing 7.7 and making it freely available on the Internet.

7.12 Testing the Java electronic mail libraries

Listing 7.8 shows a simple HTML document that can be used to start both **mwa.agent.testSendMail** and **mwa.agent.testGetMail** applets using the applet viewer program.

Listing 7.8

```
<title>Test SendMail stuff</title>
<hr>
<applet code=mwa.agent.testSendMail.class width=320 height=110>
</applet>
<applet code=mwa.agent.testGetMail.class width=370 height=190>
</applet>
<hr>
```

Listing 7.9 contains the class definition for **mwa.agent.testSendMail**, which is derived (or extended) from the Java class **mwa.gui.GUI**. All new behavior is contained in the **doRunButton( )** callback method. This test applet sends me a two-line E-mail message. Please edit the file **MWA\Agent\testSendMail.java** to change my E-mail address to your E-mail address before running this sample application. (Thank you.)

Listing 7.9

```
// Test SendMail class
//
// Copyright 1996, Mark Watson.  No rights reserved.

package mwa.agent;

import mwa.gui.GUI;

public class testSendMail extends GUI {

    public String getAppletInfo() {
        return "Test the SendMail stuff.";
    }

    public void init() {
      // Disable graphics area of standard GUI display:
      NoGraphics = true;
      NoInput = true;
      NoResetButton=true;

      super.init();
      P("testSendMail applet\n");
    }

    public void doRunButton() {
        String mailhost="pacbell.net";
        String me="mwa@pacbell.net";
        String domain="pacbell.net";
        String to="mwa@netcom.com";
        String letter="This is\n test.\n";

        SendMail mailer;
        mailer = new SendMail(mailhost, domain, me, to, letter);
        mailer = null;

    }
}
```

Listing 7.10 contains the class definition for **testGetMail**. The Java class **testGet-Mail** is derived from the class **mwa.gui.GUI** and provides the behavior for creating an applet that contains a "Run" button, an input text field, and an output text field. The method **doRunButton()** is overridden to get a user name and password from the text input field (assuming that a single space separates the user name and password) and makes a connection to a local or remote POP server to fetch any available E-mail messages. All retrieved messages are copied to the scrolling output text field.

Listing 7.10

```
// Test GetMail class
//
// Copyright 1996, Mark Watson.  No rights reserved.

package mwa.agent;

import mwa.gui.GUI;
import mwa.data.*;

public class testGetMail extends GUI {

    public String getAppletInfo() {
        return "Test the SendMail stuff.";
    }
    public void init() {
      // Disable graphics area of standard GUI display:
      NoGraphics = true;
      NoResetButton=true;
      BigText=1;

      super.init();
      P("testGetMail applet\n");
    }
    public void doRunButton() {
        String r =GetInputText();
        int space=r.indexOf(" ");
        String name=r.substring(0,space);
        String password=r.substring(space+1,r.length());
        P("name =      |" + name + "|\n");
        P("password = |" + "*******" + "|\n"); // do not print
        String mailhost="netcom.com";
        GetMail mailer = new GetMail(mailhost, name, password);
        P("Number of E-mail messages = " + mailer.NumMessages + "\n");
        for (int i=0; i<mailer.NumMessages; i++)
```

```
        P("\n" + mailer.Messages[i] + "\n******\n");
      mailer=null;
    }
}
```

Figure 7.7 shows applets **mwa.agent.testSendMail** and **mwa.agent.testGetMail**.

To test the E-mail classes, I click the **mwa.agent.testSendMail** applet "Run" button to send one or more test E-mail messages. I wait a minute or so for the remote POP server (which runs on a computer owned by my Internet service provider) to process the incoming message. I then click the "Run" button of the **mwa.agent.testGetMail** applet to fetch any available E-mail messages.

The input file for **mwa.agent.testGetMail** contains a user name and password. I entered my own user name and password, ran the program, then replaced the text with "username password" for obvious reasons.

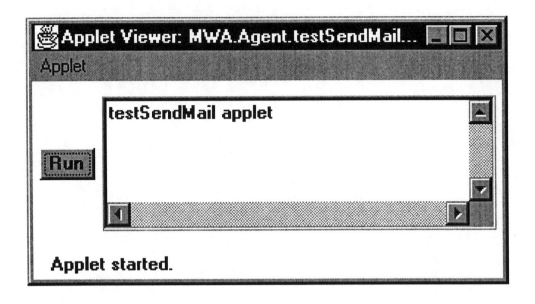

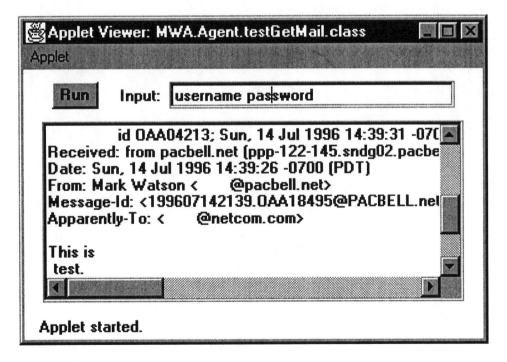

Figure 7.7   **mwa.agent.testSendMail** and **mwa.agent.testGetMail** test programs

Expert Systems 8

The application of expert systems to a wide range of problems has been one of the most useful technologies to emerge from AI research in the last 20 years. The subject of writing expert systems could fill more than one book. By necessity, this one-chapter introduction to expert system technology is tutorial in nature. After this chapter, you will be able to write simple expert systems in the CLIPS/Jess languages, but a full treatment of the syntax of these languages and all techniques for writing expert systems is not possible in such a small space. If you are interested in further study in this area, you will find references for expert systems in the Bibliography, and a search of the World Wide Web with the keywords "CLIPS expert system" will yield many examples of more advanced applications.

This chapter does not involve any Java programming. The Jess system is implemented in the Java language, but Jess programs have a syntax that is different than Java.

I prefer to refer to expert systems by a more precise name: *production systems*. Productions are rules for transforming strings. For example, given the three production rules

a => b

b => c

c => d

then if a production system is initialized with the state **a**, the state **d** can be derived by applying these three production rules in order. The form of these production rules is

<left-hand side> => <right-hand side>

It may seem like expert systems have much programming overhead; that is, it will seem excessively difficult to solve simple problems using production systems. However, for encoding large ill-structured problems for which it is difficult to develop detailed functional specifications, production systems provide a convenient notation for collecting together what would otherwise be too large of a collection of unstructured data and heuristic rules (Brownston et al. 1985).

Production systems fairly accurately model stimulus-response behavior in people. The left-hand side (LHS) terms represent environmental data that triggers a response or action represented by the right-hand side (RHS) terms in production rules. Simple stimulus-response types of production rules might be adequate for modeling simple behaviors, but our goal in writing expert systems is to encode deep knowledge and the ability to make complex decisions in a very narrow (or limited) problem domain. In order to model complex decision-making abilities, we also need to add higher-level control functionality to expert systems.

It is useful to consider how we consciously control our thought processes. From a lifetime of experience in interacting with our environment and other people, we have a very large amount of real-world knowledge. When we are faced with a specific problem—for example, finding a new friend's house if we only have the street address— we obviously use a very small percentage of the total knowledge that we have learned from childhood. To find our new friend's house, we set aside almost all of our knowledge and might only consider the following:

- Do we know where the street is? Have we been on the street before?
- If not, did the friend mention a well-known nearby cross street?
- If not, can I find an accurate street map?
    - If I have a street map, do I see the street my friend lives on?
- If not, do I have my friend's telephone number?
    - If my friend is at home, can I get better directions?

Here, I have indented subgoals and actions that we think when trying to solve a preceding goal. We have a wealth of real-world knowledge for solving many different types of problems, but we apply a high-level control process to set aside knowledge that is probably irrelevant to solving a specific problem. An expert system must be laboriously programmed to solve very specific types of problems. Even working in narrow problem areas, we will see that it is very important to support both high-level control structures and low-level stimulus-response types of rules. The high-level control structure is a set of rules that enable or disable stimulus-response rules based on the current goal(s) and/or subgoal(s) that the expert system is processing.

Production system rule interpreters that start with facts that are matched to the LHS term(s) of production rules are called *forward chaining* production systems. Production system rule interpreters that start with desired goal states that are matched to the RHS term(s) are called *backward chaining* production systems. For the introduction and tutorial for expert system technology in this chapter, we will use a forward chaining production system interpreter written in Java by Ernest Friedman-Hill of the Sandia National Laboratories that supports most of the capabilities of the "classic" expert system language OPS5 developed by Charles Forgy at Carnegie-Mellon University.

The three sample production rules listed at the beginning of this chapter look rather sparse and abstract. Please remember that production system interpreters manipulate symbols, not real-world knowledge. The three production rules could have their symbols **a**, **b**, **c**, and **d** changed to make the rules more meaningful to human readers:

```
I_am_hungry => find_food
find_food => cook_food
cook_food => eat_food
```

This substitution of symbols makes a difference for human readers, but a production system interpreter does not care. Still the form of these three rules is far too simple to encode interesting knowledge. We will extend the form of the rules by allowing

- variables in both the LHS and RHS terms of production rules
- multiple LHS and RHS terms in rules
- the ability to perform arithmetic operations in both LHS and RHS terms

The use of variables in rules is crucial since it allows us to properly generalize knowledge encoded in rules. The use of multiple LHS terms allows us to use compound tests on environmental data. In an English syntax, if we use a question mark to indicate a variable, rather than a constant, a rule might look like this:

```
If
        have food ?food_object
        ?food_object is_frozen
        ?food_object weight ?weight
        have microwave_oven
Then
        place ?food_object in microwave_oven
        set microwave_oven timer to (compute ?weight * 10)
        turn on microwave_oven
```

There is a strong similarity between the steps in this fairly complex rule and the notion of scripts seen in Section 6.6. This rule is still what I think of as a stimulus-response rule; higher-level control rules might set a goal of being hungry that would enable this rule to execute. We need to add an additional LHS term to allow higher-level control rules to set a "prepare food" goal; we can rewrite this rule and add an additional rule that could execute after the first rule (additional terms and rules are shown in italic):

```
If
        state equals I_am_hungry
        have food ?food_object
        ?food_object is_frozen
        ?food_object weight ?weight
        have microwave_oven
Then
        place ?food_object in microwave_oven
        set microwave_oven timer to (compute ?weight * 10)
        turn on microwave_oven
        set state to (I_am_hungry and food_in_microwave)
        set microwave_food to ?food_object

If
        state equals food_in_microwave
        microwave_timer? < 0
        microwave_food ?what_food_is_cooking
Then
        remove ?what_food_is_cooking from microwave
        eat ?what_food_is_cooking
```

A higher-level control rule could set an environmental variable **state** to the value **I_am_hungry**, which would allow the RHS terms of this rule to execute if the other four LHS terms matched environmental data. We have assumed that rules match their LHS terms with environmental data. This environmental data and higher-level control data is stored in *working memory*. If we use a weak analogy, production rules are like human long-term memory, and the transient data in working memory is like human short-term memory. The production rules are stored in *production memory*. We will see in the next section how the OPS5/CLIPS language supports structured working memory that is matched against the LHS terms of rules stored in production memory.

8.1   The CLIPS/OPS5 languages

The OPS5 language developed by Charles Forgy has been widely used for expert system development because it used a very efficient pattern-matching algorithm (the Rete network) and because it is freely available in source form. It is difficult to find documents about expert system technology that do not at least mention OPS5. (If you are curious, you can search for "OPS5" on the World Wide Web using your favorite search engine.)

OPS5 is written in, and available in, various dialects of LISP. (I ported OPS5 to In-terLisp-D for Xerox LISP machines and to ExperLisp for the Apple Macintosh.)

Researchers at NASA reimplemented OPS5 in the C language, renaming it CLIPS. Ernest Friedman-Hill reimplemented CLIPS in the Java language, renaming it Jess. Jess supports most of the capabilities of CLIPS and is downward-compatible; that is, any expert systems that you write for Jess will probably run with little or no modification under CLIPS. The complete implementation of Jess (including source code) is provided on the CD-ROM. A World Wide Web search on "Jess OPS5" will, in the future, point to newer versions of Jess and other interesting material.

All expert system examples and tutorial material in this chapter use the CLIPS/Jess syntax.

8.2   Using the Jess Java implementation of CLIPS/OPS5

CLIPS/Jess/OPS5 production systems consist of both conditional statements known as production rules stored in *production memory* (PM) and a global data base, the *working memory* (WM). Production rules contain at least one condition and at least one corresponding action. In Jess and CLIPS, the condition and action parts of rules are separated by the characters =>, which can be thought as representing an arrow.

The conditions are placed on the left-hand side of the characters =>, and the actions are placed on the right hand side of the =>. In expert system literature, you will often see the expressions "left-hand side" (LHS) and "right-hand side" (RHS) refer to the conditions and actions, respectively.

When every condition in the LHS of a rule is satisfied by matching data in WM, the rule is placed in the *conflict set* (CS). Conflict resolution is performed on the CS to determine which actions in the production rules are eligible to execute. The following actions are performed during this so-called *conflict resolution* phase:

- Check conditions of all production rules. Place those production rules with all conditions met into the conflict set.
- Choose one production rule from the conflict set and execute its related action(s).
- Remove the rule just executed from the conflict set.
- Update the conflict set based on the new state of working memory.

This cycle is repeated until the conflict set is empty. Production rules in the conflict set are assigned a rule *salience* or priority.

Working memory elements (WME) are structured data. We specify structure types in CLIPS and Jess using the **deftemplate** function. The notation for defining WME structure types is similar to the **mwa.data.AIframe** Java class that we developed in the package **mwa.data**. The slot values can be character strings or numbers. We might use this template in a rule to print the last names of all programmers, represented as WMEs, by using the rule **print_programmer_names** in Listing 8.1. The first thing that you will notice in Listing 8.1 is two comment lines. Comments can occur anywhere in CLIPS source code and always start with a semicolon. A **deftemplate** statement is used to define a working memory structure named **employee** with the following slot names:

- **first_name**
- **last_name**
- **age**
- **job_description**
- **phone_number**
- **phone_area_code**

CLIPS uses a LISP-style syntax: expressions are enclosed in parentheses and use a prefix functional form (function names precede the function's arguments). There are two production rules defined in Listing 8.1: **print_programmer_names** and **startup**.

The LHS terms in the production rule **print_programmer_names** will match every WME of the structure type **employee** that has a value "programmer" in the slot named **job_description**. Two matching variables, **?last** and **?first,** are used to match any values in the slots named **first_name** and **last_name**. The single RHS term in the rule **print_programmer_names** uses the built-in function **printout,** which can be used to print out any combination of string constants and variable values to a file. In this rule, we use a built-in file specifier **t,** which causes the function **printout** to write to standard output.

The CLIPS/Jess runtime system will always execute the rule **startup** because this rule has no LHS conditions, so it is always eligible to execute one time after the runtime system is reset; that is, the rule **startup** is added to the CS because it has no conditions (LHS terms). The rule **startup** will not continually execute because it is removed from the CS after it executes the first time.

Enabling debug/diagnostic output in Jess expert systems

If you have trouble understanding the runtime behavior of your expert systems, edit and then recompile the file **Rete.java**, changing the statements

```
public boolean watch_rules = false;
public boolean watch_facts = false;
```

to

```
public boolean watch_rules = true;
public boolean watch_facts = true;
```

These changes will cause the Jess system to print out any changes to WMEs and to print out which rules are executing.

Listing 8.1

```
;; File: ..\MWA\Jess\test1.clp
;; first example in CLIPS/Jess tutorial:

(deftemplate employee
    (slot first_name)
    (slot last_name)
    (slot age)
    (slot job_description
        (default programmer))
    (slot phone_number)
    (slot phone_area_code
        (default 619)))

(defrule print_programmer_names "test rule for tutorial 1"
  (employee
    (last_name ?last)
    (first_name ?first)
    (job_description programmer))
  =>
  (printout t "Programmer:" ?last ", " ?first crlf))

(defrule startup "define initial WMEs created by (reset)"
  =>
  (assert (employee
```

```
              (first_name Carol)
              (last_name Watson)
              (job_description marketing)))
  (assert (employee
              (first_name Mark)
              (last_name Watson))))
```

Executing Jess expert systems

The directory **c:\books\JavaAI\src\MWA\Jess** contains a prebuilt Jess environment for interactively running CLIPS/Jess programs using a command line interface. For example, typing **java Jess test1.clp** in a command window (assuming that you are in the directory **c:\books\JavaAI\src\MWA\Jess**) will execute the example shown in Listing 8.1. The following command line will also execute the example in Listing 8.1, adding an additional WME:

java Jess test1.clp "(employee (last_name Merril) (first_name Brad))"

Remember that since the Java class name **Jess** starts with a capital *J*, it is necessary to capitalize **Jess** when typing **java Jess test1.clp**.

Listing 8.2 shows a sample output from the example in Listing 8.1. The Java variables **watch_rules** and **watch_facts** are set to **true** values in file **Rete.java** to enable seeing changes to working memory and debug printout for the rules executing. Listing 8.2 is hand-edited to improve formatting; you will not see any indentation when you run this example.

Listing 8.2

```
C:\books\javaai\src\mwa\jess>java Jess test1.clp
No initial fact set on command line
 ==>  f-0 [Fact: initial-fact (ordered)]
(initial-fact)

FIRE [Defrule: startup "define initial WMEs created by (reset)";
            1 patterns; salience: 0] f-0,
  f-1 [Fact: employee (unordered) first_name=Carol; last_name=Watson;
            age=NIL; job_description=marketing; phone_number=NIL;
            phone_area_code=619;]
  f-2 [Fact: employee (unordered) first_name=Mark; last_name=Watson;
            age=NIL; job_description=programmer; phone_number=NIL;
            phone_area_code=619;]
```

```
FIRE [Defrule: print_programmer_names "test rule for tutorial 1";
               1 patterns;
               salience: 0] f-2,
Programmer:Watson, Mark
```

In Listing 8.2, the facts in working memory (i.e., WMEs) labeled "f-1" and "f-2" are created when the rule **startup** executes. The fact labeled "f-2" instantiates rule **print_programmer_names**.

The **deftemplate** function requires a template name and one or more slot specifications. In Listing 8.1, the template name is **employee** and the slot names are **first_name**, **last_name**, **job_description**, **phone_number**, and **phone_area_code**. The slots **job_description** and **phone_area_code** have default values specified; if we create a new WME using this template, this WME will have the default values for **job_description** and **phone_area_code** if we do not specify alternative values.

The **defrule** function is used to specify CLIPS/Jess rules. The first argument for **defrule** is a required rule name. The second argument is an optional comment string for documentation. CLIPS/Jess rules have two parts: the LHS and the RHS of the arrow characters =>. The LHS contains zero or more patterns to be matched against working memory. The RHS contains actions that are usually the following:

- Delete the WME that matched an LHS expression
- Modify the WME that matched an LHS expression
- Create a new WME
- Print to standard output

There are two new things for Java programmers to learn if they want to write effective rule-based expert systems: how the LHS of rules matches WMEs and how to add control structures to the rules in an expert system. The purpose of most of the material in the rest of this chapter is to illustrate LHS term matching against working memory and adding high-level control structures to CLIPS/Jess expert systems.

The rule **print_programmer_names** contains one LHS term that is matched against all WMEs of type **employee**:

```
(employee
    (last_name ?last)
    (first_name ?first)
    (job_description programmer))
```

The variables **?last** and **?first** will match any last or first names in a WME of type **employee**. The value of the slot **job_description** must equal (case insensitive) the string "programmer" for this LHS to match a WME of type **employee**. There are fields in the template **employee** that are not used in this rule; these fields are ignored during the matching process. CLIPS/Jess provides several useful matching operators for character and numeric data in WMEs. For example,

```
(employee (job_description ~programmer))
```
or

```
(employee (job_description ?job&~programmer))
```

will match WMEs of type **employee** where the slot **job_description** is not equal to "programmer." The first form,

```
(employee (job_description ~programmer))
```

is used if we want to test for the existence of a WME of type **employee** where the slot **job_description** does not equal "programmer." The second form,

```
(employee (job_description ?job&~programmer))
```

is used if we want to test for the existence of a WME of type **employee** where the slot **job_description** does not equal "programmer" and we want to store the **job_description** slot value in the matching variable **?job**.

With some loss of efficiency, we can also perform arithmetic operations during pattern matching, as seen in the production rule **test_salary** that is shown in Listing 8.3.

Listing 8.3

```
;; File: ..\MWA\Jess\test2.clp
;; second example in CLIPS/Jess tutorial:

(deftemplate employee
    (slot first_name)
    (slot last_name)
    (slot age)
    (slot job_description
        (default programmer))
    (slot phone_number)
    (slot salary
        (default 60000))
    (slot phone_area_code
        (default 619)))
```

```
(defrule test_salary "test for a raise"
  ?fact1 <- (employee
              (last_name ?last)
              (salary ?money&:(< ?money 40000))
              (job_description programmer))
  =>
  (printout t ?last " does not make enough: " ?money crlf)
  (modify ?fact1 (salary (+ ?money 10000))))

(defrule startup "define initial WMEs created by (reset)"
  =>
  (assert (employee
            (first_name Carol)
            (last_name Watson)
            (job_description marketing)))
  (assert (employee
            (first_name Bowsworthy)
            (last_name Howonthroth)
            (salary 22000)))
```

The variable **?fact1** is used to reference which WME actually matched the first (and only, in this example) LHS in which the value of the slot named **salary** is less than the numeric value 40,000. We then use the variable **?fact1** to modify a slot value in the WME that matched the first LHS term. The following statement in Listing 8.3 uses several useful constructs:

```
(salary ?money&:(< ?money 40000))
```

The variable **?money** matches any numeric value less than 40,000. The operator **&:** is a type of **if** statement. CLIPS/Jess expects to see a prefix (LISP-like) expression enclosed in parentheses following the **if** statement operator **&**. The operator < could also be <=, >=, or >.

The format for specifying CLIPS/Jess templates and rules uses a LISP-like syntax. Programmers with LISP programming experience find this a natural syntax; for non-LISP programmers, make sure to count parentheses when specifying both template definitions and rules. Jess provides rather sparse rule compiler errors. If you build very large expert systems in Jess, you may also want to obtain a copy of the CLIPS runtime system from the Internet (use your favorite World Wide Web search engine, and look for "CLIPS"). CLIPS provides detailed compilation errors that make it easier to correct syntax errors in both **deftemplate** and **defrule** statements.

Listing 8.4 shows the rules defined in Listing 8.3 executing. Debug printout shows changes to working memory and rule executions. Listing 8.4 is hand-edited to improve formatting; you will not see any indentation when you run this example.

Listing 8.4

```
C:\books\javaai\src\mwa\jess>java Jess test2.clp
No initial fact set on command line
 ==>  f-0 [Fact: initial-fact (ordered)]
(initial-fact)

FIRE [Defrule: startup "define initial WMEs created by (reset)";
               1 patterns; salience: 0]
f-0,
f-1 [Fact: employee (unordered) first_name=Carol;
           last_name=Watson; age=NIL;
           job_description=marketing; phone_number=NIL; salary=60000;
           phone_area_code=619;]
f-2 [Fact: employee (unordered) first_name=Bowsworthy;
           last_name=Howonthroth; age=NIL;
           job_description=programmer; phone_number=NIL;
           salary=22000; phone_area_code=619;]
FIRE [Defrule: test_salary "test for a raise"; 1 patterns; salience: 0]
f-2,

Howonthroth does not make enough: 22000
 <==  f-2 [Fact: employee (unordered) first_name=Bowsworthy;
               last_name=Howonthroth; age=NIL;
               job_description=programmer; phone_number=NIL;
               salary=22000; phone_area_code=619;]
f-3 [Fact: employee (unordered) first_name=Bowsworthy;
           last_name=Howonthroth; age=NIL; job_description=programmer;
           phone_number=NIL; salary=32000; phone_area_code=619;]
FIRE [Defrule: test_salary "test for a raise"; 1 patterns; salience: 0]
f-3,
Howonthroth does not make enough: 32000
 <==  f-3 [Fact: employee (unordered) first_name=Bowsworthy;
               last_name=Howonthroth; age=NIL;
               job_description=programmer; phone_number=NIL;
               salary=32000; phone_area_code=619;]
f-4 [Fact: employee (unordered) first_name=Bowsworthy;
           last_name=Howonthroth; age=NIL; job_description=programmer;
           phone_number=NIL; salary=42000; phone_area_code=619;]
```

In Listing 8.4, the symbol `<==` indicates that facts (or WMEs) f-2 and f-3 are removed from working memory. The creation of a new fact in working memory is represented by a fact name token like "f-4" followed by the new WME data enclosed in square brackets; for example, after fact f-3 is removed from working memory, a new fact, labeled "f-4," is created:

```
f-4 [Fact: employee (unordered) first_name=Bowsworthy;
           last_name=Howonthroth; age=NIL; job_description=programmer;
           phone_number=NIL; salary=42000; phone_area_code=619;]
```

When we modify a WME, the CLIPS/Jess runtime system removes the WME and creates a new WME that contains the modified slot values.

We will design and implement a simple expert system to diagnose medical problems related to SCUBA diving (not to be used for real medical emergencies!) in Section 8.3. In Section 8.4, we will discuss the important topic of adding control structures to expert systems for controlling which rules can fire during different phases of problem solving. The simple expert system developed in Section 8.3 is extended in Section 8.4.

Now experiment with both Jess and the tutorial files **..\MWA\Jess\test1.clp** and **..\MWA\Jess\test2.clp**. Copy these files to other file names to experiment with adding additional WMEs in the rule **startup** and additional matching terms in the sample rules. Writing production rule-based expert systems is quite different from procedural programming in languages like Java and C++. In principle, expert systems are written as sets of fairly independent rules representing often isolated facts and heuristics. We will see in Section 8.4 that as expert systems get larger (i.e., they contain more production rules), an increasingly larger effort is required to control which rules fire. The implementation of this extra control structure is achieved with *metalevel rules*. It is important for you now to actively experiment with the Jess system (or CLIPS if you would prefer to retrieve it from the Internet) before continuing working through the material in the next two sections of this chapter.

8.3 Simple Jess expert system

In this section, we will define the requirements for, and implement, a simple expert system for diagnosing SCUBA diving injuries. The expert systems developed in this section and Section 8.4 should not be used for real SCUBA diving injuries: I learned to SCUBA dive when I was 13 years old, so I learned the material that I used for these two sample expert systems over 30 years ago. The first implementation will use limited high-level control over the partitioning of rules into different groups. We will show in Section

8.4 how to manage complexity in larger sets of rules by partitioning rule sets and using control structures to enable and disable entire sets of rules.

Rules in expert systems usually execute in certain patterns that the expert system developer should recognize when designing a new system. We will use a single format for working memory elements; this WME template **goal** contains two slots: **type** and **value**.

The **type** slot of **goal** will vary, with possible values **nobreath**, **respirate**, **bleed**, and **scrape**.

The value of the **value** slot will be "Y" or "N." We use the RHS function **assert** to create new WMEs. For example:

```
(assert (goal (type scrape) (value (readline))))
```

We will use a new function **readline** in RHS terms to accept input from the user of the expert system. The function **readline** returns a quoted string, so we will use LHS matching terms like

```
(goal (type scrape) (value "Y"))
```

Figure 8.1 represents both the requirements for the sample expert system and shows how rules cause other related rules to execute (or fire). Rules are represented as labeled boxes, and arrows are labeled with the WME pattern required to instantiate another rule.

Listing 8.5 shows the first implementation of the SCUBA diving injury expert system. The rule **startup** asks the user several yes/no questions. A new **goal** WME is asserted for each question, and the return value of the **readline** function is used for the value of the slot named **value**.

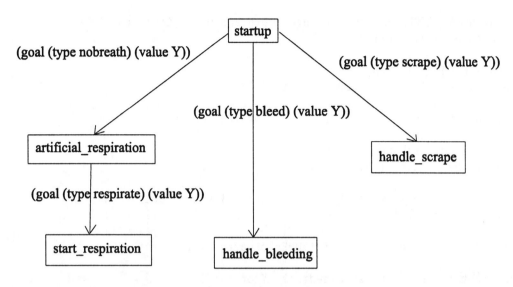

Figure 8.1 Interaction of rules in simple SCUBA diving medical diagnosis system

Listing 8.5

```
;; File: ..\MWA\Jess\diver1.clp
;; third example in CLIPS/Jess tutorial:

(deftemplate goal
 (slot type)
 (slot value (default N)))    ;; N for no, Y for yes

(defrule artificial_respiration
 ?fact1 <- (goal (type nobreath) (value "Y"))
 =>
 (printout t "Lay diver on his or her back in preparation "
  "to giving artificial respiration." crlf)
 (modify ?fact1 (value being_treated))
 (assert (goal (type respirate) (value "Y"))))


(defrule start_respiration
 ?fact <- (goal (type respirate) (value "Y"))
 =>
 (printout t "Pull chin forward." crlf)
 (printout t "Open mouth wide and pinch nostrils shut." crlf)
```

```
(printout t "REPEAT: blow air into mouth and pause to allow "
  "air to escape." crlf))

(defrule handle_bleeding
 ?fact1 <- (goal (type bleed) (value "Y"))
 =>
 (printout t "Apply pressure to stop bleeding." crlf))

(defrule handle_scrape
 (goal (type scrape) (value "Y"))
 =>
 (printout t "Gently wash the scraped area with soap and " crlf
  "clean water." crlf))

(defrule startup "define initial WMEs created by (reset)"
 =>
 (printout t "Is the diver bleeding? (Y or N):")
 (assert (goal
         (type bleed)
         (value (readline))))
 (printout t "Is the diver scraped? (Y or N):")
 (assert (goal (type scrape) (value (readline))))
 (printout t "Has the diver stopped breathing? (Y or N):")
 (assert (goal (type nobreath) (value (readline)))))
```

Listing 8.6 shows a sample output when executing the rules shown in Listing 8.5. User responses are highlighted in *italic*.

Listing 8.6

```
C:\books\javaai\src\mwa\jess>java Jess diver1.clp
No initial fact set on command line
(initial-fact)

Is the diver bleeding? (Y or N):Y
Is the diver scraped? (Y or N):N
Has the diver stopped breathing? (Y or N):N
Apply pressure to stop bleeding.
```

Listing 8.7 shows a sample output when executing the rules shown in Listing 8.5 with debug output enabled. User responses are highlighted in *italic*.

Listing 8.7

```
C:\JavaAI\Jess>java Jess diver1.clp
No initial fact set on command line
 ==> f-0 [Fact: initial-fact (ordered)]
(initial-fact)

FIRE [Defrule: startup "define initial WMEs created by (reset)";
      1 patterns; salience: 0]
f-0,
Is the diver bleeding? (Y or N):Y
 ==> f-1 [Fact: goal (unordered) type=bleed; value="Y";]
Is the diver scraped? (Y or N):N
 ==> f-2 [Fact: goal (unordered) type=scrape; value="N";]
Has the diver stopped breathing? (Y or N):N
 ==> f-3 [Fact: goal (unordered) type=nobreath; value="N";]
FIRE [Defrule: handle_bleeding 1 patterns; salience: 0] f-1,
Apply pressure to stop bleeding.
```

A common error in writing production rule systems is simple misspellings of slot names in LHS matching patterns. It is a good idea to enable debug output to quickly track down trivial misspelling bugs.

8.4 Control structures in expert systems

Production systems are best for solving problems in which problem-solving knowledge can be expressed as fairly independent sets of pattern-matching rules. Indeed, complex production systems often seem to solve subtasks in parallel. Production systems are not appropriate for problems for which there is a well-known algorithm, or that are best solved by following long sequences of tasks in order. It is quite straightforward to add control logic that forces a long sequence of production rules to execute in a specific order, but such problems should simply be coded in a procedural language like Java.

So, in general, we will try to write logically consistent subsets of rules and allow the Rete pattern-matching process to supply most of the control in our expert systems. This said, there are times when it is also important to partition expert systems into distinct subsets of rules and to tightly control which sets of rules are eligible to execute. In the last section we used (some limited) problem-solving knowledge rules; now we will also store some control knowledge in rules.

Figure 8.2 shows the interactions of rules in the extended SCUBA diving medical diagnosis system. The rule **handle_bleeding** provides some control of the possible

execution of the rules **handle_punctures** and **handle_one_puncture**. This control is
implemented by asking the user two questions and creating two new goal WMEs with the
user's response data. These two rules also provide control structure for determining if the
rules **venom_puncture**, **cone_shell_puncture**, **handle_octopus_bite**, and **han-
dle_profuse_bleeding** are eligible to execute (i.e., that they are placed in the conflict
set).

Listing 8.8 shows a refined version of the expert system seen in Listing 8.5. This
extended diagnostic system uses fairly explicit control over the order of rule firings to
serve as an example of how this is done. Two additional working memory templates are
used: **number_of_puncture_wounds** and **lacerations**.

Listing 8.8

```
;; File: ..\MWA\Jess\diver2.clp
;; third example in CLIPS/Jess tutorial:

(deftemplate goal
 (slot type)
 (slot value (default N)))    ;; N for no, Y for yes
(deftemplate number_of_puncture_wounds
 (slot value (default 0)))
(deftemplate lacerations
 (slot value (default N)))

(defrule artificial_respiration
 ?fact1 <- (goal (type nobreath) (value "Y"))
 =>
 (printout t "Lay diver on his or her back in prepration "
  "to giving artificial repiration." crlf)
 (modify ?fact1 (value being_treated))
 (assert (goal (type respirate) (value "Y")))
 (printout t "Can you see any foreign objects in the" crlf
  "diver's mouth? (Y or N):")
 (assert (goal (type unplug_mouth) (value (readline)))))
```

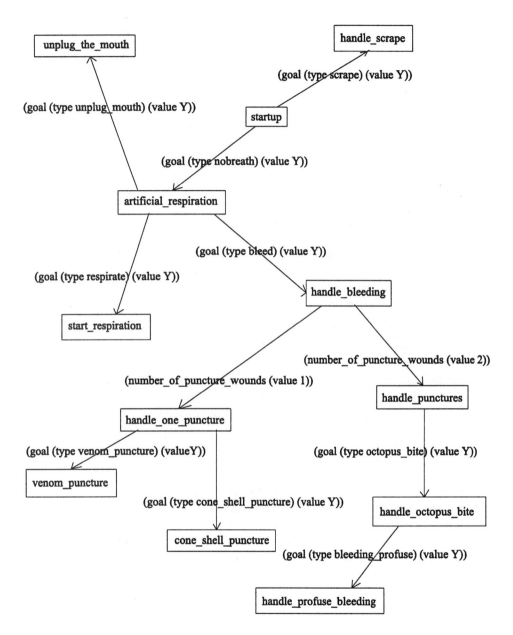

Figure 8.2   Rule interactions in extended diagnosis system

```
(defrule unplug_the_mouth
  ?fact1 <- (goal (type unplug_mouth) (value "Y"))
  =>
  (printout t "Remove foreign matter from mouth of diver" crlf)
```

```
  (modify ?fact1 (value unplugged))))

(defrule start-respiration
 ?fact <- (goal (type respirate) (value "Y"))
 =>
 (printout t "Pull chin forward." crlf)
 (printout t "Open mouth wide and pinch nostrils shut." crlf)
 (printout t "REPEAT: blow air into mouth and pause to allow "
  "air to escape." crlf))
;; (modify ?fact1 (type OK)))

(defrule handle_bleeding
 ?fact1 <- (goal (type bleed) (value "Y"))
 =>
 (printout t "Enter number of puncture wounds (0, 1, or 2):")
 (assert (number_of_puncture_wounds (value (readline))))
 (printout t "Are there any lacerations? (Y or N):")
 (assert (lacerations (value (readline)))))

(defrule handle_punctures
 ?fact1 <- (number_of_puncture_wounds (value "2"))
 =>
 (printout t "Are the two punctures lose together with "
  "surrounding redness and stinging? (Y or N):")
 (assert (goal (type octopus_bite) (value (readline)))))

(defrule handle_octopus_bite
 ?fact <- (goal (type octopus_bite) (value "Y"))
 =>
 (printout t "Diver has probably been bitten by an octopus." crlf)
 (printout t "Apply a cold compress to the wound." crlf)
 (printout t "Keep the diver lying down." crlf)
 (printout t "Get medical attention as soon as possible." crlf)
 (printout t "Is the bleeding profuse? (Y or N):")
 (assert (goal (type bleeding_profuse) (value (readline)))))

(defrule handle_profuse_bleeding
 ?fact1 <- (goal (type bleeding_profuse) (value "Y"))
 =>
 (printout t "Apply pressure to the wound to slow the "
  "flow of blood." crlf))

(defrule handle_one_puncture
 ?fact1 <- (number_of_puncture_wounds (value "1"))
```

```
=>
(printout t "Are there any muscle spasms around the" crlf
 "puncture? (Y or N)")
(assert (goal (type venom_puncture) (value (readline))))
(printout t "Is there a severe burning sensation around" crlf
 "the wound? (Y or N)")
(assert (goal (type cone_shell_puncture) (value "Y")))
(printout t "Clean the puncture and apply pressure to" crlf
 "prevent bleeding." crlf))

(defrule venom_puncture
 ?fact1 <- (goal (type venom_puncture) (value "Y"))
 =>
 (printout t "The wound was likely caused by either a:" crlf
 "     Weever fish"    crlf
 "     Scorpion fish"  crlf
 "     Rat fish"       crlf
 "     Rabbit fish"    crlf  crlf
 "Irrigate with clean water and make a small" crlf
 "incision across the wound and apply suction" crlf
 "before soaking in very hot water for 30" crlf
 "minutes.  Obtain medical care as soon as possible." crlf
 "This temporary treatment should alleviate the pain" crlf
 "and help to combat the effects of venom to prevent" crlf
 "a secondary infection." crlf))


(defrule cone_shell_puncture
 ?fact1 <- (goal (type cone_shell_puncture) (value "Y"))
 =>
 (printout t "The wound is probably a cone shell puncture." crlf
 "Keep the diver lying down and get medical care" crlf
 "immediately." crlf)
 (modify ?fact1 (value no_treatment)))

(defrule handle_scrape
 (goal (type scrape) (value "Y"))
 =>
 (printout t "Gently wash the scraped area with soap and " crlf
 "clean water." crlf))

(defrule startup "define initial WMEs created by (reset)"
 =>
 (printout t "Is the diver bleeding? (Y or N):")
```

```
(assert (goal
        (type bleed)
        (value (readline))))
(printout t "Is the diver scraped? (Y or N):")
(assert (goal (type scrape) (value (readline))))
(printout t "Has the diver stopped breathing? (Y or N):")
(assert (goal (type nobreath) (value (readline)))))
```

Listing 8.9 shows a sample output when executing the rules shown in Listing 8.8 with debug printout disabled.

Listing 8.9

```
C:\books\javaai\src\mwa\jess>java Jess diver2.clp
No initial fact set on command line
(initial-fact)

Is the diver bleeding? (Y or N):Y
Is the diver scraped? (Y or N):N
Has the diver stopped breathing? (Y or N):Y
Lay diver on his or her back in preparation to giving artificial respi-
ration.
Can you see any foreign objects in the
diver's mouth? (Y or N):Y
Remove foreign matter from mouth of diver
Pull chin forward.
Open mouth wide and pinch nostrils shut.
REPEAT: blow air into mouth and pause to allow air to escape.
Enter number of puncture wounds (0, 1, or 2):2
Are there any lacerations? (Y or N):N
Are the two punctures close together with surrounding redness and sting-
ing? (Y or N):Y
Diver has probably been bitten by an octopus.
Apply a cold compress to the wound.
Keep the diver lying down.
Get medical attention as soon as possible.
Is the bleeding profuse? (Y or N):Y
Apply pressure to the wound to slow the flow of blood.
```

Listing 8.10 shows a sample output when executing the rules shown in Listing 8.8 with debug printout enabled.

Listing 8.10

```
C:\books\javaai\src\mwa\jess>java Jess diver2.clp
No initial fact set on command line
 ==> f-0 [Fact: initial-fact (ordered)]
(initial-fact)

FIRE [Defrule: startup "define initial WMEs created by (reset)";
             1 patterns; salience: 0]
f-0,
Is the diver bleeding? (Y or N):Y
 ==> f-1 [Fact: goal (unordered) type=bleed; value="Y";]
Is the diver scraped? (Y or N):N
 ==> f-2 [Fact: goal (unordered) type=scrape; value="N";]
Has the diver stopped breathing? (Y or N):Y
 ==> f-3 [Fact: goal (unordered) type=nobreath; value="Y";]
FIRE [Defrule: artificial_respiration 1 patterns; salience: 0] f-3,
Lay diver on his or her back in preparation to giving artificial respi-
ration.
 <== f-3 [Fact: goal (unordered) type=nobreath; value="Y";]
 ==> f-4 [Fact: goal (unordered) type=nobreath; value=being_treated;]
 ==> f-5 [Fact: goal (unordered) type=respirate; value="Y";]
Can you see any foreign objects in the
diver's mouth? (Y or N):Y
 ==> f-6 [Fact: goal (unordered) type=unplug_mouth; value="Y";]
FIRE [Defrule: unplug_the_mouth 1 patterns; salience: 0] f-6,
Remove foreign matter from mouth of diver
 <== f-6 [Fact: goal (unordered) type=unplug_mouth; value="Y";]
 ==> f-7 [Fact: goal (unordered) type=unplug_mouth; value=unplugged;]
FIRE [Defrule: start_respiration 1 patterns; salience: 0] f-5,
Pull chin forward.
Open mouth wide and pinch nostrils shut.
REPEAT: blow air into mouth and pause to allow air to escape.
FIRE [Defrule: handle_bleeding 1 patterns; salience: 0] f-1,
Enter number of puncture wounds (0, 1, or 2):2
 ==> f-8 [Fact: number_of_puncture_wounds (unordered) value="2";]
Are there any lacerations? (Y or N):N
 ==> f-9 [Fact: lacerations (unordered) value="N";]
FIRE [Defrule: handle_punctures 1 patterns; salience: 0] f-8,
Are the two punctures close together with surrounding redness and sting-
ing? (Y or N):Y
 ==> f-10 [Fact: goal (unordered) type=octopus_bite; value="Y";]
FIRE [Defrule: handle_octopus_bite 1 patterns; salience: 0] f-10,
Diver has probably been bitten by an octopus.
Apply a cold compress to the wound.
```

```
Keep the diver lying down.
Get medical attention as soon as possible.
Is the bleeding profuse? (Y or N):Y
 ==>  f-11 [Fact: goal (unordered) type=bleeding_profuse; value="Y";]
FIRE [Defrule: handle_profuse_bleeding 1 patterns; salience: 0] f-11,
Apply pressure to the wound to slow the flow of blood.
```

8.5   Knowledge acquisition

Knowledge acquisition is the combined processes of understanding what we know about solving a specific type of problem and encoding that knowledge in a form that can be used in expert systems. Typically a knowledge engineer who is an expert in expert system technology works with one or more problem domain experts to create expert systems. If you want to create your own expert system, you will probably play both these roles.

The obvious first step in creating your own expert system is choosing a problem domain in which you have some expertise or at least a strong interest. Possible ideas are

- diagnostic system for troubleshooting problems with your car
- tutorial system for teaching someone how to program your VCR
- loan advisor program
- help desk expert system for employees to answer questions from customers

Whatever type of expert system you decide to build, start by doing the following:

- Write a two- or three-page description of the problem that you are trying to solve. This description contains your list of requirements.
- Write down a list of the possible types of data templates (with the slot names) that you will use for working memory elements.
- Write a simple prototype expert system that only contains the **deftemplate** definitions for working memory elements and a few test rules.
- After making sure that your simple prototype works, write a short description of which requirements still need to be satisfied.
- After experimenting with the prototype, add to the original list of requirements.
- Based on your new requirements, write a second-stage prototype by adding rules.

Part III

Projects

Using Genetic Algorithms in a Scrolling Arcade Game

9

The programming project developed in this chapter demonstrates the use of genetic algorithms to evolve more efficient control functions for enemy ships in a scrolling arcade game. This project is based on Mark Tacchi's Gamelet tool kit, a Java class library for implementing two-dimensional arcade-style games. I would like to thank Mark Tacchi and his friends (programmer Kresten Thorup and graphics artist Tim Wasko) who helped him create the Gamelet tool kit and accompanying graphics and sound files for making their work freely available. The arcade game used in this chapter as a test bed for game playing with genetic-based game agents is derived from the cool Roids game that Mark Tacchi wrote to demonstrate the capabilities of the Gamelet tool kit. I modified the Roids example game in the following ways:

- Player ship slides vertically along the left side of the screen.
- Enemy ships usually approach from the right side of the screen.
- Global state information for player and enemy ships is recorded to use in the genetic algorithm fitness function employed to breed more efficient enemy ships.
- Enemy ships alter their strategy for approaching the player ship based on the player's style of play.
- The Java genetic algorithm classes developed in Chapter 5 are used.

In the beginning of a game, the genetic-algorithm-controlled enemy spaceships have randomly assigned chromosomes. The chromosome for a ship encodes a list of 10 "machine instructions" that are used to control the ship. A program counter keeps track of which machine instruction is executing. When the last instruction is reached, this program counter returns to the first instruction in the list. These instructions either move the ship or conditionally branch based on the distance from the enemy to the player ship.

As you would expect, the behavior of the enemy ships is erratic at the beginning of a game because they effectively use randomly "written" control programs. Approximately every five seconds of game play, a fitness function is applied to all of the chromosomes controlling the enemy ships. The fitness function uses the following statistics since the last time the genetic chromosome population was updated using crossover and mutation:

- closest distance to the player
- furthest distance to the player
- average distance to the player
- number of times the ships is blown up and re-created
- maximum speed

This fitness function allows a genetic algorithm to find sequences of the machine instructions that program the enemy ships to approach the player, yet occasionally zigzag to avoid being easy targets.

9.1   Overview of the Gamelet tool kit

Mark Tacchi's Gamelet tool kit provides support for easily writing two-dimensional arcade games in Java. Figure 9.1 shows a Booch class diagram for the major Java classes in the tool kit. The **Actor** class encapsulates the data and behavior for both player- and computer-controlled opponents in arcade-style games. The appearance of an instance of class **Actor** is determined by supplying a GIF image file containing multiple views of the **Actor**; Figure 9.2 shows the GIF file created by Tim Wasko for Mark Tacchi's Roids game (which I also use in the example for this chapter). Actors use internal data to record their current position and velocity. The **Actor** method **tick( )** is called periodically to update the graphics state and position of the **Actor** object.

The class **ActorManager** is a collection class for controlling one or more actors. An instance of class **ActorManager** will notify two actors if they collide by calling their **Actor.collideWithActor(Actor theActor)** methods. The class **Gamelet** is derived from the class **java.applet.Applet**. **Gamelet** provides the behavior of creating an application window and handling user events. Each instance of class **Actor** is passed a reference to the **Gamelet** instance that is created to control the game. When the class **Gamelet** is extended (subclassed) to write a new game, game-specific data can be added to the derived class; all instances of class **Actor** (and more likely instances of classes derived from class **Actor**) can reference this game-specific data through the **Gamelet** reference passed as the first argument in their constructor argument list.

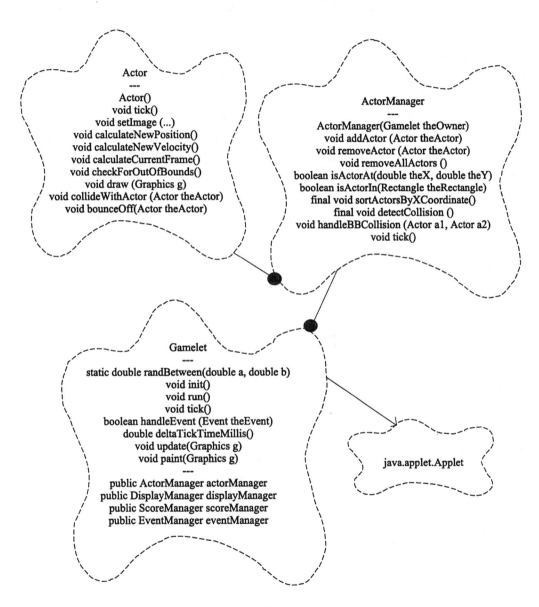

Figure 9.1   Booch class diagram for the Gamelet Java classes

You can use the following steps to create a new two-dimensional arcade game:

- Create a subclass of **Gamelet**, adding data declarations specific to your new game.
- Create a new subclass of **Actor** for each type of player- and computer-controlled object in the game.
- Write **tick( )** methods for game-specific processing for each new subclass of **Actor** for new moving objects.
- Create a GIF file like the one seen in Figure 9.2 to define the appearance of each new subclass of **Actor**.

All instances of class **Actor** are initialized with a GIF image file like the one shown in Figure 9.2. The GIF image should contain 32 views of the object. As seen in Figure 9.2, the subimages are used in row-first order:

1	2	3	4
5	6	7	8
9	10	11	12
13	14	15	16
17	18	19	20
21	22	23	24
25	26	27	28
29	30	31	32

9.2   Overview of the example program

The original Roids program written by Mark Tacchi used the following game-specific Java source files to extend the Gamelet tool kit:

- **Asteroid.java**
- **Bigoobie.java**
- **Bullet.java**
- **Explosion.java**
- **Goobie.java**
- **Javaroids.java**
- **Ship.java**

Figure 9.2   GIF file showing the multiple appearances of the **Actor** used for the enemy ships that are controlled using a program generated by a genetic algorithm

The complete Gamelet tool kit is stored on the CD-ROM in the directory **\JavaAI\game\com\next\gt**. The example program was derived from the Roids example, using the following source files:

- **Bullet.java** (unchanged from the Roids example program)
- **Explosion.java** (unchanged from the Roids example program)
- **Ship.java** (slightly modified from the Roids example program)
- **GeneticGame.java** (derived from **Roids.java**)
- **GAship.java** (mostly new code using a genetic algorithm; derived from **Asteroid.java**)

These source files are stored in the directory **\books\JavaAI\src\MWA\Game** on the CD-ROM. The files **GeneticGame.java** and **Ship.java** are not listed since they are very similar to the original Roids files and they do not contain any AI-specific code. The asteroids in the original Roids game are now the "enemy ships."

9.3   Requirements for controlling enemy ships

Moving objects in arcade games usually move by using movement templates. These templates contain a list of delta-x and delta-y values that are added one per game update cycle to the moving object's position. The advantage of this approach is that a few different movement patterns can be handcrafted to look good. The disadvantage of this approach is that after a specific movement pattern has been chosen (usually randomly), the player can often recognize the pattern and respond from his or her memory of previous games.

The use of genetic algorithms offers an interesting alternative for controlling the behavior (in this case simply the movement) of objects in arcade-style games. With an appropriate fitness function, control parameters can evolve in real time to adapt to a player's changing playing style. The disadvantage of using genetic algorithms to modify the control parameters of objects in games is that often the motion can look erratic and too unpredictable. The requirements for automatically adapting the control parameters of moving objects in the example game implemented in this chapter are the following:

- The performance of the enemy ships should noticeably improve while the game is playing.
- The overhead for adapting control parameters or a control program should not noticeably slow down the game so that it is no longer fun to play.
- A player can consciously adopt a playing style and within a minute see a different type of movement behavior of the enemy ships in the game.

9.4   Design of a genetic algorithm controller

The enemy ships are controlled by short programs written in a simple machine language that contains eight instructions. Since there are eight instructions in this machine language, we will need three bits to store each instruction. I somewhat arbitrarily chose programs with a length of 10 machine instructions to control the enemy ships, so we will need 30 bits of data for each control program. The instructions (preceded by their operation codes) are

- 0—Move toward the player.
- 1—Move away from the player.
- 2—Move in $+y$ direction (down the screen).
- 3—Move in $-y$ direction (up the screen).
- 4—If distance to player < 100 pixels, then skip next instruction.
- 5—If distance to player > 100 pixels, then skip next instruction.
- 6—If distance to player < 50 pixels, then skip next two instructions.
- 7—If distance to player > 50 pixels, then skip next two instructions.

Since the player's ship is constrained to move vertically on the left side of the screen, moving an enemy ship vertically up or down has the effect of dodging from side to side as the player ship shoots.

Given a machine language for writing control programs for the enemy ships and the requirement to move quickly toward the player's ship while zigzagging to avoid being shot, it would be fairly easy to manually write down a few reasonable control programs; for example, a reasonable 10-instruction control program might be

- Move toward the player.
- Move toward the player.
- If distance to player < 50 pixels, then skip next two instructions.
- Move in -y direction (up the screen).
- Move in -y direction (up the screen).
- Move toward the player.
- Move toward the player.
- If distance to player < 100 pixels, then skip next instruction.
- Move in +y direction (down the screen).
- Move toward the player.

After the tenth program step, the program starts over again executing the first instruction. What does this example control program do? It usually moves toward the player (half the instructions are to move toward the player), while occasionally moving up or down the screen (dodging to the right or left, respectively) if the enemy ship is not close to the player's ship. If the enemy ship is sufficiently close to the player ship, we use the "skip" instructions to avoid dodging to the left or right.

As we have just seen, an effective enemy ship controller has the following properties:

- It minimizes the probability of being hit by a bullet from the player's ship.
- It approaches the player as quickly as possible.

These properties are mutually exclusive, so an effective control program must mix both strategies. Usually, a ship moving quickly in a straight line toward the player's ship will be quickly shot. On the other hand, an enemy ship that zigzags too often cannot quickly approach the player's ship.

If the player never shot at the enemy ships, the genetic algorithm would fairly quickly evolve a population of controllers with programs simply containing the first instruction (i.e., operation code 0: move toward the player in a straight line). Assuming that the player is actively trying to shoot and blow up the enemy ships, more genetically fit control programs will contain occasional dodging maneuvers.

The 30 bits that make up each control program are represented by the 30 genes in a chromosome. As we change chromosomes with genetic crossover and mutation, we are modifying the enemy ship control programs. For testing, we will use 12 enemy ships, so the example program uses 12 distinct chromosomes. The fitness function uses the following statistics from recent play:

- closest distance to the player
- furthest distance to the player
- average distance to the player
- number of times the ships is blown up and re-created
- maximum speed

These fitness parameters were at least partially chosen because they are computationally cheap to calculate.

9.5   Implementation of the example program

Figure 9.3 shows the Booch class diagram for the new classes that are added to the Gamelet tool kit to create the sample game. The Gamelet tool kit file **EventHandler.java** specifies an interface for handling events (see Appendix A for a discussion of Java interfaces). The class **GeneticGame** implements the **EventHandler** interface and is derived (i.e., it extends) from the class **Gamelet**. An instance of class **GeneticGame** contains many instances of the class **GAship** (one for each enemy ship in the game). The class **GAship** contains a static variable for a single member of the class **ShipGenetic**. This single instance of class **ShipGenetic** contains data for playing statistics for all instances of class **GAship**; the single static member of class **ShipGenetic** is responsible for using a genetic algorithm to improve the playing ability of the enemy ships in the example game. The class **ShipGenetic** is derived from the class **mwa.ai.genetic.Genetic**.

Note on packages

The Java utility classes for implementing user interface, AI, and agent behaviors that were developed in Chapters 2 through 7 were organized in separate Java packages (see Appendix A for a discussion of packages). The Java classes developed by Mark Tacchi are located in the package **com.next.gt**. The example game is implemented using several new classes that are not placed in any specific package, so they belong to the Java default package. All classes in the default package share access to data and methods that are not specifically declared to be private or protected.

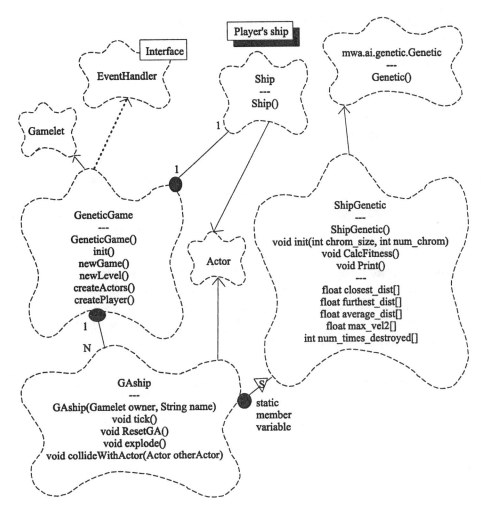

Figure 9.3   Booch class diagrams for **ShipGenetic, GeneticGame, Gaship,** and the associated Gamelet classes. A single instance of class **ShipGenetic** is used to represent the data for all enemy ships.

The class **ShipGenetic**, defined in Listing 9.1, is derived from the class **mwa.ai.genetic.Genetic**. The class **ShipGenetic** adds data specific for calculating the fitness of each chromosome. **ShipGenetic** redefines the **Genetic** method **CalcFitness( )** to use this local data that characterizes the performance of the enemy ships since the last population update (using crossover and mutation).

The class **ShipGenetic** contains the following public data for recording statistics on enemy ship performance, which is available to all instances of class **GAship**:

- **float closest_dist[]**
- **float furthest_dist[]**
- **float average_dist[]**
- **float max_vel2[]**
- **int num_times_destroyed[]**

Each of these static arrays has the same number of elements as **GAships**. This statistical data is stored in an instance of class **ShipGenetic** since it is required for the method **ShipGenetic.CalcFitness( )**. This data could alternatively have been stored in each **GAship** instance; in this case, the class **ShipGenetic** would require references to all instances of class **GAship**.

The class **ShipGenetic** is derived from the class **mwa.ai.genetic.Genetic**. The method **CalcFitness( )** is redefined to use enemy ship performance statistics to evolve a more effective population of chromosomes (which represent the machine language control programs for the instances of class **GAship**). The following methods from the superclass **mwa.ai.genetic.Genetic** are used to provide the behavior for simulating genetic algorithms:

- **void init(int chromosome_size, int num_chromosomes)**
- **void Sort()**
- **void DoCrossovers()**
- **void DoMutations()**

Listing 9.1

```
// ShipGenetic.java
//
//   How the GA works:
//
//   I invented a simple "machine language" for controlling
//   the enemy ships. There are eight instructions in this language:
//
//     0 move toward the player
//     1 move away from the player
//     2 move in +y direction (down the screen)
//     3 move in -y direction (up the screen)
//     4 if distance to player < 100 pixels, then skip next instruction
//     5 if distance to player > 100 pixels, then skip next instruction
//     6 if distance to player < 50 pixels, skip next 2 instructions
```

```
//    7 if distance to player > 50 pixels, skip next 2 instructions
//
// Each GAship has an instructon buffer that can hold 10 instructions.
// A program counter PC is used to index these instructions. When the
// program counter reaches the last instruction in the instruction
// buffer, it wraps around to the first instruction.
//
// It takes 3 bits to encode one "machine instruction," so the
// chromosome for each GAship is 30 bits long.
//
// Statistics are kept for each GAship in order to evaluate
// its genetic fitness.
//
// The storage for all chromosomes (one for each GAship instance)
// is stored as static public class data.

import java.lang.Math;

import mwa.ai.genetic.*;

import com.next.gt.*;

class ShipGenetic extends Genetic {

    // Public data for calculating a fitness function
    // (The class GeneticGame will statically allocate one
    // instance of this class. The following data is available
    // to methods in GeneticGame and GAship):
    public float closest_dist[];  // to player
    public float furthest_dist[]; // to player
    public float average_dist[];  // to player
    public float max_vel2[];      // square of the maximum velocity
    public int num_times_destroyed[];
    // (These arrays are allocated one element for each instance
    // of the class GAship.)

    float move_sq[];  // square of max distance travelled

    ShipGenetic() {
        // Call the init() function with good game defaults
        // in the constructor, so that a ShipGenetic instance can
        // be allocated statically in the GAship class:
        init(30, GAship.MAX_GA_SHIPS);
    }
```

```java
    public void init(int g, int c) {
        super.init(g, c);
        num_times_destroyed = new int[c];
        closest_dist = new float[c];   // to player
        furthest_dist = new float[c]; // to player
        average_dist = new float[c];   // to player
        max_vel2 = new float[c];
        move_sq = new float[c];
    }
    public void CalcFitness() {
        for (int i=0; i<NumChrom; i++) {
            // the distances are really distances squared.
            // take the square root to make distance
            // comparisons linear, rather than quadratic:
            average_dist[i] = (float)Math.sqrt(average_dist[i]);
            closest_dist[i] = (float)Math.sqrt(closest_dist[i]);
            furthest_dist[i] = (float)Math.sqrt(furthest_dist[i]);
            max_vel2[i] = (float)Math.sqrt(max_vel2[i]);
            move_sq[i] = (float)Math.sqrt(move_sq[i]);

            float fitness = 0.0f;
            fitness -= average_dist[i];
            fitness += 7.0f * (100.0f - closest_dist[i]);
            fitness -= 5.0f * furthest_dist[i];
            fitness -= 10 * num_times_destroyed[i];
            fitness -= max_vel2[i];
            fitness += 10.0f * move_sq[i];
            Fitness[i] = fitness;
        }
        //Print();
    }
    public void Print() {
        for (int i=0; i<NumChrom; i++) {
            System.out.print("Fitness for chromosome ");
            System.out.print(i);
            System.out.print(" is ");
            System.out.print(Fitness[i]);
            System.out.print(", average_dist=" + average_dist[i]);
            System.out.print(", closest_dist=" + closest_dist[i]);
            System.out.print(", furthest_dist=" + furthest_dist[i]);
            System.out.print(", num_times_destroyed=" +
                            num_times_destroyed[i]);
            System.out.print(", max_vel2=" + max_vel2[i]);
            System.out.println(", move_sq=" + move_sq[i]);
```

```
      }
    }
  }
```

Listing 9.2 shows the implementation of the class **GAship**. The file **GAship.java** contains the public **GAship** class and is shown in Listing 9.2. The statement

```
import mwa.ai.genetic.*;
```

allows us to reference the genetic algorithm utility class that we developed in Chapter 5. The class **GAship** (short for Genetic Algorithm ship) is derived from the Gamelet tool kit class **Actor**.

Using static class data

The Java language allows class data to be allocated for either each new instance of a class or for a single copy of data to be shared by all instances of a class by declaring the data to be static inside the class definition. The following class definition declares both instance data and static class data:

```
public class FOO {
    static int InstanceCount = 0;
    FOO() {
        InstanceCount++;
    }

    int width;
    int height;

    void main(String argv[]) {
        System.out.println("Instance count=" + InstanceCount);
        FOO f1 = new FOO();
        System.out.println("Instance count=" + InstanceCount);
}
```

If the **main()** method of class **FOO** is called, the following will be printed to standard output:

```
Instance count=0
Instance count=1
```

In this simple example, the static variable **InstanceCount** counts the number of times new **FOO** objects are created. Static class data has many uses. A good alternative to using static class data is to create a separate container class that manages (e.g., counts instances) a class.

The following static data defined in the **GAship** class allows us to share data for using the genetic algorithm utility class for all instances of the class **GAship**:

```
public static int NumGAships = 0;
public static ShipGenetic Chromosomes;
public static int Generation = 0;
```

The variable **NumGAships** counts the number of instances of class **GAship**. The class **ShipGenetic** is defined at the end of Listing 9.1. The class **ShipGenetic** is derived from the genetic algorithm class **mwa.ai.genetic.Genetic** developed in Chapter 5. The static class variable **Generation** keeps a count of the number of times we use genetic algorithm crossover and mutations to evolve the chromosome population stored in the static data **Chromosomes**.

The **GAship** class constructor takes two arguments:

- A reference to a **Gamelet** object
- The name of a GIF file used to define the appearance of the **GAship** object

The **GAship** constructor allocates storage for the 10-instruction control program in the variable **IB** and calls the method **ResetGA( )** to set the values of the instruction buffer **IB**. Each instance of class **GAship** has its local copy of the variable **MyChromosomeIndex**, which is its index in the chromosome array and the arrays used to store fitness data that is allocated in the class **ShipGenetic**:

- **float closest_dist[]**
- **float furthest_dist[]**
- **float average_dist[]**
- **float max_vel2[]**
- **int num_times_destroyed[]**

The method **ResetGA( )** fills in the values of the instruction buffer **IB** from the chromosome corresponding to this particular instance of class **GAship**. The method **tick()** updates the current **velocity_x** and **velocity_y** values (which are inherited from the base class **Agent**) based on the current instruction buffer **IB** and the index into the instruction buffer **IBindex**.

Listing 9.2

```
/**
 *
 * GAship.java     NOTE: this file was Asteroid.java
 * Originally written by Mark G. Tacchi (mtacchi@next.com)
 *
 * Mark Watson: converted Mark Tacchi's original code.
 * NOTE: modified for the Genetic Algorithm demo: we only
 *       want the smallest size of asteroids and will use
 *       these to represent the GA-controlled opponents.
 */


//
//   How the GA works:
//
//   I invented a simple "machine language" for controlling
//   the enemy ships. There are eight instructions in this language:
//
//     0 move toward the player
//     1 move away from the player
//     2 move in +y direction (down the screen)
//     3 move in -y direction (up the screen)
//     4 if distance to player < 100 pixels, then skip next instruction
//     5 if distance to player > 100 pixels, then skip next instruction
//     6 if distance to player < 50 pixels, skip next 2 instructions
//     7 if distance to player > 50 pixels, skip next 2 instructions
//
// Each GAship has an instructon buffer that can hold 10 instructions.
// A program counter PC is used to index these instructions. When the
// program counter reaches the last instruction in the instruction
// buffer, it wraps around to the first instruction.
//
// It takes 3 bits to encode one "machine instruction," so the
// chromosome for each GAship is 30 bits long.
//
// Statistics are kept for each GAship in order to evaluate
// its genetic fitness.
//
// The storage for all chromosomes (one for each GAship instance)
// is stored as static public class data.
```

```java
import java.lang.Math;

import mwa.ai.genetic.*;

import com.next.gt.*;

public class GAship extends Actor {

    // The data for the genetic algorithm:

    final static int MAX_GA_SHIPS = 14;
    public static int NumGAships = 0;

    // Change the following constant to specify
    // the number of game simulation cycles to use
    // for each machine instruction (i.e., increment
    // the "program counter" for the control programs
    // every 'NUM_TURNS_PER_INSTRUCTION' game iterations):
    final static int NUM_TURNS_PER_INSTRUCTION = 4;

    int repeat_count;


    //
    //                 Setup for GA:
    public static ShipGenetic Chromosomes = new ShipGenetic();
    public static int Generation = 0;
    public static int MyTick = 0;

    private int MyChromosomeIndex;

    // data for "machine language" instruction buffer:
    int IB[];
    int IBindex = 0;

    //
    // The filename prefix.
    //
    String                    name;

    GeneticGame GG;

float InitX, InitY;
```

```
GAship(Gamelet theOwner, String theName) {

  owner= theOwner;
  GG = (GeneticGame)theOwner;
  name= theName;

  IB = new int[10];

  MyChromosomeIndex = NumGAships++;
  if (NumGAships > MAX_GA_SHIPS) {
    System.out.println("FATAL error: too many GAships created.");
    NumGAships--;
  }

  // Copy the chromosome data to the instruction buffer 'IB':
  ResetGA();

  IBindex=0;

  // Randomize the initial repeat count for the different ships:
  repeat_count = (int)((NUM_TURNS_PER_INSTRUCTION - 1)
                  * Math.random());

  // Setup for graphics:

  java.awt.Image theImage;

  // Define the initial position and velocity:
  x= (Math.random()*200) + owner.size().width/2;
  InitX = (float)x;
  y= (Math.random()*100) + owner.size().height/2;
  InitY = (float)y;
  velocity_x= (double)((int)Gamelet.randBetween(0.5,1.5)*2 - 1)
            * Gamelet.randBetween(8.,32.);
  velocity_y= (double)((int)Gamelet.randBetween(0.5,1.5)*2 - 1)
            * Gamelet.randBetween(8.,32.);

  theImage = owner.getImage(owner.getCodeBase(),
                            "images/" +theName + "S" + ".gif");
  setImage (theImage, 4, 32);

  currentFrame= (int)Gamelet.randBetween(0, numFrames);
```

```java
} /*GAship()*/

public void tick() {  // override Actor class tick function

  // update the fitness statistics in the ShipGenetic object for
  // this particular instance of class GAship:
  float temp_sq =
      (float)((x - InitX)*(x - InitX) + (y - InitY)*(y - InitY));
  if (Chromosomes.move_sq[MyChromosomeIndex] < temp_sq)
    Chromosomes.move_sq[MyChromosomeIndex] = temp_sq;

  float dist2 = (float)((x - GG.player.x)*(x - GG.player.x) +
                        (y - GG.player.y)*(y - GG.player.y));
  if (dist2 < Chromosomes.closest_dist[MyChromosomeIndex])
    Chromosomes.closest_dist[MyChromosomeIndex] = dist2;
  if (dist2 > Chromosomes.closest_dist[MyChromosomeIndex])
    Chromosomes.furthest_dist[MyChromosomeIndex] = dist2;
  if (MyTick > 0) {
    float d1 = Chromosomes.average_dist[MyChromosomeIndex];
    float d2 = (float)(Math.sqrt(dist2) + MyTick * d1);
    d2 /= (float)MyTick;
    Chromosomes.average_dist[MyChromosomeIndex] = d2;
  }
  if (Chromosomes.max_vel2[MyChromosomeIndex] <
      velocity_x*velocity_x + velocity_y*velocity_y)
      Chromosomes.max_vel2[MyChromosomeIndex] =
         (float)(velocity_x*velocity_x + velocity_y*velocity_y);

  if (MyChromosomeIndex == 0) { // only for first GAship object
    // check for time to process all chromosomes for all GAships:
    if (MyTick++ > 500) {  // yup, time to update chromosomes
      Chromosomes.CalcFitness();
      Chromosomes.Sort();
      Chromosomes.DoCrossovers();
      Chromosomes.DoMutations();
      MyTick = 0;
      Generation++;
    }
  }

  // use instruction buffer to set velocity components:
  float del_x, del_y, scale;
  switch (IB[IBindex]) {
      case 0: // move toward player
```

```
            del_x = 0.5f * (float)(x - GG.player.x);
            del_y = (float)(y - GG.player.y);
            scale = 2000.0f / (0.001f + del_x*del_x + del_y*del_y);
            del_x *= scale;
            del_y *= scale;
            velocity_x -= del_x;
            velocity_y -= 2*del_y;
            break;
        case 1: // move away from player
            del_x = (float)(x - GG.player.x);
            del_y = (float)(y - GG.player.y);
            scale = 900.0f / (0.001f + del_x*del_x + del_y*del_y);
            del_x *= scale;
            del_y *= scale;
            velocity_x -= del_x;
            velocity_y -= del_y;
            break;
        case 2: // move in +y direction (down screen)
            velocity_y += 80;
            break;
        case 3: // move in -y direction (up screen)
            velocity_y -= 80;
            break;
        case 4: // if dist to player < 100 skip 1 instruction
            del_x = (float)(x - GG.player.x);
            del_y = (float)(y - GG.player.y);
            if (del_x*del_x + del_y*del_y < 100.0f*100.0f) {
                if (repeat_count > NUM_TURNS_PER_INSTRUCTION)
                    IBindex += 1;
            }
            break;
        case 5: // if dist to player > 100 skip 1 instruction
            del_x = (float)(x - GG.player.x);
            del_y = (float)(y - GG.player.y);
            if (del_x*del_x + del_y*del_y > 100.0f*100.0f) {
                if (repeat_count > NUM_TURNS_PER_INSTRUCTION)
                    IBindex += 1;
            }
            break;
        case 6: // if dist to player < 50 skip 2 instructions
            del_x = (float)(x - GG.player.x);
            del_y = (float)(y - GG.player.y);
            if (del_x*del_x + del_y*del_y < 50.0f*50.0f) {
                if (repeat_count > NUM_TURNS_PER_INSTRUCTION)
```

```
                    IBindex += 2;
                }
            break;
        case 7: // if dist to player > 50 skip 2 instructions
            del_x = (float)(x - GG.player.x);
            del_y = (float)(y - GG.player.y);
            if (del_x*del_x + del_y*del_y > 50.0f*50.0f) {
                if (repeat_count > NUM_TURNS_PER_INSTRUCTION)
                    IBindex += 2;
            }
            break;
        default:
            System.out.println("Illegal GAship instruction: " +
                            IB[IBindex] +
                            " at program counter " + IBindex);
            break;
    }

    if (repeat_count++ > NUM_TURNS_PER_INSTRUCTION) {
      repeat_count = 0;
      IBindex++;
      if (IBindex > 9)  IBindex -= 9;
    }

    // do not allow this ship to leave visible screen area:
    //if (x < 30) x = 30;
    if (x < 10) x = owner.size().width - 45;
    if (x > (owner.size().width - 45)) x = owner.size().width - 45;
    if (y < 80) y = 80;
    if (y > (owner.size().height - 100)) y = owner.size().height - 100;

    if (velocity_x > 40)  velocity_x = 40;
    if (velocity_x <-40)  velocity_x =-40;
    if (velocity_y > 40)  velocity_y = 40;
    if (velocity_y <-40)  velocity_y =-40;

    // call Actor.tick() for normal processing:
    super.tick();
}

void ResetGA() {
  currentFrame=0; // inherited from class Agent
  Chromosomes.num_times_destroyed[MyChromosomeIndex] = 0;
  Chromosomes.closest_dist[MyChromosomeIndex]=9999f*9999f; // to player
```

```
Chromosomes.furthest_dist[MyChromosomeIndex]=0; // to player
Chromosomes.average_dist[MyChromosomeIndex]=0;  // to player
Chromosomes.max_vel2[MyChromosomeIndex]=0;
Chromosomes.move_sq[MyChromosomeIndex]=0;

    // refill instruction buffer IB based on the
    // contents of this GAship's chromosome:
    int gene=0;
    for (int i=0; i<10; i++) {
      IB[i]=0;
      if (Chromosomes.GetGene(MyChromosomeIndex, gene++))
          IB[i]+=1;
      if (Chromosomes.GetGene(MyChromosomeIndex, gene++))
          IB[i]+=2;
      if (Chromosomes.GetGene(MyChromosomeIndex, gene++))
          IB[i]+=4;
    }
    x= (Math.random()*200) + owner.size().width/2;
    y= (Math.random()*100) + owner.size().height/2;
    velocity_x= (double)((int)Gamelet.randBetween(0.5,1.5)*2 - 1)
              * Gamelet.randBetween(8.,32.);
    velocity_y= (double)((int)Gamelet.randBetween(0.5,1.5)*2 - 1)
              * Gamelet.randBetween(8.,32.);
}

/**
 * Explode GAship.
 */
public void explode()
{
  Explosion anExplosion;

  anExplosion= new Explosion(owner, this);
  owner.actorManager.addActor(anExplosion);
  owner.play(owner.getCodeBase(), "sounds/explode1.au");

  //
  // The GAship is destroyed. Update statistics
  // for calculating the GA fitness function and
  // restart this ship off-screen:
  //

  float dist2 = (float)((x - GG.player.x)*(x - GG.player.x) +
                        (y - GG.player.y)*(y - GG.player.y));
```

```
    if (dist2 > 70*70) { // dist2 is distance squared
        Chromosomes.num_times_destroyed[MyChromosomeIndex] += 1;
    }

    x= (Math.random()*200) + owner.size().width/2;
    y= (Math.random()*100) + owner.size().height/2;
    velocity_x= (double)((int)Gamelet.randBetween(0.5,1.5)*2 - 1)
                * Gamelet.randBetween(8.,32.);
    velocity_y= (double)((int)Gamelet.randBetween(0.5,1.5)*2 - 1)
                * Gamelet.randBetween(8.,32.);

} /*explode*/



/**
 * Handle collision with an actor.
 */
protected void collideWithActor (Actor theActor)
{
    String theActorClassName= theActor.getClass().getName();

    if (theActorClassName.equals("Bullet") ||
        theActorClassName.equals("Ship") ) {
        explode();
    } /*endif*/

} /*collideWithActor*/

} /*GAship*/
```

The file **GeneticGame.java** is shown in Listing 9.3. The class **GeneticGame** was created by copying Mark Tacchi's **Roid** class and adding support for using the genetic algorithm classes. The method **GeneticGame.init( )** performs the following tasks:

- Call **GeneticGame.NewGame( )** to initialize player and enemy ships.
- Register this instance of class **GeneticGame** to receive keyboard events from the **EventManager** interface for restarting the game when the F1 key is pressed.
- Load the background GIF image in the game window.

The methods **newGame( )**, **createActors( )**, and **createPlayer( )** use the member variable **actorManager** (class **com.next.gt.ActorManager**) inherited from the **Gamelet** superclass to manage the player and enemy ships.

Listing 9.3

```
/**
 * Genetic algorithm demo game.
 *
 * BASED ON:
 *
 * Roids.java
 * @author    Mark G. Tacchi (mtacchi@next.com)
 * @version   0.8
 * Mar 27/1996
 *
 *
 * Changes by Mark Watson for using a genetic algorithm
 * to dynamically modify enemy ship behaviors.
 *
 */



import java.applet.AudioClip;
import java.lang.Math;
import java.awt.*;

import com.next.gt.*;

import mwa.ai.genetic.*;


public class GeneticGame extends Gamelet
                         implements EventHandler {

    public Ship        player;
    public int         numShips;
    public int         badGuyCount;

    //
    // Genetic algorithm generation # label.
    //
    private Label      myLabel;

    /**
     * Initialize.
     */
    public void init() {
      //
```

```
    // cache images
    //
    new ImageManager(this);

    myLabel =
        new Label(" GA generation: " + GAship.Generation + "     ");
    add("South",myLabel);

    this.newGame();

    //
    // register for events
    //
    eventManager.
      registerForSingleEventNotification(this,
                                   Event.KEY_ACTION_RELEASE);

    //
    // paint background image
    //
    displayManager.setBackgroundTile(getImage(getCodeBase(),
                                "images/background.gif"));

} /*init*/



/**
 * Set up the new game.
 */
public void newGame() {
  numShips= 15;
  badGuyCount= 0;
  player= null;
  actorManager.removeAllActors();
  this.createActors();
} /*newGame*/


/**
 * Create the actors for this scene.
 */
public void createActors() {
  for (int i= 0; i< (numShips - 1); i++) {
```

```
      actorManager.addActor (new GAship(this, "gumball"));
        badGuyCount++;
  } /*nexti*/
  this.createPlayer();
} /*createActors*/


/**
 * Create the player object.
 */
public void createPlayer() {
  if (player!=null) {
    actorManager.removeActor(player);
  } /*endif*/
  player= new Ship(this);
  actorManager.addActor (player);
} /*createPlayer*/


/**
 * Handle keyboard events to restart game.
 */
public boolean handleRequestedEvent (Event theEvent) {
  switch(theEvent.id) {
  case Event.KEY_ACTION_RELEASE:
    switch(theEvent.key) {
        case Event.F1:
      this.newGame();
          return true;
    } /*endSwitch*/
  } /*endSwitch*/
  return false;
} /*handleRequestedEvent*/




/**
 * Override paint to display genetic algorithm
 * generation # printout
 */
public void paint(Graphics g) {
  super.paint(g);
  myLabel.setText(" GA generation: " + GAship.Generation);
} /*paint*/
```

```
} /*GeneticGame*/
```
Figure 9.4 shows a captured screen shot of a game in progress. The number of genetic algorithm generations (i.e., the number of times we have updated the chromosome population using crossover and mutation) is shown at the top of the screen. The colors have been reversed in this image; the background in the game is solid black with white stars. The player ship appears on the left side of the screen and can be moved vertically by using the up/down arrow keys. The left/right arrow keys affect the direction of the ship. The space key fires bullets.

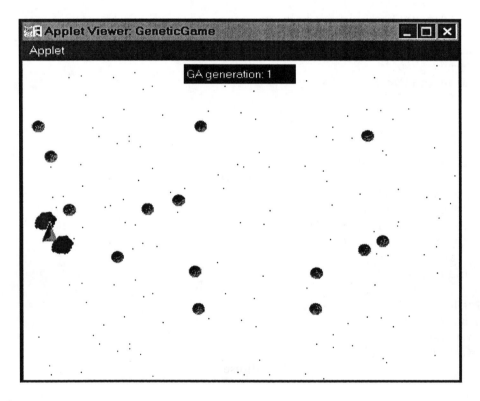

Figure 9.4   View of the game in progress

Neural Network for Real-Time Handwriting Recognition

A Java neural network class library was developed in Chapter 4. In this chapter, we will use the classes in packages **mwa.ai.neural** and **mwa.gui** to build an effective handwriting recognition application. The purpose of this example program is to demonstrate embedding a neural network in an application. In Chapter 11, we will write Java utility classes to optimize neural network training data using greedy algorithms, and in Chapter 12, we will write Java utility classes to optimize both training data and the structure of neural networks using genetic algorithms. The example application developed in this chapter will be extended in Chapters 11 and 12 to use this new technology.

10.1 Requirements for handwriting recognition

In order to recognize handwritten characters, we need to digitize the position of the path of a drawing tool on a writing surface. We will use a mouse to draw characters in the window of the example application. We will not use the order of pen or mouse strokes to create characters, although a handwriting recognition system that uses temporal information will be more accurate than a system that uses a simple digital representation of the lines used to draw characters.

A primary requirement of a handwriting recognition system is to allow handwriting anywhere on a writing surface and characters of any size. The sample program requires a user to draw one or more copies of each character. After training a neural network using these hand-drawn characters, the same user can write anywhere in the sample application's window. The system must be retrained for new users. Figure 10.1 shows sample training characters being drawn in the lower left corner of the application window.

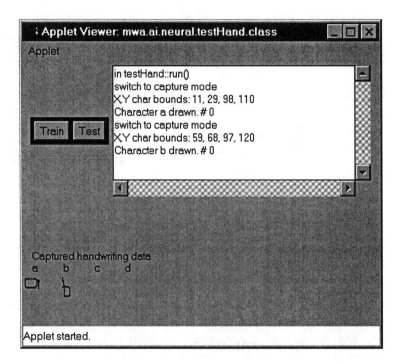

Figure 10.1   Training characters are drawn in vertical columns in the lower left part of the application window. The sample program has been configured in demo mode to recognize the four characters *a*, *b*, *c*, and *d*.

10.2 Design of a program for handwriting recognition

As characters are drawn or written, bounding rectangles are calculated for each character. A hand-drawn character can be of any size because the bounding rectangle is used to normalize the image of the character to fit into a small two-dimensional grid that is used for input to a neural network. Each input grid point represents the value of an input neuron in a neural network. Three primary modes of operation are supported:

- Capturing training data
- Training the neural network
- Testing handwriting recognition

10.2.1 Capturing training data

Usually multiple training cases per character are required for training. As we increase the number of characters that the sample program recognizes, we must also increase the number of training examples per character. As seen in Figure 10.1, the characters to be recognized are printed in a row in the bottom left of the application window. The program user draws training characters in any order below the printed characters. The data collection software can use the screen *x*-coordinate range of each hand-drawn training character to determine which training character is currently being drawn.

Hand-drawn characters can be of any size, but they are down-sampled to a specific size of grid. Constants **XSIZE** and **YSIZE** are used to specify the size of this input grid. The number of input neurons will be **XSIZE * YSIZE**. The sample program is configured by setting the following parameters:

- **XSIZE**—horizontal size of mapped characters in units of screen pixels
- **YSIZE**—vertical size of mapped characters in units of screen pixels
- **NUM**—number of distinct characters to be recognized
- **NUM_EX**—maximum number of training examples per character

As characters are drawn, they are down-sampled onto an **XSIZE** by **YSIZE** grid and stored in the integer array **Inputs[NUM][NUM_EX][XSIZE][YSIZE]**.

The size of the constants **XSIZE** and **YSIZE** affects the fidelity of the down-sampled data. If the values of **XSIZE** and **YSIZE** are too small, similar characters like *a* and *e* might be mapped into the same pattern. If the values of **XSIZE** and **YSIZE** are too large, then the neural network will take longer to train, with more training cases required to differentiate the characters in the training data set. The array **Count[NUM]** is used to record the number of training examples per character type.

The sample program must determine when the program user is done drawing an individual character. This determination is made by recording the current time in milliseconds when each mouse down movement is recorded. After no mouse down movements have occurred for 400 milliseconds, it is assumed that a training character is no longer being drawn and the following processing steps are executed:

- Calculate the *x* and *y* minimum and maximum screen coordinates of the hand drawn character.
- Determine which column, if any, of training data contains the character. This column index determines the first array index of the multidimensional array **Inputs**.
- Scale the hand-drawn character to the **XSIZE** by **YSIZE** grid, and store the character in the array **Inputs**.

- Increase by one the array element of array **Count** indexed by the character type. The array **Count** is used for properly calculating the second array index of the multidimensional array **Inputs**.

Figure 10.2 shows the sample application after two training examples have been captured for each of four distinct characters, and the neural network is being trained.

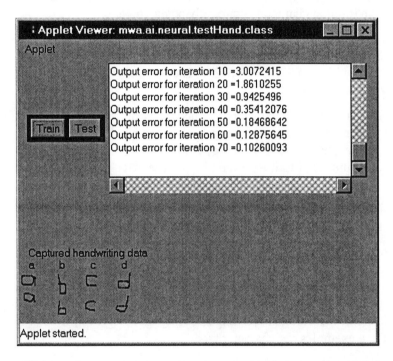

Figure 10.2   Application after recording training data and clicking the button "Train"

10.2.2 Training the neural network

The following method of class **mwa.ai.neural.Neural** is used for training the neural network: **float train(float ins[], float outs[], int num_cases)**. Method **train** returns a training error, which should, on average, get smaller as we repeatedly call method **train**.

The neural network class **Neural** expects input training data to be a linear, one-dimensional array (or a vector). For example, if the input grid size is set to **XSIZE = 5** and **YSIZE = 6**, then we fill the neural network input vector in this order:

1	7	13	19	25
2	8	14	20	26
3	9	15	21	27
4	10	16	22	28
5	11	17	23	29
6	12	18	24	30

The elements of the multidimensional array **Inputs** have values of zero or one. When the neural network input training vector is filled, we map zero values in the **Inputs** array to the value -0.4, and we map the value one to the input neuron value +0.4.

The output neuron training data is represented by a vector with **NUM** elements. For each training case, an output neuron target training value for character type N is set to

- -0.4 if the vector index is not equal to N
- +0.4 if the vector index is equal to N

The number of times that the method **train** needs to be called depends on the number of distinct characters to be recognized. For learning four distinct characters, calling method **train** about 60 times is sufficient. For learning ten distinct characters, method **train** will probably need to be called over 500 times before the training error starts to approach zero. Each time the "Train" button is clicked (see Figure 10.2), method **train** is called up to 3000 times. In practice, however, the method **train** is called fewer times since the training process ends when the cumulative error over all training examples is less than 0.1.

In Chapters 11 and 12, we will develop powerful techniques using both greedy algorithms and genetic algorithms to improve both training data and the actual structure of a neural network. The example application developed in this chapter will be extended to support many more distinct characters in Chapters 11 and 12.

10.2.3 Testing handwriting recognition

After the neural network has been trained, the "Test" button on the application can be pressed to switch the program mode to testing. The same logic is used for capturing characters, except that now we can allow the program user to draw a character anywhere on the application window. Figure 10.3 shows the sample application after drawing a test character. The correct recognition is printed in the text output field.

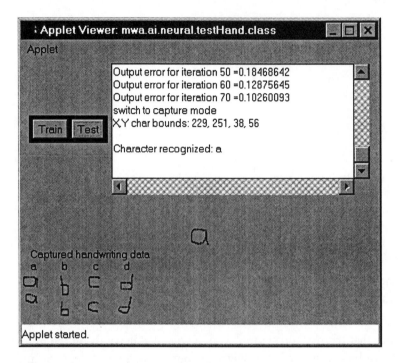

Figure 10.3   Testing character recognition

After a character has been drawn, the following steps are followed:

- Down-sample the pixels in the hand-drawn character to an **XSIZE** by **YSIZE** grid.
- Fill the neural network input vector (as in the training process).
- Copy the neural network input vector to the public array **mwa.ai.neural.Neural.Inputs[]**.
- Call the method **mwa.ai.neural.Neural.ForwardPass( )**.
- Examine the array **mwa.ai.neural.Neural.Inputs[]** to determine the largest value. The index of the largest value identifies the character that was just drawn on the application window.

10.3 Implementation of the handwriting recognition program

Listing 10.1 shows the implementation of the handwriting recognition program. This program is relatively short and simple because the Java classes **mwa.gui.GUI** and

mwa.ai.neural.Neural provide the behavior for application control of a neural network simulation.

The class **testHand** implements the **Runnable** interface since it creates a thread. Classes that implement the **Runnable** class must define a method **run( )** that is used by the **Thread** class. See Appendix A for a discussion of threaded applications.

In Listing 10.1, the method **mwa.ai.neural.testHand.init( )** initializes the application window by calling **super.init( )** (i.e., the method **mwa.gui.GUI.init( )**) and then creates a thread to handle mouse input in the application window. An instance of class **mwa.ai.neural.Neural** is created and is referenced by the class variable **mwa.ai.neural.testHand.network**.

The method **mwa.ai.neural.train( )** uses captured mouse data (representing hand-drawn characters and stored in the array **Inputs**) to train the neural network object referenced by the variable **mwa.ai.neural.testHand.network**. The array **Inputs** is a four-dimensional array whose dimensions represent

- index on the type of character (i.e., 0 index for *a*, an index value of 1 for *b*, etc.)
- index on the training example number
- index for the *x*-coordinate in the neural network two-dimensional input grid
- Index for the *y*-coordinate in the neural network two-dimensional input grid

The method **mwa.ai.neural.testHand.run( )** is called automatically when the mouse event thread is started in the method **mwa.ai.neural.testHand.init( )**. The **run( )** method uses the class variable **mwa.ai.neural.testHand.MouseState** to determine if mouse down events should be captured for training data. The method **mwa.ai.neural.testHand.PutChar( )** is a utility method used by the **run( )** method for storing mouse event data. Method **PutChar( )** provides the following behavior:

- Calculates the *x*- and *y*-coordinate ranges of recently captured data.
- Tests for the special case for testing handwriting recognition. If the program is in test mode, then the recently captured mouse event data is copied into a neural network input array and the trained neural network referenced by the variable **network** is used to determine what character has been drawn.
- If the program is not in the test mode, then the recently captured mouse event data is copied to the four-dimensional **Inputs** array for future use in training the neural network.

Listing 10.1

```
// testHand.java
//
```

```java
// NeuralNet Java classes: tester for handwriting recognition
//
// Copyright 1996, Mark Watson.  All rights reserved.
// www.markwatson.com
//

package mwa.ai.neural;

import java.awt.*;

import mwa.gui.GUI;

public class testHand extends GUI implements Runnable {

    // define the size of two-dimensional neural
    // input array:
    final static int XSIZE=5;
    final static int YSIZE=6;

    // define the Mode: 0 for training mode,
    // 1 for testing mode:
    public int Mode = 0;

    // Number of characters of each type to use
    // for training data:
    final static int NUM_EX=2;   // number of examples

    // Number of characters to learn:
    final static int NUM = 4;
    String Chars[] = {"a", "b", "c", "d"};;
    // Data for partitioning GUI display for capturing
    // individual characters:
    int X_Pos[] = {20, 60, 100, 140};
    int Y_Pos = 90;
    int Inputs[][][][] = new int[NUM][NUM_EX][XSIZE][YSIZE];

    // Count[NUM] is used for counting drawn chars
    int Count[] = {0, 0, 0, 0};

    // data for determining when a new character
    // is being drawn:
    long TimeLastMouse = -1;   // in milliseconds
    // MouseState: 0=>no capture, 1=>currently capturing
    int MouseState = 0;
```

```
    int MousePointIndex = 0; // at the start of capture data


    int num_cap=0;
    int cap_x[] = new int[20000];
    int cap_y[] = new int[20000];

    int active = 0;  // if 1, then train network

    // Neural network:
    Neural network;

    public String getAppletInfo() {
        return "Neural Network Simulator by Mark Watson";
    }

    private Thread MouseThread = null;

    public void init() {

        Count    = new int[NUM];
        for (int i=0; i<NUM; i++) Count[i] = 0;

        NoInput = true;  // we do not need an input text field
        BigText=1;

        network = new Neural(XSIZE * YSIZE, 10, NUM);
        //network.MyGUI = this;

        RunLabel = new String("Train");
        ResetLabel = new String("Test");

        super.init();

        if (MouseThread==null) {
         MouseThread = new Thread(this);
         MouseThread.start();
        }
    }

    public void train() {
      P("Starting to train network..wait..\n");
      int sum = 0, ic=0, oc=0;
      for (int i=0; i<NUM; i++)  sum += Count[i];
```

```
    float ins[] = new float[sum*XSIZE*YSIZE];
    float outs[] = new float[sum*NUM];
    for (int i=0; i<NUM; i++) {
      for (int j=0; j<Count[i]; j++) {
        for (int x=0; x<XSIZE; x++) {
          for (int y=0; y<YSIZE; y++) {
            if (Inputs[i][j][x][y] == 0) {
              ins[ic++] = -0.4f;
            } else {
              ins[ic++] = +0.4f;
            }
          }
        }
      }
      for (int k=0; k<NUM; k++)
        if (k!=i) outs[oc++] = -0.4f;
        else      outs[oc++] = +0.4f;
      }
    }
    for (int i=0; i<3000; i++) {
      float error = network.Train(ins, outs, sum);
      if ((i % 10) == 0) {
        P("Output error for iteration " +
          i + " =" + error + "\n");
      }
      if (error < 0.1f)  break;  // done training
    }
  }

  public void paintToDoubleBuffer(Graphics g) {
    g.drawString("Captured handwriting data",
                          X_Pos[0], Y_Pos - 15);

    for (int m=0; m<NUM; m++) {
      g.drawString(Chars[m], X_Pos[m], Y_Pos);
    }
    setForeground(Color.black);
    g.setColor(getForeground());
    for (int i=0; i<num_cap; i++) {
      g.drawLine(cap_x[i],
                 cap_y[i],
                 cap_x[i],
                 cap_y[i]+1);
    }
  }
```

```
public void run() {
    P("in testHand::run()\n");
    while (true)  {
        try {
            if (MouseState==1) {
                long mtime =
                    java.lang.System.currentTimeMillis();
                if (TimeLastMouse < mtime - 800) {
                    MouseState=0;
                    PutChar();
                }
            }
        }  catch (Exception e) {} ;
        try {Thread.sleep(20);} catch (Exception ex) { };
    }
}

public void doRunButton() {
    train();
 }
public void doResetButton() {
    Mode = 1;  // switch to test mode
}

public void PutChar() {
    int x_min=9999, x_max=-9999;
    int y_min=9999, y_max=-9999;
    for (int i=MousePointIndex; i<num_cap; i++) {
        if (cap_x[i] < x_min) x_min = cap_x[i];
        if (cap_x[i] > x_max) x_max = cap_x[i];
        if (cap_y[i] < y_min) y_min = cap_y[i];
        if (cap_y[i] > y_max) y_max = cap_y[i];
    }
    if (x_min+1 > x_max)  { x_min--; x_max++; }
    P("X,Y char bounds: " + x_min + ", " + x_max +
      ", " + y_min + ", " + y_max + "\n");

    // Special case:Mode==1 for testing:
    if (Mode==1) {
        int ic = 0;
        for (int x=0; x<XSIZE; x++) {
            for (int y=0; y<YSIZE; y++) {
                network.Inputs[ic++] = -0.4f;
            }
```

```
        }
        for (int i=MousePointIndex; i<num_cap; i++) {
            float xx = (float)(cap_x[i] - x_min)
                        / (float)(x_max - x_min);
            xx *= XSIZE;
            float yy = (float)(cap_y[i] - y_min)
                        / (float)(y_max - y_min);
            yy *= YSIZE;
            int ix=(int)xx;
            int iy=(int)yy;
            if (ix<0) ix=0;
            if (ix>=XSIZE) ix=XSIZE-1;
            if (iy<0) iy=0;
            if (iy>=YSIZE) iy=YSIZE-1;
            network.Inputs[ix*YSIZE+iy] = +0.4f;
        }
        // Propagate input neuron values through
        // to the hidden, then output neuron layer:
        network.ForwardPass();
        // Find the largest output neuron value:
        int index=0;
        float maxVal=-99f;
        for (int i=0; i<NUM; i++) {
            if (network.Outputs[i]>maxVal) {
                maxVal = network.Outputs[i];
                index = i;
            }
        }
        P("\nCharacter recognized: " + Chars[index] + "\n");
        return;
    }

    // Find which character is drawn by the x coord:
    int char_type = -1;
    for (int i=0; i<NUM; i++) {
        if (x_min - 10 < X_Pos[i] &&
            x_max + 10 > X_Pos[i]) {
                char_type = i;
            }
    }
    if (char_type==-1) {
        P("Error: character is not drawn in correct position\n");
        MousePointIndex = num_cap;
        return;
```

```
        }
        P("Character " + Chars[char_type] + " drawn. # "
          + Count[char_type] + "\n");
        if (Count[char_type] > (NUM_EX-1)) {
            P("Too many examples for this char type: ignoring!\n");
            MousePointIndex = num_cap;
            return;
        }
        for (int x=0; x<XSIZE; x++) {
            for (int y=0; y<YSIZE; y++) {
                Inputs[char_type][Count[char_type]][x][y] = 0;
            }
        }
        for (int i=MousePointIndex; i<num_cap; i++) {
            float xx = (float)(cap_x[i] - x_min)
                        / (float)(x_max - x_min);
            xx *= XSIZE;
            float yy = (float)(cap_y[i] - y_min)
                        / (float)(y_max - y_min);
            yy *= YSIZE;
            int ix=(int)xx;
            int iy=(int)yy;
            if (ix<0) ix=0;
            if (ix>=XSIZE) ix=XSIZE-1;
            if (iy<0) iy=0;
            if (iy>=YSIZE) iy=YSIZE-1;
            Inputs[char_type][Count[char_type]][ix][iy] = 1;
        }
        MousePointIndex = num_cap;
        Count[char_type] += 1;
    }

    public void doMouseDown(int x, int y) {
        long mtime = java.lang.System.currentTimeMillis();
        if (MouseState==0) { // not yet in capture mode
            P("switch to capture mode\n");
            MouseState=1;
            MousePointIndex = num_cap;
        }

        TimeLastMouse = mtime;

        //System.out.println("Mouse x: " + x + ", y: " + y);
        if (num_cap<19999) {
```

```
            cap_x[num_cap] = x;
            cap_y[num_cap] = y;
            num_cap++;
            repaint();
        }
    }
}
```

Figure 10.4 shows the test application running in test mode. The method **doReset-Button( )** is executed when the button labeled "Test" is clicked with the mouse. This method sets the class variable **mwa.ai.neural.testHand.Mode** to the value 1, which is a flag for method **PutChar( )** to run in test mode.

The example program in Listing 10.1 is reused and modified in Chapters 11 and 12, so it is worth the effort now to carefully read it.

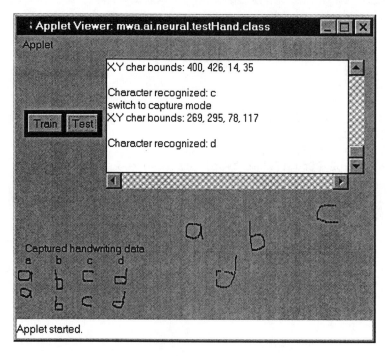

Figure 10.4   After correctly recognizing all character types

Using a Greedy Algorithm to Optimize Neural Networks

11

As we discussed in Chapter 4, one of the most difficult problems that need to be solved in the application of neural network technology is creating a good set of training data. I have been using backwards error propagation neural networks for 10 years. The utilities developed in this chapter are based on my experience hand-tuning neural network training data. In Chapter 12, we will extend these capabilities of improving training data by using genetic algorithms to discard bad training cases and to change the structure of neural networks.

A greedy algorithm is defined by its inability to retract any action. Based on a current situation, an action is chosen without the possibility of undoing this action. A greedy algorithm thus differs from search techniques that allow backtracking.

11.1 Requirements for a greedy algorithm for optimizing neural network training data

Conflicting training cases make it impossible for a neural network to learn to recognize all training examples. A neural network with **NumInputs** input layer neurons has an input space that is a **NumInputs**-dimensional hypercube. For example, if a neural network has two input layer neurons, then the input space is bounded by the square centered at the origin with both width and height equal to one (i.e., a hypercube of dimension two; a normal cube is a hypercube of dimension three). Any point inside this square region is a valid input for the neural network. If the neural network also has two output layer neurons, then the output of the neural network can also be characterized by a point inside the unit square centered at the origin. Two conflicting training cases might be

- inputs: -0.3, 0.4; outputs: 0.1, -0.2
- inputs: -0.28, 0.399; outputs: -0.2, -0.3

The two inputs are very close together, while the target output values are very different. It will not be possible for a neural network to recognize both of these training patterns. The greedy algorithm will keep the first conflicting training case that it finds and discard the second conflicting training case.

Another fault often found in training data occurs when a large portion of the possible input space is not covered by training examples. For the example of a neural network with two input layer neurons, an uncovered region would be any relatively large region of the unit square centered at the origin that did not contain any training examples. For some applications, it is fine to have large uncovered regions of the input space, but for other types of applications, problems will occur when using the trained neural network in an application. For example, if a simple neural network was used to control a steam boiler, it might have two input neurons:

- the current boiler pressure normalized to the range -0.5 to +0.5
- the current outer boiler temperature normalized to the range -0.5 to +0.5

It would be very important to train this neural network with training data that covered all regions of the input space that could possibly occur in any realistic situation.

The second utility developed in this chapter searches the input space for large regions that do not contain any training examples. This utility adds training cases to the output file generated by an instance of the class **mwa.ai.neural.NNfile**; the output values for these added cases are set to 9999.9 as an indication to the system developer either to define reasonable output neuron values for these cases or to remove them because the corresponding area of the input space will never be used in the final application that uses the neural network.

11.2 Design of a greedy algorithm for optimizing neural network training data

The class **mwa.ai.neural.NNgreedy** contains an instance of class **mwa.ai.neural.NNfile** that is used to manage the data for specifying both the structure and training data for a neural network. Figure 11.1 shows the Booch class diagram containing the public interface for the class **mwa.ai.neural.NNgreedy** and the relationships with classes **mwa.ai.neural.NNfile** and **mwa.ai.neural.Neural**.

The Java class **mwa.ai.neural.NNfile** (defined in Chapter 4) is used to save and load neural networks to and from disk files. A neural network file is ASCII data containing the following information:

- Number of layers (currently this is always three)
- Number of neurons in the input layer
- Number of neurons in the hidden layer
- Number of neurons in the output layer
- A flag indicating if previously calculated weights are stored in the file
- A flag indicating if any special application-specific data is stored in the file (a nonzero value indicates the number of special data values in the file)
- The number of training cases in the file
- Input-layer-to-hidden-layer weights (optional)
- Hidden-layer-to-output-layer weights (optional)
- Application-specific data (optional)
- Training data (optional)

Instances of the class **mwa.ai.neural.NNgreedy** use the utility class **mwa.ai.neural.NNfile** to both read existing input neural network description files and to write output neural network description files.

An instance of class **mwa.ai.neural.NNgreedy** is created by specifying the name of a data file used to construct an instance of class **mwa.ai.neural.NNfile**. The class **mwa.ai.neural.NNgreedy** has three public member functions:

- **RemoveExtraData**—removes all conflicting training data cases
- **FindEmptyRegion**—attempts to find one empty region each time that it is called
- **Save**—writes a file that can be used later to create a new **NNfile** object

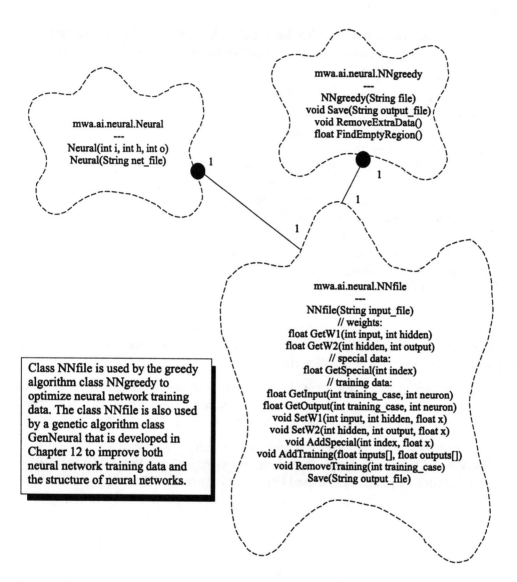

Figure 11.1   Booch class diagram for **NNgreedy**

11.3 Implementation of a greedy algorithm for optimizing data

The class **mwa.ai.neural.NNgreedy** is implemented in this chapter as a utility for improving training data sets for neural networks. The class **mwa.ai.neural.NNgreedy** uses the class **mwa.ai.neural.NNfile** that was implemented in Chapter 4.

Listing 11.1 shows the implementation of the class **mwa.ai.neural.NNgreedy**. The method **RemoveExtraData** removes training cases that have very similar input neuron values. While it is useful to have different training examples for each output classification, there are two reasons to remove extra training cases whose inputs almost exactly match the input values of another training case:

- To reduce training time without adversely affecting the quality of the trained network
- To prevent training cases with almost identical inputs that have very different output values

The method **RemoveExtraData** uses the class **mwa.ai.neural.NNfile** to maintain the data for the training cases. A training case can be removed by using the method **mwa.ai.neural.NNfile.RemoveTrainingData**.

The method **FindEmptyRegion** generates a fairly large number of random points inside the hypercube representing the input space of the neural network. The distance to the closest input training case is calculated for each of these random points. The random point that is furthest from any input training case is added to the training data maintained by the contained instance of **NNfile**. The output neuron values of the added training data set are set to 9999.9 to indicate that they must be manually set. The method **RemoveExtraData** is very useful for quickly checking the coverage of a set of training data.

Listing 11.1

```
// NNgreedy class: parses neural network input files
// using the class NNfile and reports areas of input
// data space that contain no training examples and
// also uses a greedy algorithm to remove conflicting
// training examples

package mwa.ai.neural;

import java.applet.Applet;
import java.io.*;
import java.net.URL;
```

```java
import java.util.*;


public class NNgreedy {

  public NNfile NeuralFile = null;

  public NNgreedy() {
     System.out.println("\n\nError: NNgreedy constructor " +
                        "requires a file name.\n");
  }

  public NNgreedy(String input_file) {
    NeuralFile = new NNfile(input_file);
  }

  public void Save(String file) {
    NeuralFile.Save(file);
  }

  void RemoveExtraData() {
     if (NeuralFile==null) return;
     for (int m=0; m<NeuralFile.NumTraining; m++) {
        for (int k=m+1; k<NeuralFile.NumTraining; k++) {
           float dist = 0.0f;
           for (int i=0; i<NeuralFile.NumInput; i++) {
              float x = NeuralFile.GetInput(m, i) -
                        NeuralFile.GetInput(k, i);
              dist += x*x;
           }
           if (dist < 0.005f) { // adjustable threshold
              // Remove training data item # k:
              NeuralFile.RemoveTraining(k);
              System.out.println("Deleted training case " + k);
              break;
           }
        }
     }
     System.out.println("Done deleting redundant training cases.");
  }

  float FindEmptyRegion() {
     int iter = NeuralFile.NumInput*NeuralFile.NumOutput*100;
     float max_dist = 0.000001f;
```

```
    float inputs[] = new float[NeuralFile.NumInput];
    float best_inputs[] = new float[NeuralFile.NumInput];
    for (int i=0; i<iter; i++) {
        for (int j=0; j<NeuralFile.NumInput; j++) {
            inputs[j] = (float)(Math.random() - 0.5f);
        }
        int best_index = 0;
        for (int m=0; m<NeuralFile.NumTraining; m++) {
            float x = 0;
            for (int ii=0; ii<NeuralFile.NumInput; ii++) {
                float z = inputs[ii] - NeuralFile.GetInput(m, ii);
                x += z*z;
            }
            if (x > max_dist) {
                max_dist = x;
                best_index = i;
                for (int k=0; k<NeuralFile.NumInput; k++) {
                    best_inputs[k]=inputs[k];
                }
            }
        }
    }
    float outputs[] = new float[NeuralFile.NumOutput];
    for (int o=0; o<NeuralFile.NumOutput; o++)
        outputs[o] = 99999.9f;
    NeuralFile.AddTraining(best_inputs, outputs);
    return max_dist;
  }

}
```

11.4 Testing the classes NNfile and NNgreedy

Listing 11.2 contains a short test application for testing the class **mwa.ai.neural.NNfile**. An instance of the neural network class **mwa.ai.neural.Neural** is created in the method **mwa.ai.neural.testNeuralFile.init( )** using the neural network specification file **test.dat**.

The method **mwa.ai.neural.testNeuralFile.doRunButton( )** is called every time the application's "Run" button is clicked with the mouse. This method executes 30 neural network training cycles. The graphics display in the application window is updated after this method executes.

The method **mwa.ai.neural.testNeuralFile.doResetButton( )** is called each time the application's "Reset" button is clicked with the mouse.   This method adds six application-specific "special" values to the **NNfile** object, deletes the third training example, and saves the contents of the **NNfile** object (i.e., the network size, weights, special data, and training data cases) to a new neural network specification file **test2.dat**.

Listing 11.2

```
// NeuralNet Java classes
//
// Copyright 1996, Mark Watson.  All rights reserved.

package mwa.ai.neural;

import java.awt.*;

import mwa.gui.GUI;
import mwa.data.*;

public class testNeuralFile extends GUI {

    Neural network;

    float Errors[];
    int NumErrors = 0;
    int width = 380;
    int height = 260;

    // For training:
    private float outs[];
    private float ins[];
    private float error = -9999.9f;

    public String getAppletInfo() {
        return "Neural Network Simulator by Mark Watson";
    }

    public void init() {

        NoInput = true;  // we do not need an input text field
        //ResetLabel = new String("Save file");

        Errors = new float[512];
```

```
    NumErrors = 0;

    super.init();

    network = new Neural("test.dat");
    network.MyGUI = this;
}

private void paintNeuronLayer(Graphics g, int x, int y,
                             String title, float values[],
                             int num) {
    for (int i=0; i<num; i++) {
        paintGridCell(g, x+60 + i*12, y, 10, values[i],
                      -0.5f, 0.5f);
    }
    g.drawString(title, x, y+10);
}

private void paintWeights(Graphics g, int x, int y, String title,
                          float values[][], int num1, int num2) {
    for (int i=0; i<num1; i++) {
        for (int j=0; j<num2; j++) {
            paintGridCell(g, x+60 + i*12, y + j * 12, 10,
                          values[i][j], -1.5f, 1.5f);
        }
    }
    g.drawString(title, x, y+10);
}

public void paintToDoubleBuffer(Graphics g) {
    // Draw the input/hidden/output neuron layers:
    paintNeuronLayer(g, 170, 10, "Inputs:",
                     network.Inputs, network.NumInputs);
    paintNeuronLayer(g, 170, 80, "Hidden:",
                     network.Hidden, network.NumHidden);
    paintNeuronLayer(g, 170, 140, "Outputs:",
                     network.Outputs, network.NumOutputs);
    paintWeights(g, 170, 30, "Weights 1:",
                 network.W1, network.NumInputs,
                 network.NumHidden);
    paintWeights(g, 170, 100, "Weights 2:", network.W2,
                 network.NumHidden, network.NumOutputs);
    // Draw a plot of error summed over output neurons:
    g.drawString("Cumulative error summed over output neurons",
```

```
                              10, height - 10);
    if (NumErrors < 2)  return;
    int x1= 0, x2;
    int y1 = height - (int)(100.0f * Errors[0]), y2;
    setForeground(Color.red);
    g.setColor(getForeground());
    for (int i=1; i<NumErrors-1; i++) {
        x2 = 2*i;
        y2 = height - (int)(100.0f * Errors[i]);
        g.drawLine(x1, y1, x2, y2);
        x1 = x2;
        y1 = y2;
    }
}


public void doRunButton() {
    for (int i=0; i<30; i++) {
        Errors[NumErrors++] = error = network.Train();
        P("Output error=" + error + "\n");
        repaint();
    }
}

public void doResetButton() {
    ClearOutput();
    P("Weights saved to file test2.dat\n");
    network.NeuralFile.AddSpecial(1001.0f);
    network.NeuralFile.AddSpecial(1002.0f);
    network.NeuralFile.AddSpecial(1003.0f);
    network.NeuralFile.AddSpecial(1004.0f);
    network.NeuralFile.RemoveTraining(2);
    network.NeuralFile.AddSpecial(1005.0f);
    network.NeuralFile.AddSpecial(1006.0f);
    network.Save("test2.dat");
}
}
```

Figure 11.2 shows the test program in Listing 11.2 after training a neural network for 90 training cycles (i.e., the "Run" button was pressed three times).

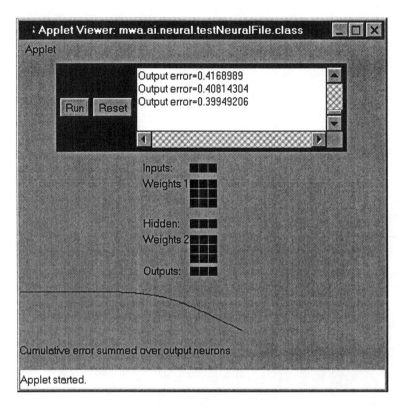

Figure 11.2   Testing the class **NNfile**

Listing 11.3 shows the neural network specification file **test.dat** that was used to construct a new **NNfile** object in the test program in Listing 11.2.

Listing 11.3

```
#  Neural network data written by NNfile

3  # number of neuron layers
3  # neurons in layer 0
3  # neurons in layer 1
3  # neurons in layer 2
0  # weight flag
0  # special data flag
3  # number of training cases in file


# Training data originally in file:
```

```
-0.4 0.4 0.4     0.4 -0.4 0.4
0.4 -0.4 0.4     0.4 0.4 -0.4
0.4 0.4 -0.4     -0.4 0.4 0.4
```

Figure 11.3 shows the same test application seen in Figure 11.2 after pressing the "Reset" button to use the method **mwa.ai.neural.NNfile.Save( )** to create a new neural network specification file **test2.dat**.

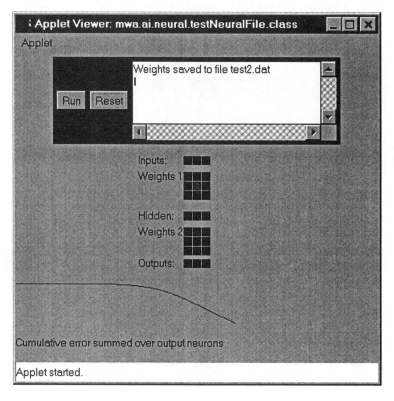

Figure II.3   Testing the class **NNfile**

Listing 11.4 shows the output file **test2.dat** created by an instance of class **NNfile** in the test program in Listing 11.2.

Listing 11.4

```
#  Neural network data written by NNfile

3  # number of neuron layers
3  # neurons in layer 0
3  # neurons in layer 1
3  # neurons in layer 2
1  # weight flag
6  # special data flag
2  # number of training cases in file

# Input layer to hidden layer weights:

-0.530072 -0.990389 1.95141
0.477923 -1.10085 -1.57668
0.341271 2.19913 -0.387759

# Hidden layer to output layer weights:

0.658675 -1.13095 0.930056
4.94609 -2.39832 -2.59064
-0.87859 4.53115 -3.46121

# Special network data:

1001
1002
1003
1004
1005
1006

# Training data:

-0.4 0.4 0.4    0.4 -0.4 0.4
0.4 -0.4 0.4    0.4 0.4 -0.4
```

Notice that the new neural network specification file seen in Listing 11.4 only has two training cases because the third original training case was deleted by calling **NNfile.RemoveTraining(2)**.

Listing 11.5 shows a test program for testing the class **NNgreedy**. The class **mwa.ai.neural.testGreedy** is derived from the class **mwa.gui.GUI** and creates an application window containing a "Run" button and a scrolling text output field. The method **mwa.ai.neural.testGreedy.doRunButton( )** is called when there is a mouse click on the "Run" button. This method performs the following tasks:

- Create a new instance of class **mwa.ai.neural.NNgreedy** using the neural network specification file **test3.dat**.
- Remove extraneous training data from the **NNgreedy** object.
- Attempt to find 10 empty input data regions in the training data.
- Save the modified network (i.e., the original network specification with the new modified training data) to the file **test.net**.

Listing 11.5

```
// Neural Net Java class for testing greedy algorithm
//
// Copyright 1996, Mark Watson.  All rights reserved.

package mwa.ai.neural;

import java.awt.*;

import mwa.gui.GUI;
import mwa.data.*;

public class testGreedy extends GUI {

    int width = 410;
    int height = 310;

    public String getAppletInfo() {
        return "Neural Network training data tool by Mark Watson";
    }

    // Initialize the application window, turning
    // off the default creation of reset button,
    // input text field, and graphics pane:
    public void init() {
        NoResetButton = true;
        NoInput = true;
        NoGraphics=true;
        super.init();
    }
```

```
public void doRunButton() {
    // Remove redundant or overlapping data and
    // try to find 10 areas in the input space that
    // do not contain any training cases:
    P("Input file is test3.dat\n");
    NNgreedy g = new NNgreedy("test3.dat");
    g.RemoveExtraData();
    for (int i=0; i<10; i++)
        g.FindEmptyRegion();
    g.Save("test.net");
    P("Output file is 'test.net'\n");
}

}
```

Listing 11.6 shows the input neural network description file **test3.dat**. The last training example will be removed by the example program in Listing 11.5.

Listing 11.6

```
#  Neural network data written by NNfile

3  # number of neuron layers
3  # neurons in layer 0
3  # neurons in layer 1
3  # neurons in layer 2
1  # weight flag
0  # special data flag
4  # number of training cases in file

# Input layer to hidden layer weights:

0.0112542 -0.0432932 -0.00623174
-0.04761 -0.0225022 -0.0375257
0.0359218 -0.012686 0.038833

# Hidden layer to output layer weights:

0.0278448 0.026646 0.0411143
-0.0158825 -0.00881048 0.0295604
-0.00206302 0.0208291 0.0424572

# Training data:
```

```
-0.4 0.4 0.4     0.4 -0.4 0.4
0.4 -0.4 0.4     0.4 0.4 -0.4
0.4 0.4 -0.4     -0.4 0.4 0.4
0.4 -0.4 0.41    0.4 0.4 -0.41
```

Figure 11.4 shows the class **NNgreedy** test application running.

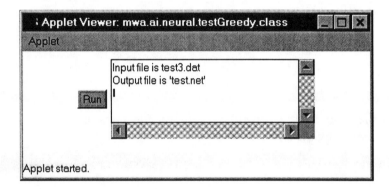

Figure 11.4   Testing the class **NNgreedy**

Listing 11.7 shows the new neural network description file **test.net**.

Listing 11.7

```
#  Neural network data written by NNfile

3  # number of neuron layers
3  # neurons in layer 0
3  # neurons in layer 1
3  # neurons in layer 2
1  # weight flag
0  # special data flag
13  # number of training cases in file

# Input layer to hidden layer weights:

0.0112542 -0.0432932 -0.00623174
-0.04761 -0.0225022 -0.0375257
0.0359218 -0.012686 0.038833
```

```
# Hidden layer to output layer weights:

0.0278448 0.026646 0.0411143
-0.0158825 -0.00881048 0.0295604
-0.00206302 0.0208291 0.0424572

# Training data:

-0.4 0.4 0.4      0.4 -0.4 0.4
0.4 -0.4 0.4      0.4 0.4 -0.4
0.4 0.4 -0.4      -0.4 0.4 0.4
-0.484226 0.458321 -0.412629     99999.9 99999.9 99999.9
0.456366 -0.385337 0.495334      99999.9 99999.9 99999.9
-0.492569 0.47867 -0.46566       99999.9 99999.9 99999.9
0.489574 -0.30845 0.447695       99999.9 99999.9 99999.9
0.488156 -0.481084 0.495302      99999.9 99999.9 99999.9
0.461447 -0.481688 0.486265      99999.9 99999.9 99999.9
0.484642 -0.425916 0.440737      99999.9 99999.9 99999.9
0.361771 -0.491258 0.457077      99999.9 99999.9 99999.9
-0.449985 0.49086 -0.441872      99999.9 99999.9 99999.9
0.449695 -0.47361 0.457023       99999.9 99999.9 99999.9
```

The function **NNgreedy.FindEmptyRegion( )** was called 10 times to find regions of the input space that were not covered by the original training data.

Optimizing Neural Networks with Genetic Algorithms

12

This chapter presents a few original ideas for optimizing the structure of neural networks using genetic algorithms. The modified structure of a neural network will depend on a specific set of training data. The Java class library **mwa.ai.neural.GenNeural** developed in this chapter uses the classes **mwa.ai.neural.Neural** and **mwa.ai.neural.NNfile** developed in Chapter 4. The class **mwa.ai.neural.GenNeural** is intended to be a complete wrapper for automatically producing optimized neural networks given a set of training data.

12.1 Requirements for a genetic algorithm for optimizing the structure of neural networks

There are two neural network structural elements that will be modified by the **mwa.ai.neural.GenNeural** class:

- The size of the hidden neuron layer
- An exclusion map of input neurons to ignore

It is fairly straightforward to calculate a reasonable size for the hidden layer, but it is possible to fine-tune this size based on the training data. For some applications, it is important to optimize the runtime performance of a network by reducing the number of neurons and connection weights. Also, neural networks with too many hidden layer neurons will memorize all training patterns instead of learning which specific features differentiate input patterns. For example, in Chapter 10 we wrote a handwriting recognition program that allows a user to draw several copies of each character to learn to recognize. In Figure 10.4 in Chapter 10, there were two copies of the hand-drawn characters *a*, *b*, *c*, and *d* in the lower left part of the application window. By minimizing the number of hidden layer neurons, we prevent the neural network from memorizing every detail for the two training examples for each letter. When we extend the handwriting recognition example by using both greedy and genetic algorithm optimization of the neural network, we will configure a new version of the handwriting optimization program to learn all the letters of the alphabet; it will be necessary to provide many training examples for each letter.

If a neural network has too many hidden neurons, it will almost exactly learn, or memorize, the training examples, but it will not perform as well recognizing new data after the training process is complete. If a neural network has too few hidden neurons, it will have insufficient memory capacity to learn all the different types of training examples (e.g., the different letters of the alphabet in the handwriting recognition program).

I have been using neural networks for 10 years. Before I wrote the software tools for automatic optimization in Chapter 11 and this chapter, I used the following procedure to calculate a reasonable number of hidden layer neurons for an application:

- Estimate the maximum number of unique output classifications in the training data (e.g., in the handwriting recognition program, how many letters will be recognized).
- Calculate the logarithm (base two) of the number of training examples and add one.
- Train a network with the application-specific training data, checking that it has learned all the output classifications.
- Keep reducing the number of hidden layer neurons until the network cannot differentiate all output classifications in the training data.

The genetic algorithm optimization tools that we will implement in the next section effectively implement this procedure, optimizing the number of hidden layer neurons and also discovering any input neurons that can be left unused. For example, we might be training a network to recognize a set of hand-drawn characters that never use a point on the input grid that we map hand-drawn characters onto. It would be better (more efficient) not to show the neural network unused values (for specific training data sets), reducing the number of input neurons and thus the number of weights in the network.

12.2 Requirements for a genetic algorithm for removing training data

The most difficult task in effectively using neural networks in an application is developing a good set of training data that is specific to that application. In Chapter 11, we used a greedy algorithm to discard conflicting training data sets. We develop an alternative method for discarding bad training data sets in this chapter using a genetic algorithm. The requirements for this genetic algorithm are

- to eliminate training cases that make it difficult for a neural network to differentiate all output classifications
- to avoid discarding training data

The fitness function used for the genetic algorithm must be able to combine these two conflicting requirements.

12.3 Design of a genetic algorithm for optimizing neural networks

The neural network class **mwa.ai.neural.Neural** developed in Chapter 4 contains two member variables that are used, respectively, for ignoring training data cases and input neuron values: **boolean IgnoreTraining[]** and **boolean IgnoreInput[]**.

Typically, both these variables are initialized to the value null and are not used in the neural network simulation code. In order to optimize the structure of a neural network using a genetic algorithm, we must first decide what application-specific information will be encoded into a chromosome, then what fitness function will yield a population of chromosomes that represent an efficient structure for a neural network.

We want to encode both bit flags for ignoring input neurons and the number of hidden layer neurons in a chromosome. To make the code a little easier to write and understand, we assume that we will use at most 15 hidden layer neurons; this value can be encoded in four bits. We also need one bit in the chromosome to represent each input layer neuron. Since an instance of the Java class **mwa.ai.neural.Neural** has **Neural.NumInputs** input neurons, we can design the format of the chromosome to have the following genes, where each gene is represented by a single bit:

- **Neural.NumInputs** genes. A true value indicates that the corresponding input neuron value should be ignored.
- Four genes. This encodes a value of zero to 15 hidden layer neurons.

Neural networks are defined by creating an instance of the utility class **mwa.ai.neural.NNfile**. The constructor for **NNfile** reads a network description file. It is required that a network description file specify at least 15 hidden layer neurons in order to produce a neural network object with sufficient storage space for up to 15 hidden layer neurons.

The fitness function for the genetic algorithm performs the following calculations for each chromosome in the population:

- Use the last four genes (bits) in the chromosome to calculate the number of hidden layer neurons. Set the variable **Neural.NumHidden** to this new value.
- Each instance of class **Neural** contains a reference to a Boolean array **IgnoreInput[]**. The values of this array are set to the first **Neural.NumInputs** gene values in the chromosome.
- Count the number of inputs that are ignored.
- Train the neural network for 500 learning cycles. Sum the training error for the last 40 cycles.
- Calculate the fitness value for a chromosome based on the cumulative learning error, the number of input neurons that are ignored, and the number of hidden layer neurons.

The fitness function should minimize the training error, the number of hidden neurons, and the number of input neurons that are ignored. Figure 12.1 shows the Booch class diagram for the **GenNeural** class. The design of this class is specified in both this section and Section 12.4; the class is implemented in Section 12.5. We will rewrite the example handwriting program to use the **GenNeural** class in Section 12.7.

12.4 Design of a genetic algorithm for removing training data

The neural network class **mwa.ai.neural.Neural** developed in Chapter 4 contains two member variables that are used, respectively, for ignoring training data cases and input neuron values: **boolean IgnoreTraining[] and boolean IgnoreInput[]**. We will use these member variables to disable the use of training data in a neural network input file and to disable the use of specific input neurons.

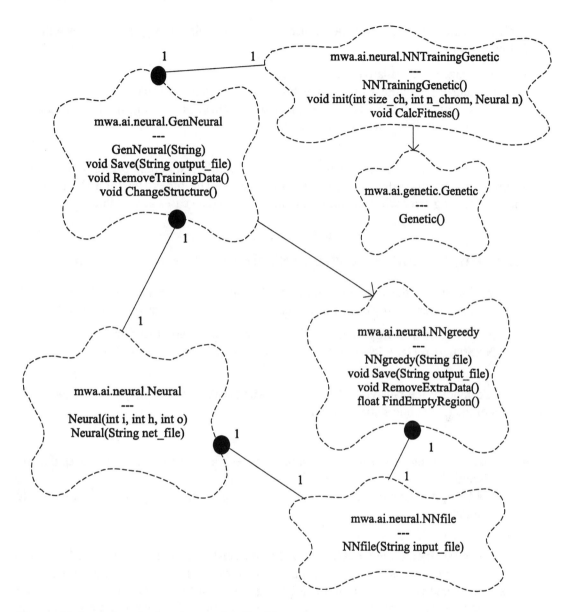

Figure 12.1   Booch class diagram for **GenNeural**

When an instance of class **mwa.ai.neural.Neural** is created, a **String** file name is passed to the constructor. This constructor creates an instance of the utility class **mwa.ai.neural.NNfile** that is contained in the instance of class **Neural**. The chromosome contains one gene (or bit of information) for each training case contained in an instance of class **NNfile**. The fitness function must produce a population of chromosomes with the following properties:

- Minimize the cumulative training error.
- Maximize the number of original training cases that are used. We do not want to indiscriminately discard training cases unless there is a strong likelihood that the data in the training case is not correct.

It should be noted that these properties are in conflict: we could certainly reduce the training error by discarding all but one training case! The fitness function should minimize the training error while keeping as many training data cases as possible.

12.5 Implementating the optimizing genetic algorithm

Listing 12.1 shows the implementation of the Java class **mwa.ai.neural.GenNeural**. Two additional classes are defined in the same file that defines class **GenNeural**:

- **NNTrainingGenetic** — extends the class **mwa.ai.genetic.Genetic**
- **NNStructureGenetic** — extends the class **mwa.ai.genetic.Genetic**

To modify the behavior of class **mwa.ai.neural.GenNeural**, you can change the values of the two public static class variables:

- **GAINtraining**—increasing this value reduces the number of training cases that are discarded
- **GAINinputs**—increasing this value reduces the number of input neurons that are ignored

The class **mwa.ai.neural.GenNeural** also adjusts the number of hidden layer neurons, but it is not necessary to have a separate control parameter for this adjustment. The class **GenNeural** constructor requires a **String** argument that specifies a file name for a neural network specification file. The class **mwa.ai.neural.NNgreedy** did not require an instance of class **mwa.ai.neural.Neural** to optimize training data. The class **GenNeural** requires an instance of **mwa.ai.neural.Neural** since a neural network is trained receptively as part of both genetic algorithms used in this class. The class constructor builds a single instance of class **Neural** that is reused by the fitness functions of both genetic algorithms.

The method **mwa.ai.neural.GenNeural.RemoveTrainingData( )** has the same purpose as method **mwa.ai.neural.NNgreedy.RemoveExtraData( )** that was developed in Chapter 11. The method **mwa.ai.neural.GenNeural.RemoveTrainingData( )** uses a different approach for solving this problem:

- Create a Boolean array for **mwa.ai.neural.Neural.IgnoreTraining**. This array is set by the fitness function contained in the class **NNTrainingGenetic**.

- The chromosome used by the class **NNTrainingGenetic** is modified using the genetic crossover and mutation operations to evolve a population of chromosomes that represent sets of training data with specific cases removed that prevented the neural network from learning all cases.

The fitness function in class **NNTrainingGenetic** tries to maximize the number of training cases (i.e., avoids discarding training cases except when absolutely necessary) and tries to reduce the neural network training error.

The method **GenNeural.ChangeStructure( )** uses an instance of class **NNStructureGenetic** to find a population of chromosomes that specify which input neurons can be ignored and encode a reasonable number of hidden layer neurons. When a fit chromosome is found, the last four genes (i.e., bits) in the chromosome are used to specify the number of hidden layer neurons. The number of hidden neurons in the **NNfile** object (which is contained in the instance of class **Neural** that is contained and used by the class **GenNeural**) is reset, and application-specific data is added to the same instance of class **NNfile** to indicate which input neurons can be ignored for this application.

Listing 12.1

```
// GenNeural class: parses neural network input files
// using the class NNfile and uses a genetic algorithm
// to optimize both the structure and training data for
// a neural network.

// Copyright 1996, Mark Watson

package mwa.ai.neural;


public class GenNeural extends NNgreedy {

  Neural MyNeural = null;

  // Increasing the GAINtraining reduces the number of training
  // cases that are discarded:
```

```
static public float GAINtraining = 3.4f;

// Increasing GAINinputs reduces the number of
// input neurons that are ignored:
static public float GAINinputs = 2.5f;

public GenNeural() {
    System.out.println("\n\nError: GenNeural constructor " +
                       "requires a file name.\n");
}

public GenNeural(String input_file) {
  MyNeural = new Neural(input_file);
  NeuralFile = MyNeural.NeuralFile;
}

public void Save(String file) {
  NeuralFile.Save(file);
}

void RemoveTrainingData() {
  if (NeuralFile==null) return;
  // we need to refresh the active training cases from
  // the NNfile object into the Neural object:
  MyNeural.LoadTrainingCases();

  // Build a chromosome containing one bit for
  // each training case:
  MyNeural.IgnoreTraining = new boolean[NeuralFile.NumTraining];
  MyNeural.IgnoreInput=null;
  NNTrainingGenetic g = new NNTrainingGenetic();
  g.init(NeuralFile.NumTraining, 20, MyNeural);

  // The fitness functon is determined by:
  //
  //    How low the training error is
  //    Maximize # of training cases (i.e., we
  //    really want to avoid tossing out training
  //    cases unless they adversely affect the
  //    final training error):

  // Remove any bad training cases from the
  // NNfile object:
```

```
    for (int i=0; i<16; i++) {
      g.CalcFitness();
      g.Sort();
      if ((i%5)==0) {
          System.out.println("Generation " + i);
          g.Print();
      }
      g.DoCrossovers();
      g.DoCrossovers();
      g.DoCrossovers();
      g.DoCrossovers();
      g.DoCrossovers();
      g.DoCrossovers();
      g.DoMutations();
    }
    int num = NeuralFile.NumTraining;
    for (int i=num-1; i>=0; i--) {   // remove in reverse order!!!
      if (g.GetGene(0, i)) {
          System.out.println("Removing training case # " + i);
          NeuralFile.RemoveTraining(i);
      }
    }
    NeuralFile.Save("test_gen.trn");
  }

  void ChangeStructure() {
    if (NeuralFile==null) return;
    if (NeuralFile.NumHidden < 15) {
        System.out.println("WARNING: GenNeural.ChangeStructure " +
                           "requires a network with room for at");
        System.out.println("least 15 neurons.\n\n");
        return;
    }

    // Build a chromosome containing one bit for each
    // input neuron, and 4 bits to encode an
    // optimal number of hidden layer neurons:

    MyNeural.IgnoreTraining = null;
    MyNeural.IgnoreInput = new boolean[MyNeural.NumInputs];
    NNStructureGenetic g = new NNStructureGenetic();
    g.init(NeuralFile.NumInput + 4, 20, MyNeural);

    for (int i=0; i<16; i++) {
```

```java
        g.CalcFitness();
        g.Sort();
        if ((i%5)==0) {
            System.out.println("Generation " + i);
            g.Print();
        }
        g.DoCrossovers();
        g.DoCrossovers();
        g.DoCrossovers();
        g.DoCrossovers();
        g.DoCrossovers();
        g.DoCrossovers();
        g.DoMutations();
    }

    // When done, add 'special' application-specific
    // data values to mark input neurons as "don't
    // care" inputs that are ignored, and modify the
    // parameter specifying the number of hidden layer
    // neurons:

    int numh = 0;
    int POW2[] = {1, 2, 4, 8};
    for (int i=0; i<4; i++) {
        if (g.GetGene(0, NeuralFile.NumInput + i)) {
          numh += POW2[i];
        }
    }
    NeuralFile.NumHidden = numh;
    System.out.println("Reset the number of hidden neurons to " +
                        numh);

    for (int i=0; i<NeuralFile.NumInput; i++) {
        if (g.GetGene(0, i)) {
            System.out.println("Disabling input neuron " + i);
            NeuralFile.AddSpecial((float)i);
        }
    }
    NeuralFile.Save("test_gen.inp");
  }

}

class NNTrainingGenetic extends mwa.ai.genetic.Genetic {
```

```java
Neural MyNeural;

NNTrainingGenetic() {
    System.out.println("Entered NNTrainingGenetic()\n");
}
public void init(int g, int c, Neural neural) {
    super.init(g, c);
    for (int j=0; j<g; j++)
      for (int i=0; i<c; i++)
        SetGene(i, j, false);
    MyNeural = neural;
}
public void CalcFitness() {
    for (int i=0; i<NumChrom; i++) {
        float fitness = 40.0f;
        int OnCount = 0;
        for (int j=0; j<NumGenes; j++) {
            MyNeural.IgnoreTraining[j] = GetGene(i, j);
            if (GetGene(i, j)) OnCount++;
        }
        for (int iter=0; iter<500; iter++) {
            float x = MyNeural.Train();
            if (iter > 460)  fitness -= x;
        }
        Fitness[i] =
            fitness - GenNeural.GAINtraining * (float)OnCount;
    }
}
public void Print() {
    for (int i=0; i<NumChrom; i++) {
        System.out.print("Fitness for chromosome ");
        System.out.print(i);
        System.out.print(" is ");
        System.out.print(Fitness[i] + ": ");
        for (int j=0; j<NumGenes; j++) {
            if (GetGene(i, j)) System.out.print("1 ");
            else               System.out.print("0 ");
        }
        System.out.println("");
    }
}
}
```

```java
class NNStructureGenetic extends mwa.ai.genetic.Genetic {
    Neural MyNeural;

    NNStructureGenetic() {
        System.out.println("Entered NNStructureGenetic()\n");
    }
    public void init(int g, int c, Neural neural) {
        super.init(g, c);
        for (int i=0; i<g; i++) {
          for (int j=0; j<c; j++) {
            if (i < (g - 4)) SetGene(j, i, false);
            else            SetGene(j, i, true); // # hidden neurons
          }
        }
        MyNeural = neural;
    }

    public void CalcFitness() {
        for (int i=0; i<NumChrom; i++) {
            float fitness = 100.0f;

            int numh = 0;
            int POW2[] = {1, 2, 4, 8};
            for (int j=NumGenes-4; j<NumGenes; j++) {
                if (GetGene(i, j)) {
                  numh += POW2[j - (NumGenes - 4)];
                }
            }
            MyNeural.NumHidden = numh;
            MyNeural.randomizeWeights();

            int OnCount = 0;
            for (int j=0; j<MyNeural.NumInputs; j++) {
                MyNeural.IgnoreInput[j] = GetGene(i, j);
                if (GetGene(i, j)) OnCount++;
            }
            for (int iter=0; iter<500; iter++) {
                float x = MyNeural.Train();
                if (iter > 460)  fitness -= x;
            }
            Fitness[i] = fitness - 30.0f * (float)numh
                            - GenNeural.GAINinputs * OnCount;
            if (numh < 3) Fitness[i] -= 100000.0f;
        }
```

```
    }
    public void Print() {
        for (int i=0; i<NumChrom; i++) {
            System.out.print("Fitness for chromosome ");
            System.out.print(i);
            System.out.print(" is ");
            System.out.print(Fitness[i] + ": ");
            for (int j=0; j<NumGenes-4; j++) {
                if (GetGene(i, j)) System.out.print("1 ");
                else               System.out.print("0 ");
            }
            System.out.print(" | ");

            // hard-coded to allow 2^4 = 16 hidden neurons:
            for (int j=NumGenes-4; j<NumGenes; j++) {
                if (GetGene(i, j)) System.out.print("1 ");
                else               System.out.print("0 ");
            }
            System.out.println("");
        }
    }
}
```

12.6 Testing the optimizing genetic algorithm

Listing 12.2 contains an application for testing the class **mwa.ai.neural.GenNeural**. There are two options for this application that are triggered by the application's "Training" and "Structure" buttons:

- Use the method **GenNeural.RemoveTrainingData( )** to read the neural network specification file **test10.dat** and write out a new specification file **test_gen.trn**.
- Use the method **GenNeural.ChangeStructure( )** to read the neural network specification file **test10.dat** and write out a new specification file **test_gen.str**.

Each of these options takes about 10 minutes of processing time on a Pentium-class PC. The default labels in the **mwa.gui.GUI** class are "Run" and "Reset"; these default labels are changed in Listing 12.2 to "Training" and "Structure."

Listing 12.2

```
// Neural Net Java class for testing GenNeural class
//
```

```java
// Copyright 1996, Mark Watson.  All rights reserved.

package mwa.ai.neural;

import java.awt.*;

import mwa.gui.GUI;
import mwa.data.*;

public class testGenNeural extends GUI {

    int width = 410;
    int height = 310;

    public String getAppletInfo() {
        return "Neural Network training data tool by Mark Watson";
    }

    GenNeural gen = null;

    public void init() {
        NoInput = true;
        NoGraphics=true;
        RunLabel   = new String("Training");
        ResetLabel = new String("Structure");
        super.init();
     }

    public void doRunButton() {
        P("Starting genetic algorithm for training data.\n");
        gen = new GenNeural("test10.dat");
        gen.RemoveTrainingData();
        gen = null;
        P("Output file is 'test_gen.trn'\n");
        gen.Save("test_gen.trn");
    }

    public void doResetButton() {
        P("Starting genetic algorithm for structure.\n");
        gen = new GenNeural("test10.dat");
        gen.ChangeStructure();
        P("Output file is 'test_gen.str'\n");
        gen.Save("test_gen.str");
        gen = null;
```

```
    }

}
```

Figure 12.2 shows the class **mwa.ai.neural.GenNeural** test application running.

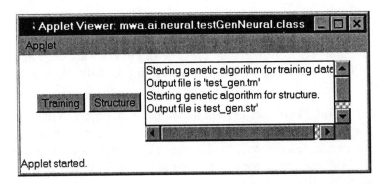

Figure 12.2   Testing the class **mwa.ai.neural.GenNeural**. Each option takes about 10 minutes to run.

12.7 Improving the handwriting recognition program

We will improve the handwriting recognition program developed in Chapter 10 by using both greedy and genetic algorithms to adjust the training data for recognizing all 26 characters of the alphabet. We will use a genetic algorithm to adjust the structure of the neural network. We will create three separate test applications implemented in the files:

- **testHand_2.java**—implements class **testHand_2**, which uses the input file **hand_1.dat** to specify the initial size of a network and writes the files **hand_2.dat**, containing captured training data, and **hand_3.dat**, containing both captured training data and trained weights
- **testHand_3.java**—implements class **testHand_3**, which reads the neural network description file **hand_3.dat** and uses the **GenNeural** class to produce an optimized neural network description file **hand_4.dat**
- **testHand_4.java**—implements class **testHand_4**, which reads the network description file **hand_4.dat** and allows the program user to test this optimized neural network

Listing 12.3 shows the file **testHand_2.java**. This file is a modified version of Listing 10.1. The constants **XSIZE** and **YSIZE** determine the size of the two-dimensional input array to the neural network. The variable **Mode** has a zero value when collecting training data and is set to the value of one when the "Test" button is pressed, causing the program to switch to a mode where characters can be drawn (and recognized) anywhere in the application window. The constant **NUM_EX** specifies the maximum number of training examples that can be captured for any character.

The method **test_Hand2.init( )** creates a new neural network object (instance of class **mwa.ai.neural.Neural**) and stores a reference to this object in the variable **network**. The "Run" and "Reset" buttons from the base class **mwa.gui.GUI** are renamed "Train" and "Test" before calling **super.init( )** (which is **mwa.gui.GUI.init( )**). A new thread is created and started.

The method **test_Hand2.train( )** saves the current neural network object to the file **hand_2.dat** and then uses the method **Neural.LoadTrainingCases( )** to set the training cases from data in a neural network description file. The neural network is trained for 20,000 training cycles (or until the training error has a value less than 0.2). The trained neural network object is saved to the file **hand_3.dat**.

The method **test_Hand2.run( )** is called automatically because we created and started a thread object. This method has the responsibility for capturing user mouse events in the application window. The method **test_Hand2.doRunButton( )** calls the method **test_Hand2.train( )**; this method is called when the application's "Train" button is clicked. The method **test_Hand2.doResetButton( )** is called when the application's "Test" button is clicked and sets the variable **Mode** to the value of one. The method **test_Hand2.PutChar( )** copies a complete hand-drawn character to the input array of the neural network when in "Test" mode and copies this data to the array **Inputs** when collecting training data.

The class **testHand_2** implements the **Runnable** interface since it creates a thread. Classes that implement the **Runnable** class must define a method **run( )** that is used by the **Thread** class.

Listing 12.3

```
// NeuralNet Java classes: tester for handwriting recognition
//
// Copyright 1996, Mark Watson.  All rights reserved.

package mwa.ai.neural;

import java.awt.*;
```

```
import mwa.gui.GUI;

public class testHand_2 extends GUI implements Runnable {

    // define the size of two-dimensional neural
    // input array:
    final static int XSIZE=5;
    final static int YSIZE=6;

    // define the Mode: 0 for training mode,
    // 1 for testing mode:
    public int Mode = 0;

    // Number of characters of each type to use
    // for training data:
    final static int NUM_EX=2;  // number of examples

    // Number of characters to learn:
    final static int NUM = 26;
    String Chars[] = {"a", "b", "c", "d", "e", "f", "g", "h", "i", "j",
                      "k", "l", "m", "n", "o", "p", "q", "r", "s", "t",
                      "u", "v", "w", "x", "y", "z"};
    // Data for partitioning GUI display for capturing
    // individual characters:
    int X_Pos[];
    int Y_Pos = 90;
    int Inputs[][] = new int[XSIZE][YSIZE];

    // Count[NUM] is used for counting drawn chars
    int Count[];

    // data for determining when a new character
    // is being drawn:
    long TimeLastMouse = -1;  // in milliseconds
    // MouseState: 0=>no capture, 1=>currently capturing
    int MouseState = 0;
    int MousePointIndex = 0; // at the start of capture data


    int num_cap=0;
    int cap_x[] = new int[50000];
    int cap_y[] = new int[50000];
```

```java
int active = 0;  // if 1, then train network

// Neural network:
Neural network;

public String getAppletInfo() {
    return "Neural Network Simulator by Mark Watson";
}

private Thread MouseThread = null;

public void init() {

    Count    = new int[NUM];
    for (int i=0; i<NUM; i++) Count[i] = 0;

    NoInput = true;  // we do not need an input text field
    BigText=1;

    network = new Neural("hand_1.dat");
    //network.MyGUI = this;

    RunLabel = "Train";
    ResetLabel = "Test";

    X_Pos = new int[27];
    for (int i=0; i<27; i++) X_Pos[i] = 20 + 22 * i;

    super.init();

    if (MouseThread==null) {
     MouseThread = new Thread(this);
     MouseThread.start();
    }
}

public void train() {
  P("Saving training data to file hand_2.dat\n");
  network.Save("hand_2.dat");
  // we need to refresh the active training cases from
  // the NNfile object into the Neural object:
  network.LoadTrainingCases();
  P("Starting to train network..wait..\n");
```

```java
        for (int i=0; i<20000; i++) {
          float error = network.Train();
          if ((i % 10) == 0) {
            P("Output error for iteration " +
              i + " =" + error + "\n");
          }
          if (error < 0.2f)  break;  // done training
          if (i > 5000 && error < 0.5f) break;
          if (i > 10000 && error < 0.9f) break;
        }
        // Save the training cases and the new weights:
        network.Save("hand_3.dat");
      }

      public void paintToDoubleBuffer(Graphics g) {
          g.drawString("Captured handwriting data",
                                X_Pos[0], Y_Pos - 15);

          for (int m=0; m<NUM; m++) {
              g.drawString(Chars[m], X_Pos[m], Y_Pos);
          }
          setForeground(Color.black);
          g.setColor(getForeground());
          for (int i=0; i<num_cap; i++) {
              g.drawLine(cap_x[i],
                      cap_y[i],
                      cap_x[i],
                      cap_y[i]+1);
          }
      }
      public void run() {
          P("in testHand::run()\n");
          while (true)  {
              try {
                  if (MouseState==1) {
                      long mtime =
                        java.lang.System.currentTimeMillis();
                      if (TimeLastMouse < mtime - 1500) {
                          MouseState=0;
                          PutChar();
                      }
                  }
              } catch (Exception e) {} ;
              try {Thread.sleep(20);} catch (Exception ex) { };
```

```java
        }
    }

    public void doRunButton() {
        train();
    }
    public void doResetButton() {
        P("Resetting to test mode.\n");
        Mode = 1;  // switch to test mode
    }

    public void PutChar() {
        int x_min=9999, x_max=-9999;
        int y_min=9999, y_max=-9999;
        for (int i=MousePointIndex; i<num_cap; i++) {
            if (cap_x[i] < x_min) x_min = cap_x[i];
            if (cap_x[i] > x_max) x_max = cap_x[i];
            if (cap_y[i] < y_min) y_min = cap_y[i];
            if (cap_y[i] > y_max) y_max = cap_y[i];
        }
        if (x_min+1 > x_max)  { x_min--; x_max++; }
        P("X,Y char bounds: " + x_min + ", " + x_max +
          ", " + y_min + ", " + y_max + "\n");

        // Special case:Mode==1 for testing:
        if (Mode==1) {
            int ic = 0;
            for (int x=0; x<XSIZE; x++) {
                for (int y=0; y<YSIZE; y++) {
                    network.Inputs[ic++] = -0.4f;
                }
            }
            for (int i=MousePointIndex; i<num_cap; i++) {
                float xx = (float)(cap_x[i] - x_min)
                        / (float)(x_max - x_min);
                xx *= XSIZE;
                float yy = (float)(cap_y[i] - y_min)
                        / (float)(y_max - y_min);
                yy *= YSIZE;
                int ix=(int)xx;
                int iy=(int)yy;
                if (ix<0) ix=0;
                if (ix>=XSIZE) ix=XSIZE-1;
                if (iy<0) iy=0;
```

```
            if (iy>=YSIZE) iy=YSIZE-1;
            network.Inputs[ix*YSIZE+iy] = +0.4f;
    }
    // Propagate input neuron values through
    // to the hidden, then output neuron layer:
    network.ForwardPass();
    // Find the largest output neuron value:
    int index=0;
    float maxVal=-99f;
    for (int i=0; i<NUM; i++) {
        if (network.Outputs[i]>maxVal) {
            maxVal = network.Outputs[i];
            index = i;
        }
    }
    P("\nCharacter recognized: " + Chars[index] + "\n");
    return;
}

// Capture training data: find which character is
// drawn by checking the range of the x coordinates:
int char_type = -1;
for (int i=0; i<NUM; i++) {
    if (x_min - 5 < X_Pos[i] &&
        x_max + 5 > X_Pos[i] &&
        x_max + 5 < X_Pos[i + 1]) {
            char_type = i;
        }
}
if (char_type==-1) {
    P("Error: character is not drawn in correct position\n");
    MousePointIndex = num_cap;
    return;
}
P("Character " + Chars[char_type] + " drawn. # "
  + Count[char_type] + "\n");
if (Count[char_type] > (NUM_EX-1)) {
    P("Too many examples for this char type: ignoring!\n");
    MousePointIndex = num_cap;
    return;
}
for (int x=0; x<XSIZE; x++) {
    for (int y=0; y<YSIZE; y++) {
        Inputs[x][y] = 0;
```

```
        }
    }
    for (int i=MousePointIndex; i<num_cap; i++) {
        float xx = (float)(cap_x[i] - x_min)
                 / (float)(x_max - x_min);
        xx *= XSIZE;
        float yy = (float)(cap_y[i] - y_min)
                 / (float)(y_max - y_min);
        yy *= YSIZE;
        int ix=(int)xx;
        int iy=(int)yy;
        if (ix<0) ix=0;
        if (ix>=XSIZE) ix=XSIZE-1;
        if (iy<0) iy=0;
        if (iy>=YSIZE) iy=YSIZE-1;
        Inputs[ix][iy] = 1;
    }
    float inputs[] = new float[XSIZE*YSIZE];
    float outputs[]= new float[26];

    int c = 0;
    for (int x=0; x<XSIZE; x++) {
        for (int y=0; y<YSIZE; y++) {
          if (Inputs[x][y] == 0) {
            inputs[c++] = -0.4f;
          } else {
            inputs[c++] = +0.4f;
          }
        }
    }
    for (int i=0; i<26; i++) outputs[i] = -0.4f;
    outputs[char_type] = +0.4f;
    network.NeuralFile.AddTraining(inputs, outputs);

    MousePointIndex = num_cap;
    Count[char_type] += 1;
}

public void doMouseDown(int x, int y) {
    long mtime = java.lang.System.currentTimeMillis();
    if (MouseState==0) { // not yet in capture mode
        P("switch to capture mode\n");
        MouseState=1;
        MousePointIndex = num_cap;
```

```
        }

        TimeLastMouse = mtime;

        //System.out.println("Mouse x: " + x + ", y: " + y);
        if (num_cap<19999) {
            cap_x[num_cap] = x;
            cap_y[num_cap] = y;
            num_cap++;
            repaint();
        }
    }
}
```

Figures 12.3, 12.4, and 12.5 show the test program implemented by class **mwa.ai.neural.test_Hand2**.

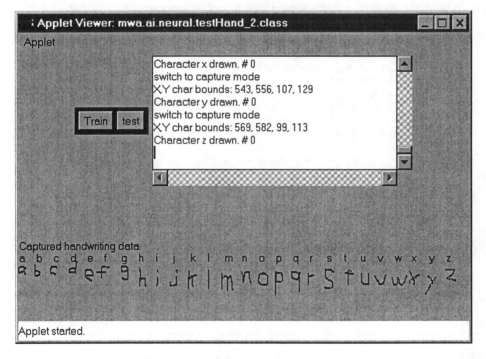

Figure 12.3   Testing the class **testHand_2**. All 26 letters of the alphabet have been captured.

Listing 12.4 shows the implementation of the class **testHand_3**. This class reads the neural network description file produced by the program in Listing 12.3 and writes an optimized neural network description to file **hand_4.dat**.

The method **mwa.ai.neural.testHand_3.init( )** turns off the default input text field and graphics display area usually created by the superclass **mwa.gui.GUI** and renames the "Run" and "Reset" buttons to "Training data" and "Structure/Save." A new instance of class **mwa.ai.neural.GenNeural** is created, and a reference to this object is stored in the class variable **gen**.

The method **mwa.ai.neural.testHand_3.doRunButton( )** is called when the "Training data" button is clicked and calls the **mwa.ai.neural.GenNeural** class methods **RemoveExtraData( )** and **RemoveTrainingData( )**.

The method **GenNeural.RemoveTrainingData( )** is hard-coded to save the **Gen-Neural** object to a local file **test_gen.trn** after using a genetic algorithm to search for training data cases to discard.

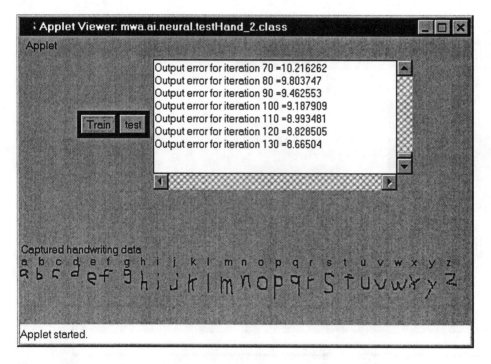

Figure 12.4   Testing the class **testHand_2**. Training the neural network.

The method **mwa.ai.neural.testHand_3.doResetButton( )** is called when the "Structure/Save" button is clicked. A new **GenNeural** object is created from the file **test_gen.trn**. The processing steps for the "Training data" and "Structure/Save" operations are separate because both are very time-consuming; breaking the optimization process into these two steps allows the **testHand_3** program to be run twice, once for "Training data" and once for "Structure/Save" optimizations. The following **mwa.ai.neural.Neural** and **mwa.ai.neural.GenNeural** class methods are called:

- **Neural.LoadTrainingCases()**
- **GenNeural.ChangeStructure()**
- **Neural.LoadTrainingCases()**
- **Neural.Train()**
- **Neural.Save("hand_4.dat")**

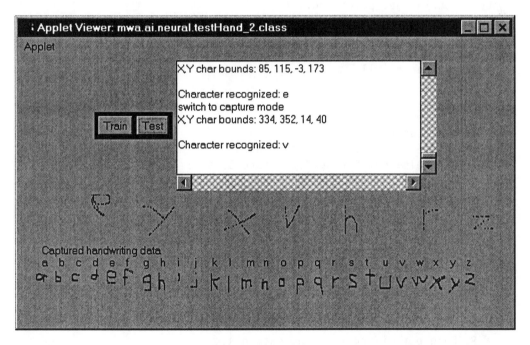

Figure 12.5   Testing the class **testHand2**. The characters e, y, x, v, h, r, and z have been drawn in the application window after clicking the "Test" button.

Listing 12.4

```
// Neural Net Java class for testing GenNeural class
//
// Copyright 1996, Mark Watson.  All rights reserved.
```

```
package mwa.ai.neural;

import java.awt.*;

import mwa.gui.GUI;
import mwa.data.*;

public class testHand_3 extends GUI {

    int width = 410;
    int height = 310;

    public String getAppletInfo() {
        return "Neural Network training data tool by Mark Watson";
    }

    GenNeural gen = null;

    public void init() {
       NoInput = true;
       NoGraphics=true;
       RunLabel   = new String("Training data");
       ResetLabel = new String("Structure/Save");
       super.init();
       gen = new GenNeural("hand_3.dat");
     }

    public void doRunButton() {
       P("Starting greedy algorithm for training data.\n");
       gen.RemoveExtraData();
       P("Starting genetic algorithm for training data.\n");
       gen.RemoveTrainingData();
       gen = null;
       P("Done optimizing training data\n");
    }

    public void doResetButton() {
       P("Starting genetic algorithm for structure.\n");
       // reload from the saved results of the "Run"
       // button:
       gen = new GenNeural("test_gen.trn");
       // we need to refresh the active training cases from
```

```
                  // the NNfile object into the Neural object:
                  gen.MyNeural.LoadTrainingCases();
                  gen.ChangeStructure();
                  P("Output file is 'hand_4.dat'\n");
                  P("Retrain the network...\n");
                  // we need to refresh the active training cases from
                  // the NNfile object into the Neural object:
                  gen.MyNeural.LoadTrainingCases();
                  for (int i=0; i<5000; i++) {
                    float error = gen.MyNeural.Train();
                    if ((i % 10) == 0) {
                      P("Output error for iteration " +
                        i + " =" + error + "\n");
                    }
                    if (error < 0.2f)  break;  // done training
                    if (i > 2000 && error < 0.5f) break;
                    if (i > 3000 && error < 0.9f) break;
                  }

                  gen.MyNeural.Save("hand_4.dat");
                  gen = null;
           }


       }
```

Figure 12.6 shows the test program **testHand_3** seen in Listing 12.4. This program splits the processing into two tasks: using a greedy algorithm to prune test data and using a genetic algorithm to prune test data cases based on multiple training cycles.

Listing 12.5 shows the implementation of the class **testHand_4**. This program uses a previously optimized and trained neural network to recognize hand-drawn characters. This program does not capture new training data; it is only used to test previously trained neural networks.

The method **testHand_4.init( )** creates a new **mwa.ai.neural.Neural** object and stores the reference to this object in the class variable **network**. A thread object is created and started to process user mouse events.

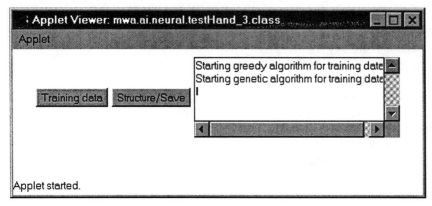

Figure 12.6   Testing the program in Listing 12.4. Both greedy and genetic algorithms are used to optimize the training data and neural network structure. This program takes approximately three hours to run on a Pentium-class PC.

The method **testHand_4.run( )** is called when the mouse-handling thread is started. The **run( )** method calls the **PutChar( )** method after 0.8 second elapses without a mouse event occurring. The **PutChar( )** method is similar to the **PutChar( )** methods in the classes **testHand** and **testHand_1**, except that captured character data is assumed here to be in "Test" mode; that is, no training data is captured by this program. The method **PutChar( )** calls the method **mwa.ai.neural.Neural.ForwardPass( )** after copying the captured data to the neural network's input array. The neural network's output array (i.e., values of the output layer neurons) are examined after calling **Neural.ForwardPass( )** to determine which character the user has drawn on the application window using the mouse.

The class **testHand_4** implements the **Runnable** interface since it creates a thread. Classes that implement the **Runnable** class must define a method **run()** that is used by the **Thread** class.

Listing 12.5

```
// NeuralNet Java classes: tester for handwriting recognition
//
// Copyright 1996, Mark Watson.  All rights reserved.

package mwa.ai.neural;

import java.awt.*;

import mwa.gui.GUI;
```

```
public class testHand_4 extends GUI implements Runnable {

    // define the size of two-dimensional neural
    // input array:
    final static int XSIZE=5;
    final static int YSIZE=6;

    int Inputs[][] = new int[XSIZE][YSIZE];

    // data for determining when a new character
    // is being drawn:
    long TimeLastMouse = -1;   // in milliseconds
    // MouseState: 0=>no capture, 1=>currently capturing
    int MouseState = 0;
    int MousePointIndex = 0; // at the start of capture data

    int num_cap=0;
    int cap_x[] = new int[20000];
    int cap_y[] = new int[20000];

    // Neural network:
    Neural network;

    public String getAppletInfo() {
        return "Neural Network Simulator by Mark Watson";
    }

    private Thread MouseThread = null;
    // Number of characters to learn:
    final static int NUM = 26;
    String Chars[] = {"a", "b", "c", "d", "e", "f", "g", "h",
                      "i", "j", "k", "l", "m", "n", "o", "p",
                      "q", "r", "s", "t", "u", "v", "w", "x",
                      "y", "z"};

    public void init() {

        NoInput = true;  // we do not need an input text field
        BigText=1;
        NoRunButton=true;
        NoResetButton=true;

        network = new Neural("hand_4.dat");
```

```
    super.init();

    if (MouseThread==null) {
     MouseThread = new Thread(this);
     MouseThread.start();
    }
}

public void paintToDoubleBuffer(Graphics g) {
    setForeground(Color.black);
    g.setColor(getForeground());
    for (int i=0; i<num_cap; i++) {
        g.drawLine(cap_x[i],
                   cap_y[i],
                   cap_x[i],
                   cap_y[i]+1);
    }
}
public void run() {
    P("in testHand::run()\n");
    while (true)  {
        try {
          if (MouseState==1) {
            long mtime =
              java.lang.System.currentTimeMillis();
            if (TimeLastMouse < mtime - 800) {
                MouseState=0;
                PutChar();
            }
          }
        } catch (Exception e) {} ;
        try {Thread.sleep(20);} catch (Exception ex) { };
    }
}

public void PutChar() {
    int x_min=9999, x_max=-9999;
    int y_min=9999, y_max=-9999;
    for (int i=MousePointIndex; i<num_cap; i++) {
        if (cap_x[i] < x_min) x_min = cap_x[i];
        if (cap_x[i] > x_max) x_max = cap_x[i];
        if (cap_y[i] < y_min) y_min = cap_y[i];
        if (cap_y[i] > y_max) y_max = cap_y[i];
    }
```

```
        if (x_min+1 > x_max)  { x_min--; x_max++; }
        P("X,Y char bounds: " + x_min + ", " + x_max +
          ", " + y_min + ", " + y_max + "\n");

        int ic = 0;
        for (int x=0; x<XSIZE; x++) {
            for (int y=0; y<YSIZE; y++) {
                network.Inputs[ic++] = -0.4f;
            }
        }
        for (int i=MousePointIndex; i<num_cap; i++) {
            float xx = (float)(cap_x[i] - x_min)
                       / (float)(x_max - x_min);
            xx *= XSIZE;
            float yy = (float)(cap_y[i] - y_min)
                       / (float)(y_max - y_min);
            yy *= YSIZE;
            int ix=(int)xx;
            int iy=(int)yy;
            if (ix<0) ix=0;
            if (ix>=XSIZE) ix=XSIZE-1;
            if (iy<0) iy=0;
            if (iy>=YSIZE) iy=YSIZE-1;
            network.Inputs[ix*YSIZE+iy] = +0.4f;
        }
        // Propagate input neuron values through
        // to the hidden, then output neuron layer:
        network.ForwardPass();
        // Find the largest output neuron value:
        int index=0;
        float maxVal=-99f;
        for (int i=0; i<NUM; i++) {
            if (network.Outputs[i]>maxVal) {
                maxVal = network.Outputs[i];
                index = i;
            }
        }
        P("\nCharacter recognized: " + Chars[index] + "\n");
        return;
    }

public void doMouseDown(int x, int y) {
    long mtime = java.lang.System.currentTimeMillis();
    if (MouseState==0) { // not yet in capture mode
```

```
        P("switch to capture mode\n");
        MouseState=1;
        MousePointIndex = num_cap;
    }

    TimeLastMouse = mtime;

    //System.out.println("Mouse x: " + x + ", y: " + y);
    if (num_cap<19999) {
        cap_x[num_cap] = x;
        cap_y[num_cap] = y;
        num_cap++;
        repaint();
    }
    }
}
```

Figure 12.7 shows the execution of program **testHand_4** seen in Listing 12.5. This program reads a trained neural network from a neural network description file. The program **testHand_4** provides an example for using pretrained embedded neural networks in Java programs.

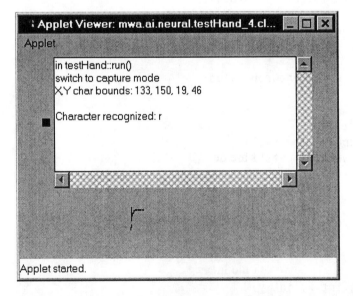

Figure 12.7   Testing the class **testHand_4** by recognizing hand-drawn characters using a previously trained neural network

Supporting Natural Language Queries in a World Wide Web Document

13

This chapter uses the natural language processing classes developed in Chapter 6 for a program to answer history questions. The frame data structures developed in Chapter 2 are used to store data dealing with historical events, places, and people, and the object (frame) server developed in Chapter 3 is used to place the history database in a separate server program that can run on any computer in a local area network or the Internet. Figure 13.1 shows the distributed nature of this example system.

13.1 Requirements for a distributed natural language processing system

Successful natural language processing systems are designed and built for specific topics. The example programs (both client and server) developed in this chapter have the following requirements:

- Historical data for people, places, and events are stored as **AIframe** data objects.
- The people, place, and event objects are stored in a separate server application. This application can execute on the same machine as the client program, or on any other computer on a local area network or the Internet.

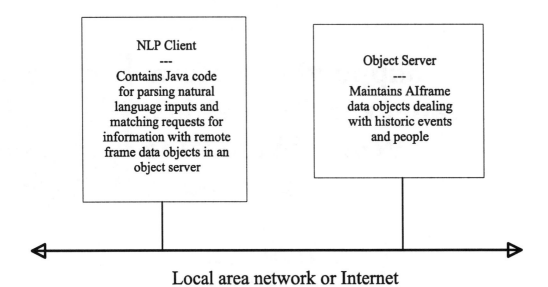

Figure 13.1 Process architecture of the distributed client/server NLP history system

- The client program allows a user to type natural language requests for information stored on a remote object server.
- The client program caches (or stores locally) some information from the server program in order to reduce the frequency of information requests between the client and server programs. This caching results in quicker response to the user data queries when using the client program.
- The client program attempts to understand queries for data; if this attempt fails, the system degrades "gracefully" by recognizing proper names, names of places, and words used in event descriptions. All (possibly) relevant data is retrieved from the server program and displayed for the user in a scrolling text field in the client program.

Data for places, events, and people is stored using the class **mwa.data.AIframe**. A slot named **type** has one of the following values that identifies the type of information in the **AIframe** object:

- **place**
- **event**
- **type**

AIframe objects containing information about places contain two additional slots in addition to the **type** slot:

- **name (String)**
- **description (String)**

AIframe objects containing information about events contain the following slots in addition to the **type** slot:

- **year (int)**
- **person (AIframe)**
- **place (AIframe)**
- **action (String)**
- **description (String)**

AIframe objects containing information about people contain the following slots in addition to the **type** slot:

- **last (String)**—the last name of the person
- **first (String)**—the first name of the person
- **event (AIframe)**

This data format for storing places, events, and people is fairly simple; however, because **AIframe** objects can refer to other **AIframe** objects in slot values, this scheme will work well for storing facts about history.

13.2 Distributed natural language processing system design

Figure 13.2 shows the Booch class diagram for the example distributed natural language processing system that is developed in this chapter. Three new Java classes are used to implement this distributed natural language processing demonstration system:

- **mwa.ai.nlp.HistoryAIframeServer**
- **mwa.ai.nlp.History**
- **mwa.ai.nlp.HistoryParser**

The class **mwa.ai.nlp.HistoryAIframeServer** contains an instance of the class **mwa.agent.AIframeServer** that provides the necessary behavior for accepting remote data requests for **AIframe** objects that are stored in the **AIframeServer**. The only new behavior required by the derived class **HistoryAIframeServer** is the creation of the

AIframe objects that encode the historical data of events, people, and places; this behavior is provided by the method **HistoryAIframeServer.AddData( )**, which is called from the method **HistoryAIframeServer.init( )**. The class **HistoryAIframeServer** is derived from the class **mwa.gui.GUI**, which provides the data and behavior for creating a Java application.

The class **mwa.ai.nlp.History** is also derived from the class **mwa.gui.GUI** and implements the client program for accessing historic data stored on the object server program. The class **mwa.ai.nlp.History** provides the following application-specific behavior:

- Sets up an input text field for queries and a scrolling output text field.
- Provides utility behavior in the methods **GetPlaces( )**, **GetPeople( )**, and **GetEvents( )** for fetching from a remote server the names of places, people, and events and caching them (i.e., storing them locally) for future use.
- Creates an instance of the class **mwa.agent.Client** for handling data requests to the server program. This instance is static so that it is accessible by instances of the class **mwa.ai.nlp.HistoryParser**.
- Provides a static utility method **GetFrameFromServer( )**, which fetches an **AIframe** object from the server program.
- Creates a single instance of the class **mwa.ai.nlp.HistoryParser**, which is used to process a user's queries to the historical database.

13.3　Implementation of a distributed natural language processing system

The example distributed natural language processing interface to a historical database is implemented as two separate programs. The server-side program is implemented in Section 13.3.1, and the client-side program is implemented in Section 13.3.2.

13.3.1 Implementation of the AIframeServer for historical data

Listing 13.1 shows the implementation of the class **mwa.ai.nlp.HistoryAIframeServer**, which is derived from the class **mwa.gui.GUI**. The **HistoryAIframeServer** class contains an instance of the class **mwa.agent.AIframeServer**, which is used to manage incoming socket connections and provide the following services:

- Return a list of **AIframe** names of a specified type
- Return the value of an **AIframe**, given its name

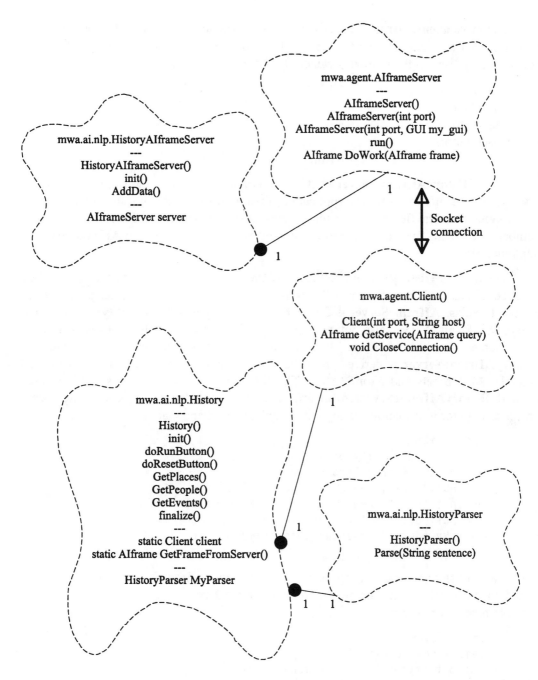

Figure 13.2 Booch class diagram for the classes **History** and **HistoryAIframeServer**

The **mwa.agent.AIframeServer** class, which was implemented in Chapter 3, also provides other services that this application does not use. The method **HistoryAIframe-Server.init( )** disables the following standard **GUI** class components:

- Graphics area
- Input field
- Run button
- Reset button

The **HistoryAIframeServer.init( )** method calls the superclass method **mwa.gui.GUI.init()** to set up the application, then allocates a new instance of the class **AIframeServer**. The first argument for the class **AIframeServer** constructor is a socket number; specifying a value of zero uses a default value that is set in the **AIframeServer** implementation.

The method **HistoryAIframeServer.AddData()** is used to initialize the data in the instance of class **AIframeServer** with example historical data for people, places, and events. The class **AIframeServer** defines a protected array **MyObjects** of type **AIframe**. The class **AIframeServer** also defines a protected integer variable **NumObjects**, which is a counter for the number of elements in the array **MyObjects**. Since the class **HistoryAIframeServer** is derived from the class **AIframeServer**, it has access to the variables **MyObjects** and **NumObjects**. The following Java statements show how the method **HistoryAIframeServer.AddData( )** adds new **AIframe** objects to the local object storage for information dealing with people, events, and places:

```
AIframe place;
// Place object: city of Knossos
place = new AIframe("Knossos_0");
place.put("type", new AIframedata("place"));
place.put("name", new AIframedata("Knossos"));
place.put("description", new AIframedata("city"));
server.MyObjects[server.NumObjects++]=place;
```

Notice that all slot values are instances of the class **AIframedata**. Other **AIframe** objects added to the local object storage can refer to this **AIframe** object referenced in the variable **place**. For example,

```
AIframe event;
event = new AIframe("Knossos_2");
event.put("type", new AIframedata("event"));
event.put("description",
          new AIframedata("Destruction of Knossos"));
event.put("place", new AIframedata("!!" + place.getName()));
```

```
event.put("action", new AIframedata("destruction"));
event.put("year", new AIframedata(-1400)); // negative for BC
server.MyObjects[server.NumObjects++]=event;
```

There is something mysterious about this example! In the statement

```
event.put("place", new AIframedata("!!" + place.getName()));
```

a new slot value (defined as **AIframedata**) is created with the name of the "place" **AIframe** object with the string "!!" prepended to indicate to the **AIframedata** class constructor that the argument refers to the name of an **AIframe** object, not a standard Java **String**.

Figure 13.3 shows the execution of the server program implemented with the class **mwa.ai.nlp.HistoryAIframeServer**.

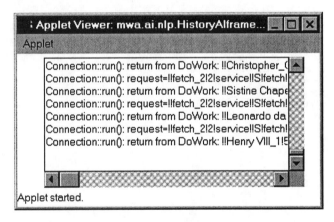

Figure 13.3   The Java class **mwa.ai.nlp.HistoryAIframeServer**

The class **mwa.ai.nlp.HistoryAIframeServer** contains a reference to an instance of the class **mwa.agent.AIframeServer**, which is stored in the class variable **server**. This instance of class **mwa.agent.AIframeServer** provides all of the required behavior for interfacing with client applications.

Most of the code in Listing 13.1 consists of adding person, place, and event **AIframe** data objects to the data server. The method **HistoryAIframeServer.init( )** disables the default graphics area, input text field, "Run" button, and "Reset" button that are usually created by the superclass **mwa.gui.GUI.init( )** method. The method **HistoryAIframeServer.init( )** calls the method **HistoryAIframeServer.AddData( )** to add the person, place, and event **AIframe** objects to the server. These objects are stored in the array **mwa.agent.AIframeServer.MyObjects** that is referenced through the class variable **server**.

Listing 13.1

```
// Test server classes
//
// Copyright 1996, Mark Watson.  All rights reserved.

package mwa.ai.nlp;

import java.awt.*;
import java.applet.Applet;
import java.lang.*;
import java.util.*;

import mwa.gui.*;
import mwa.agent.*;
import mwa.data.*;


public class HistoryAIframeServer extends GUI {

    AIframeServer server;

    public String getAppletInfo() {
        return "Test the agent stuff.  By Mark Watson";
    }

    public void init() {
      // Disable all standard GUI display components except output:
      NoGraphics    = true;
      NoInput       = true;
      NoRunButton   = true;
      NoResetButton = true;
      BigText=1;

      super.init();
      P("testServer applet");

      server = new AIframeServer(0, this);  // use default port

      AddData();
```

```
}

//public void run() {
//     System.out.println("in testServer::run()\n");
//     super.run();  '
//}

// Add the data procedurally:
private void AddData() {
  AIframe place, event, person;
  // Place object: city of Knossos
  place = new AIframe("Knossos_0");
  place.put("type", new AIframedata("place"));
  place.put("name", new AIframedata("Knossos"));
  place.put("description", new AIframedata("city"));
  server.MyObjects[server.NumObjects++]=place;
  // Event object: founding of city of Knossos
  event = new AIframe("Knossos_1");
  event.put("type", new AIframedata("event"));
  event.put("place", new AIframedata("!!" + place.getName()));
  event.put("description",
            new AIframedata("Founding of Knossos"));
  event.put("action", new AIframedata("founding"));
  event.put("year", new AIframedata(-2500)); // negative for BC
  server.MyObjects[server.NumObjects++]=event;
  // Event object: destruction of city of Knossos
  event = new AIframe("Knossos_2");
  event.put("type", new AIframedata("event"));
  event.put("description",
            new AIframedata("Destruction of Knossos"));
  event.put("place", new AIframedata("!!" + place.getName()));
  event.put("action", new AIframedata("destruction"));
  event.put("year", new AIframedata(-1400)); // negative for BC
  server.MyObjects[server.NumObjects++]=event;
  // Person object: Buddha
  person = new AIframe("Buddha_0");
  person.put("last", new AIframedata("Buddha"));
  person.put("type", new AIframedata("person"));
  server.MyObjects[server.NumObjects++]=person;
  // Event object: birth of Buddha
  event = new AIframe("Buddha_1");
  event.put("type", new AIframedata("event"));
  event.put("person", new AIframedata("!!" + person.getName()));
  event.put("description",
```

```
                new AIframedata("Birth of the Buddha"));
event.put("year", new AIframedata(-563));
server.MyObjects[server.NumObjects++]=event;

// Place object: city of Rome
place = new AIframe("Rome_0");
place.put("type", new AIframedata("place"));
place.put("name", new AIframedata("Rome"));
place.put("description", new AIframedata("city"));
server.MyObjects[server.NumObjects++]=place;
// Event object: founding of city of Rome
event = new AIframe("Rome_1");
event.put("type", new AIframedata("event"));
event.put("place", new AIframedata("!!" + place.getName()));
event.put("action", new AIframedata("founding"));
event.put("description",
            new AIframedata("Founding of the city of Rome"));
event.put("year", new AIframedata(-753)); // negative for BC
server.MyObjects[server.NumObjects++]=event;
// Event object: deposition of last Roman Emperor
event = new AIframe("Roman_Emperor_0");
event.put("type", new AIframedata("event"));
event.put("place", new AIframedata("!!" + place.getName()));
event.put("action", new AIframedata("deposition"));
event.put("year", new AIframedata(+476)); // positive for AD
event.put("description",
    new AIframedata("Deposition of the last emperor of Rome"));
server.MyObjects[server.NumObjects++]=event;
// Place object: city of Byzantium
place = new AIframe("Byzantium_0");
place.put("type", new AIframedata("place"));
place.put("name", new AIframedata("Byzantium"));
place.put("description", new AIframedata("city"));
server.MyObjects[server.NumObjects++]=place;
// Event object: founding of city of Byzantium
event = new AIframe("Byzantium_1");
event.put("type", new AIframedata("event"));
event.put("place", new AIframedata("!!" + place.getName()));
event.put("action", new AIframedata("founding"));
event.put("year", new AIframedata(-660)); // negative for BC
event.put("description",
            new AIframedata("Founding of the city of Byzantium"));
server.MyObjects[server.NumObjects++]=event;
// Place object: empire of Sumeria
```

```
place = new AIframe("Sumeria_0");
place.put("type", new AIframedata("place"));
place.put("name", new AIframedata("Sumeria"));
place.put("description", new AIframedata("empire"));
server.MyObjects[server.NumObjects++]=place;
// Event object: founding of empire of Sumeria
event = new AIframe("Sumeria_1");
event.put("type", new AIframedata("event"));
event.put("place", new AIframedata("!!" + place.getName()));
event.put("action", new AIframedata("founding"));
event.put("year", new AIframedata(-2350)); // negative for BC
event.put("description",
          new AIframedata("Founding of the empire of Sumeria"));
server.MyObjects[server.NumObjects++]=event;
// Place object: city of Troy
place = new AIframe("Troy_0");
place.put("type", new AIframedata("place"));
place.put("name", new AIframedata("Troy"));
place.put("description", new AIframedata("empire"));
server.MyObjects[server.NumObjects++]=place;
// Event object: destruction of city of Troy
event = new AIframe("Troy_1");
event.put("type", new AIframedata("event"));
event.put("place", new AIframedata("!!" + place.getName()));
event.put("action", new AIframedata("destruction"));
event.put("year", new AIframedata(-1193)); // negative for BC
event.put("description",
          new AIframedata("destruction of the city of Troy"));
server.MyObjects[server.NumObjects++]=event;
// Place object: Egypt
place = new AIframe("Egypt_0");
place.put("type", new AIframedata("place"));
place.put("name", new AIframedata("Egypt"));
place.put("description", new AIframedata("pyramid"));
server.MyObjects[server.NumObjects++]=place;
// Event object: first pyramid built in Egypt
event = new AIframe("pyramid");
event.put("type", new AIframedata("event"));
event.put("place", new AIframedata("!!" + place.getName()));
event.put("action", new AIframedata("built"));
event.put("year", new AIframedata(-2780)); // negative for BC
event.put("description",
          new AIframedata("first pyramid built in Egypt"));
server.MyObjects[server.NumObjects++]=event;
```

```
// Person object: Confucius
person = new AIframe("Confucius_0");
person.put("last", new AIframedata("Confucius"));
server.MyObjects[server.NumObjects++]=person;
// Event object: birth of Confucius
event = new AIframe("Confucius_1");
event.put("type", new AIframedata("event"));
event.put("action", new AIframedata("birth"));
event.put("person", new AIframedata("!!" + person.getName()));
event.put("year", new AIframedata(-551));
event.put("description",
          new AIframedata("birth of Confucius"));
server.MyObjects[server.NumObjects++]=event;
// Person object: Caligula
person = new AIframe("Caligula_0");
person.put("last", new AIframedata("Caligula"));
server.MyObjects[server.NumObjects++]=person;
// Event object: Caligula becomes Emperor of Rome
event = new AIframe("Emperor_1");
event.put("type", new AIframedata("event"));
event.put("place", new AIframedata("!!" + place.getName()));
event.put("action", new AIframedata("becomes"));
event.put("year", new AIframedata(+37)); // positive for AD
event.put("description",
   new AIframedata("Caligula becomes emperor of Rome"));
server.MyObjects[server.NumObjects++]=event;
// Person object: Jesus
person = new AIframe("Jesus_0");
person.put("last", new AIframedata("Jesus"));
person.put("type", new AIframedata("person"));
server.MyObjects[server.NumObjects++]=person;
// Event object: birth of Jesus
event = new AIframe("Jesus_1");
event.put("type", new AIframedata("event"));
event.put("action", new AIframedata("birth"));
event.put("person", new AIframedata("!!" + person.getName()));
event.put("year", new AIframedata(-5));
event.put("description",
          new AIframedata("birth of Jesus"));
server.MyObjects[server.NumObjects++]=event;
// Person object: Muhammad
person = new AIframe("Muhammad_0");
person.put("last", new AIframedata("Muhammad"));
server.MyObjects[server.NumObjects++]=person;
```

```
// Place object: Mecca
place = new AIframe("Mecca");
place.put("type", new AIframedata("place"));
place.put("name", new AIframedata("Mecca"));
server.MyObjects[server.NumObjects++]=place;
// Event object: birth of Muhammad at Mecca
event = new AIframe("Muhammad_1");
event.put("type", new AIframedata("event"));
event.put("action", new AIframedata("birth"));
event.put("person", new AIframedata("!!" + person.getName()));
event.put("place", new AIframedata("!!" + place.getName()));
event.put("year", new AIframedata(+570));
event.put("description",
          new AIframedata("birth of Muhammad"));
server.MyObjects[server.NumObjects++]=event;
// Place object: Hastings
place = new AIframe("Hastings_0");
place.put("type", new AIframedata("place"));
place.put("name", new AIframedata("Hastings"));
server.MyObjects[server.NumObjects++]=place;
// Event object: battle of Hastings
event = new AIframe("Hastings_1");
event.put("type", new AIframedata("event"));
event.put("place", new AIframedata("!!" + place.getName()));
event.put("action", new AIframedata("battle"));
event.put("year", new AIframedata(+1066));
event.put("description",
          new AIframedata("battle of Hastings"));
server.MyObjects[server.NumObjects++]=event;
// Event object: Magna Carta
event = new AIframe("Magna Carta_0");
event.put("type", new AIframedata("event"));
event.put("place", new AIframedata("!!" + place.getName()));
event.put("year", new AIframedata(+1215));
event.put("description",
          new AIframedata("king of England signs Magna Carta"));
server.MyObjects[server.NumObjects++]=event;
// Place object: Europe
place = new AIframe("Europe_0");
place.put("type", new AIframedata("place"));
place.put("name", new AIframedata("Hastings"));
server.MyObjects[server.NumObjects++]=place;
// Event object: Hundred Years War
event = new AIframe("Hundred Years War_0");
```

```
event.put("type", new AIframedata("event"));
event.put("place", new AIframedata("!!" + place.getName()));
event.put("year", new AIframedata(+1338));
event.put("description",
          new AIframedata("hundred year war"));
server.MyObjects[server.NumObjects++]=event;
// Event object: Black Death ravages Europe
event = new AIframe("Black Death_0");
event.put("type", new AIframedata("event"));
event.put("place", new AIframedata("!!" + place.getName()));
event.put("year", new AIframedata(+1348));
server.MyObjects[server.NumObjects++]=event;
// Place object: Carthage
place = new AIframe("Carthage_0");
place.put("type", new AIframedata("place"));
place.put("name", new AIframedata("Carthage"));
server.MyObjects[server.NumObjects++]=place;
// Event object: destruction of Carthage by Arabs
event = new AIframe("Carthage_1");
event.put("type", new AIframedata("event"));
event.put("place", new AIframedata("!!" + place.getName()));
event.put("action", new AIframedata("destruction"));
event.put("year", new AIframedata(+697));
event.put("description",
          new AIframedata("destruction of Carthage by Arabs"));
server.MyObjects[server.NumObjects++]=event;
// Place object: Tenochtitlan
place = new AIframe("Tenochtitlan_0");
place.put("type", new AIframedata("place"));
place.put("name", new AIframedata("Tenochtitlan"));
place.put("description", new AIframedata("city"));
server.MyObjects[server.NumObjects++]=place;
// Event object: founding of Tenochtitlan by Aztecs
event = new AIframe("Tenochtitlan_1");
event.put("type", new AIframedata("event"));
event.put("place", new AIframedata("!!" + place.getName()));
event.put("action", new AIframedata("founding"));
event.put("year", new AIframedata(+1325));
event.put("description",
          new AIframedata("founding of Tenochtitlan by Aztecs"));
server.MyObjects[server.NumObjects++]=event;
// Place object: Peru
place = new AIframe("Peru_0");
place.put("type", new AIframedata("place"));
```

```
place.put("name", new AIframedata("Peru"));
place.put("description", new AIframedata("city"));
server.MyObjects[server.NumObjects++]=place;
// Event object: Inca Empire established in Peru
event = new AIframe("Peru_1");
event.put("type", new AIframedata("event"));
event.put("place", new AIframedata("!!" + place.getName()));
event.put("action", new AIframedata("established"));
event.put("person", new AIframedata("Incas"));
event.put("year", new AIframedata(+1438));
event.put("description",
          new AIframedata("Inca empire founded in Peru"));
server.MyObjects[server.NumObjects++]=event;
// Place object: West Indies
place = new AIframe("West Indies_0");
place.put("type", new AIframedata("place"));
place.put("name", new AIframedata("West Indies"));
place.put("description", new AIframedata("West Indies"));
server.MyObjects[server.NumObjects++]=place;

// Person object: Christopher Columbus
person = new AIframe("Columbus_0");
person.put("last", new AIframedata("Columbus"));
person.put("first", new AIframedata("Christopher"));
person.put("type", new AIframedata("person"));
server.MyObjects[server.NumObjects++]=person;
// Event object: Christopher Columbus discovers West Indies
event = new AIframe("West_Indies_1");
event.put("type", new AIframedata("event"));
event.put("place", new AIframedata("!!" + place.getName()));
event.put("action", new AIframedata("discovers"));
event.put("person", new AIframedata("!!" + person.getName()));
event.put("year", new AIframedata(+1492));
event.put("description",
 new AIframedata("Christopher Columbus discovers West Indies"));
server.MyObjects[server.NumObjects++]=event;
// Event object: Christopher Columbus dies in poverty
event = new AIframe("Christopher_Columbus_3");
event.put("type", new AIframedata("event"));
event.put("action", new AIframedata("dies"));
event.put("person", new AIframedata("!!" + person.getName()));
event.put("year", new AIframedata(+1506));
event.put("description",
    new AIframedata("Christopher Columbus dies in poverty"));
```

```
server.MyObjects[server.NumObjects++]=event;

// Place object: Rome
place = new AIframe("Rome_0");
place.put("type", new AIframedata("place"));
place.put("name", new AIframedata("Rome"));
place.put("description",
 new AIframedata("Early seat of Roman empire " +
                 "and capital of Italy"));
server.MyObjects[server.NumObjects++]=place;
// Person object: Giovanni de Dolci
person = new AIframe("Giovanni_de_Dolci_0");
person.put("last", new AIframedata("Dolci"));
person.put("first", new AIframedata("Giovanni"));
person.put("type", new AIframedata("person"));
server.MyObjects[server.NumObjects++]=person;
// Event object: Sistine Chapel built by Giovanni de Dolci
event = new AIframe("Sistine Chapel_0");
event.put("type", new AIframedata("event"));
event.put("place", new AIframedata("!!" + place.getName()));
event.put("action", new AIframedata("built"));
event.put("person", new AIframedata("!!" + person.getName()));
event.put("year", new AIframedata(+1473));
event.put("description",
  new AIframedata("Sistine Chapel built by Giovanni de Dolci"));
server.MyObjects[server.NumObjects++]=event;
// Person object: Leonardo da Vinci
person = new AIframe("Leonardo_da_Vinci_0");
person.put("last", new AIframedata("Vinci"));
person.put("first", new AIframedata("Leonardo"));
person.put("type", new AIframedata("person"));
server.MyObjects[server.NumObjects++]=person;
// Event object: birth of Leonardo da Vinci
event = new AIframe("Leonardo da Vinci_1");
event.put("type", new AIframedata("event"));
event.put("action", new AIframedata("birth"));
event.put("person", new AIframedata("!!" + person.getName()));
event.put("year", new AIframedata(+1475));
event.put("description",
          new AIframedata("birth of Leonardo da Vinci"));
server.MyObjects[server.NumObjects++]=event;
// Person object: Henry VIII, King of England
person = new AIframe("Henry_VIII_0");
person.put("last", new AIframedata("Henry VIII"));
```

```
person.put("type", new AIframedata("person"));
server.MyObjects[server.NumObjects++]=person;
// Event object: Henry VIII, King of England, dies
event = new AIframe("Henry VIII_1");
event.put("type", new AIframedata("event"));
event.put("person", new AIframedata("!!" + person.getName()));
event.put("year", new AIframedata(1547));
event.put("action", new AIframedata("dies"));
event.put("description",
          new AIframedata("Henry VIII, King of England dies"));
server.MyObjects[server.NumObjects++]=event;


    }

}
```

Suggested project

The class **HistoryAIframeServer** implemented in Listing 13.1 contains explicit Java code for initializing the historical data for the sample programs in this chapter. Modify the class **HistoryAIframeServer** to read an input file containing **AIframe** data for people, events, and places. Write another application that allows interactive editing of historical data. Add a new command button to the **HistoryAIframeServer** application to reload the historical database from a file.

13.3.2 Implementation of the natural language processing client program

The client program contains a text input field where the program user can type queries dealing with history. These queries are processed using both cached data and by using dynamic (i.e., on demand as required) queries to the remote historical data object server program. Results of the queries are displayed in a scrolling text output field.

Figure 13.2 showed the Booch class diagram for the class **mwa.ai.nlp.History** and a partial class diagram for the class **mwa.ai.nlp.HistoryParser**. Figure 13.4 shows a more detailed Booch class diagram for the class **mwa.ai.nlp.HistoryParser**.

Listing 13.2 shows the implementation of the class **mwa.ai.nlp.History**, which is derived from the class **mwa.gui.GUI** and contains an instance of the class **mwa.ai.nlp.HistoryParser**, which is derived from the class **mwa.ai.nlp.Parser**. The method **HistoryParser.init( )** performs the following application setup tasks:

- Turn off graphics support in the **mwa.gui.GUI** base class and increase the default size of the scrolling output text field.
- Override the default values for the "Run" and "Reset" comand button labels, setting them, respectively, to "Process input" and "Toggle debug on/off."

- Create an instance of the class **mwa.agent.Client** for communication with the remote object server application.
- Call the superclass method **mwa.gui.GUI.init( )** to perform inherited application setup behavior.
- Create an instance of the class **HistoryParser** for use in parsing user requests for information.
- Fetch the names of places, people, and events from the remote object server and store them locally.

The static method **History.GetFrameFromServer** is used by methods both in the **History** and **HistoryParser** classes for retrieving **AIframe** objects from the remote object server application. Remote queries require a new **AIframe** object with a slot named **service** and a slot value of an **AIframedata** object created with the **String** "fetch". The instance of class **mwa.agent.Client** created in the **History.init( )** method is used to send this request to the remote server and wait for the response. The **mwa.agent.Client.GetService( )** method returns a valid **AIframe** object or the value **null** if there is any error in accessing the remote data.

The method **Histroy.doRun( )**, which overrides the behavior defined in the base class method **mwa.gui.GUI.doRunButton( )**, reads the text in the input data field and processes any requests that the **HistoryParser** object can process. The **doRun( )** method is also executed if the user hits a return key while typing in the application's input text field. In addition to requests for data, the program user can simply type "help" in the input text field to get directions for running the application and hints on the types of data requests that can be successfully processed (see Figure 13.5 for an example of using the "help" option).

mwa.ai.nlp.HistoryParser

HistoryParser()
int synonymIndex(String s)
void SortFuzzy()
void AddFuzzy(AIframe person,
AIframe event,
float value)
int MaxFuzzy()
boolean noiseWord()
Parse(String sentence)
void DoWHwords()
void GetPersonFromEvent(AIframe event, float value)
float FuzzyMatch(String s1, String s2)
void GetPersonFromEventDescription(String description)
void DoVerb()
boolean ProperName(String name)
boolean Place(String name)
boolean Event(String name)
void DoObject()

String synonyms[]
int NumFuzzy
float FuzzyValues[]
AIframe FuzzyPersonFrames[]
AIframe FuzzyEventFrames[]

Figure 13.4   Detailed Booch class diagram of **HistoryParser**

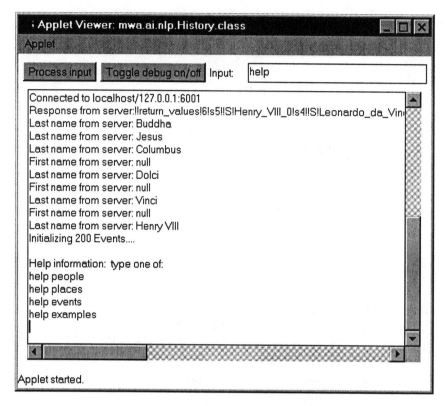

Figure 13.5   The user has typed "help" to get directions for running the sample application.

The "help" commands are useful for both new users of the example program and for development; typing "help people" will fetch the **AIframe** data for every person object on the remote object server and print the data in the text output field. In the same way, typing "help places" and "help events" fetches all remote data for places and events and prints in the scrolling output text field. If the user types "help examples" in the input text field, the method **doHistory.RunButton( )** prints out several example queries that the user can try; these examples indicate to the user the types of questions that the **HistoryParser** class can process (see Figure 13.6).

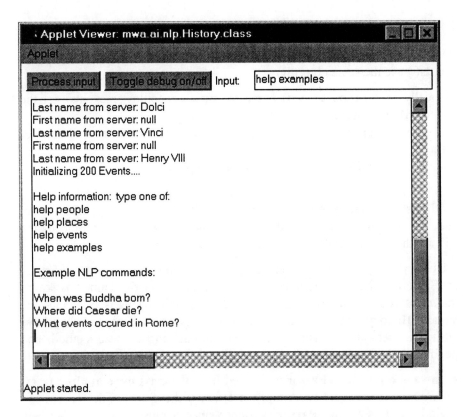

Figure 13.6   The user has typed "help examples" to see examples of the types of data requests that can be processed.

The **History.doRun( )** method first checks for simple "help" messages, which it processes itself. If the contents of the input text field is not a simple "help" message, then the method **History.doRunButton( )** calls the method **HistoryParser.Parse( )** with the contents of the input text field. The class **History** uses a single instance of the class **HistoryParser** for all parsing operations in the same way that a single instance of the class **mwa.agent.Client** is used repeatedly for all remote data requests to the remote object server application.

The **History** class utility methods **History.GetPlaces( )**, **History.GetPeople( )**, and **History.GetEvents( )** use the same algorithm:

- For each locally stored (i.e., cached) name for places, people, or events, get the locally stored **AIframe** object name.
- Send each **AIframe** object name to the remote object server to retrieve all data for that **AIframe**.
- Print out the retrieved information in the scrolling output text field.

The method **History.finalize( )** is called automatically by the Java runtime system when an instance of the **History** class is destroyed. This **finalize( )** method closes the socket connection with the remote object server.

The file **History.java**, seen in Listing 13.2, also contains the definition of class **HistoryParser**. Since the class **HistoryParser** is not defined in a file named **History-Parser.java**, the class **HistoryParser** cannot be declared public. This is fine since the classes **History** and **HistoryParser** are in the same package **mwa.ai.nlp**, so they have complete access to the methods and data in the other class as long as these methods and data are not specifically declared to be private or protected.

The class **mwa.ai.nlp.HistoryParser** is derived from the class **mwa.ai.nlp.Parser**. The base class **Parser** is fairly short, simply providing the framework for parsing sentences. The derived class **HistoryParser** is longer since it must define the data and behavior required for parsing application-specific English sentences. The derived class adds several new behaviors to the base class **Parser**:

- Specifically looks for "WH" words (i.e., WHen, WHere, WHat, and WHo)
- Determines if a word is a proper name by using the array of locally stored (or cached) proper names from the remote object server
- Adds data and support for "fuzzy" matches between words, and for words located inside long event descriptions
- Discards noise words like *a*, *the*, etc.
- Gets a person's name from a "fuzzy" event description by retrieving all event data from the remote object server and matching event words in the sentence with the event description stored on the remote server

Regardless of whether the parser can properly interpret the user's query as an English sentence, the method **HistoryParser.Parse( )** prints out information obtained from the remote object server that has a high likelihood of being relevant to the user's interest. If the parsing operation fails, the example program at least degrades gracefully;

that is, the user is still shown some information that is likely to be of relevance to the original query. If the parsing operation is successful, after the method **History-Parser.Parse( )** prints out relevant information, it returns as its value an **AIframe** object containing a conceptual-dependency type frame containing relevant information. The method **HistoryParser.Parse( )** performs the following operations:

- Breaks the sentence stored as a single **String** object into an array of **String** objects (one **String** per word).
- Identifies a query type by looking for the WH words: WHen, WHere, WHat, and WHo.
- Identifies the verb in the sentence and instantiates a conceptual dependency **AIframe** object for the verb. This **AIframe** object is stored in an array of **AIframe** objects: **sentences[]**.
- Identifies who the actor is in the sentence and fills in the actor slot in the conceptual dependency **AIframe** object.
- Identifies what the object is in the sentence and fills in the object slot in the conceptual dependency **AIframe** object.
- Tries to set the time frame for the sentence. The time can also be set when identifying the verb in the sentence.
- Performs special WH word processing, which results in (probably) relevant information being printed in the scrolling text output field of the client application. Fuzzy word match data is used to estimate what information is most relevant to the user.

Listing 13.2

```
// NLP Java classes: test program and new subclass of Parser
//
// Copyright 1996, Mark Watson.  All rights reserved.
// http://www.markwatson.com

package mwa.ai.nlp;

import java.awt.*;
import java.applet.Applet;
import java.lang.*;
import java.util.*;

import mwa.gui.GUI;
import mwa.data.*;
import mwa.agent.*;

public class History extends GUI {
```

```java
// use subclass defined at end of this file
HistoryParser MyParser;

static Client client = null;

public String getAppletInfo() {
    return "NLP history of the world demo by Mark Watson";
}

public void init() {
    NoGraphics=true;
    BigText=3;
    RunLabel   = new String("Process input");
    ResetLabel = new String("Toggle debug on/off");

    client = new Client();

    super.init();

    MyParser = new HistoryParser();
    MyParser.MyGUI = this;
    MyParser.MyGUI.SetInputText("help");

    // Cache the current place names and places from the server:
    GetPlaces();
    GetPeople();
    GetEvents();
}

// The following utility is static so that the HistoryParser
// class can use it:
synchronized static
public AIframe GetFrameFromServer(String frame_name) {
    // send a new frame to the AIframeServer:
    AIframe frame=new AIframe("test_query_frame");
    frame.put("service", new AIframedata("fetch"));
    frame.put("name", new AIframedata(frame_name));

    AIframe response = client.GetService(frame);
    // NOTE: response may be 'null' if frame not on server.
    frame=null;
    // NOTE: uncomment the following line for debug printout:
    //if (response!=null)  response.PP();
```

```
      return response;
   }

   synchronized public void doRunButton() {
      String input = GetInputText().trim();
      if (input.equals("help") || input.equals("Help")) {
         P("\nHelp information:  type one of:\n");
         P("help people\n");
         P("help places\n");
         P("help events\n");
         P("help examples\n");
         return;
      }

      if (input.equals("help people")) {
         P("\nPeople defined on remote AIframeServer:\n\n");
         for (int i=0; i<NumPeople; i++) {
           AIframe p = GetFrameFromServer(PeopleFrame[i]);
           if (p!=null) {
              p.PP(this);
           }
         }
         return;
      }

      if (input.equals("help places")) {
         P("\nPlaces defined on remote AIframeServer:\n\n");
         for (int i=0; i<NumPlaces; i++) {
           AIframe p = GetFrameFromServer(PlacesFrame[i]);
           if (p!=null) {
              p.PP(this);
           }
         }
         return;
      }

      if (input.equals("help events")) {
         P("\nEvents defined on remote AIframeServer:\n\n");
         for (int i=0; i<NumEvents; i++) {
           AIframe p = GetFrameFromServer(EventsFrame[i]);
           if (p!=null) {
              p.PP(this);
           }
         }
```

```
        return;
    }

    if (input.equals("help examples")) {
        P("\nExample NLP commands:\n\n");
        P("When was Buddha born?\n");
        P("Where did Caesar die?\n");
        P("What events occurred in Rome?\n");
        return;
    }


    MyParser.Parse(input);
    // Fetch out the semantic info from the last parse:
    AIframe cd_form = MyParser.sentences[MyParser.num_sentences-1];
    String actor = "";
    AIframedata fd = cd_form.get("actor");
    if (fd!=null) {
        if (fd.type==AIframedata.STRING) {
            if (fd.string.length() > 1) actor=fd.string;
        }
    }
    String action= "";
    fd = cd_form.get("action");
    if (fd!=null) {
        if (fd.type==AIframedata.STRING) {
            if (fd.string.length() > 1) action=fd.string;
        }
    }
    String object= "";
    fd = cd_form.get("object");
    if (fd!=null) {
        if (fd.type==AIframedata.STRING) {
            if (fd.string.length() > 1) object=fd.string;
        }
    }
    String recipient= "";
    fd = cd_form.get("recipient");
    if (fd!=null) {
        if (fd.type==AIframedata.STRING) {
            if (fd.string.length() > 1) recipient=fd.string;
        }
    }
    String place = "";
    fd = cd_form.get("place");
```

```
      if (fd!=null) {
         if (fd.type==AIframedata.STRING) {
            if (fd.string.length() > 1) place=fd.string;
         }
      }
      float time=0.0f;
      fd = cd_form.get("time");
      if (fd!=null) {
         if (fd.type==AIframedata.NUMBER) {
            time=fd.number;
         }
      }

      P("\n");
      if (!actor.equals("")) P("\nactor=" + actor + " ");
      if (!object.equals("")) P("object=" + object + " ");
      if (!recipient.equals("")) P("recipient=" + recipient + " ");
      if (!place.equals("")) P("place=" + place + " ");
      if (time != 0.0f) P("time=" + time);
      P("\n");

   }
   synchronized public void doResetButton() {
      ClearOutput();
   }
   // Utilities for getting information from
   // the remote object (frame) server:

   //    PLACES:

   static int NumPlaces=0;
   static String Places[]=null;
   static String PlacesFrame[]=null;
   static final int MAX_PLACES=200;

   synchronized private void GetPlaces() {
      if (Places==null) {
         P("Initializing " + MAX_PLACES + " Places....\n");
         Places = new String[MAX_PLACES];
         PlacesFrame = new String[MAX_PLACES];
         NumPlaces=0;
      }
      // Send request to AIframeServer:
      //Client client = new Client();
```

```
String r = client.GetInfo();
P(r + "\n");

// send a new frame to the AIframeServer:
AIframe frame=new AIframe("testframe1");
frame.put("service", new AIframedata("get_names"));
frame.put("type", new AIframedata("place"));
AIframe response = client.GetService(frame);
if (response!=null) {
   String res = response.toString();
   P("Response from server:" + res + "\n");
   for (int i=0; i<MAX_PLACES; i++) {
     String slot_name = new String("s" + i);
     AIframedata place_val = response.get(slot_name);
     if (place_val==null)  break; // we are done...
     // Still more places:
     if (place_val.type==AIframedata.STRING) {
        if (NumPlaces < (MAX_PLACES-1)) {
          // Capture the frame name (although we
          // may not save it):
          PlacesFrame[NumPlaces]=place_val.string;
          AIframe frame2 = new AIframe("fetch_2");
          frame2.put("service", new AIframedata("fetch"));
          frame2.put("name", new AIframedata(place_val.string));
          AIframe response2 = client.GetService(frame2);
          if (response2!=null) {
             AIframedata place_name_slot =
                            response2.get("name");
             if (place_name_slot!=null) {
               if (place_name_slot.type==AIframedata.STRING) {
                 Places[NumPlaces] =
                   new String(place_name_slot.string);
                 P("Place from server: " +
                   Places[NumPlaces] + "\n");
                 NumPlaces++;
               }
             }
          }
        }
     }
   }
} else {
   P("No response from server\n");
}
```

```
        //if (client!=null) client.CloseConnection();
}


//    PEOPLE:

static public int NumPeople=0;
static public String PeopleLast[]=null;
static public String PeopleFirst[]=null;
static public String PeopleFrame[]=null;
static public final int MAX_PEOPLE=200;

synchronized private void GetPeople() {
    if (PeopleLast==null) {
        P("Initializing " + MAX_PEOPLE + " People....\n");
        PeopleLast = new String[MAX_PEOPLE];
        PeopleFirst = new String[MAX_PEOPLE];
        PeopleFrame = new String[MAX_PEOPLE];
        NumPeople=0;
    }
    // Send request to AIframeServer:
    //Client client = new Client();
    String r = client.GetInfo();
    P(r + "\n");

    // send a new frame to the AIframeServer:
    AIframe frame=new AIframe("testframe1");
    frame.put("service", new AIframedata("get_names"));
    frame.put("type", new AIframedata("person"));
    AIframe response = client.GetService(frame);
    if (response!=null) {
        String res = response.toString();
        P("Response from server:" + res + "\n");
        for (int i=0; i<MAX_PEOPLE; i++) {
          String slot_name = new String("s" + i);
          AIframedata person_val = response.get(slot_name);
          if (person_val==null)  break; // we are done...
          // Still more places:
          if (person_val.type==AIframedata.STRING) {
             if (NumPeople < (MAX_PEOPLE-1)) {
                // Capture the frame name (although we
                // may not save it):
                PeopleFrame[NumPeople]=person_val.string;
                AIframe frame2 = new AIframe("fetch_2");
```

```
                    frame2.put("service", new AIframedata("fetch"));
                    frame2.put("name",
                                new AIframedata(person_val.string));
                    AIframe response2 = client.GetService(frame2);
                    if (response2!=null) {
                        // last name:
                        AIframedata person_name_slot =
                                        response2.get("last");
                        if (person_name_slot!=null) {
                            if (person_name_slot.type==AIframedata.STRING) {
                                PeopleLast[NumPeople] =
                                    new String(person_name_slot.string);
                                P("Last name from server: " +
                                            PeopleLast[NumPeople] + "\n");
                                NumPeople++;
                            }
                        } else {
                            break;   // we are done...
                        }
                        // first name:
                        person_name_slot = response2.get("first");
                        if (person_name_slot!=null) {
                            if (person_name_slot.type==AIframedata.STRING) {
                                // We have already incremented the
                                // counter 'NumPeople'
                                PeopleFirst[NumPeople-1] =
                                    new String(person_name_slot.string);
                                P("First name from server: " +
                                    PeopleFirst[NumPeople] + "\n");
                            }
                        }
                    }
                }
            }
        }
    } else {
        P("No response from server\n");
    }
}


//    EVENTS:

static public int NumEvents=0;
```

```
static public String Events[]=null;
static public String EventsFrame[]=null;
static public final int MAX_EVENTS=200;

synchronized private void GetEvents() {
    if (Events==null) {
        P("Initializing " + MAX_EVENTS + " Events....\n");
        Events = new String[MAX_EVENTS];
        EventsFrame = new String[MAX_EVENTS];
        NumEvents=0;
    }

    // send a request frame to the AIframeServer:
    AIframe frame=new AIframe("testframe1");
    frame.put("service", new AIframedata("get_names"));
    frame.put("type", new AIframedata("event"));
    AIframe response = client.GetService(frame);
    if (response!=null) {
        String res = response.toString();
        for (int i=0; i<MAX_EVENTS; i++) {
            String slot_name = new String("s" + i);
            AIframedata event_val = response.get(slot_name);
            if (event_val==null)  break;
            // Still more events:
            if (event_val.type==AIframedata.STRING) {
                if (NumEvents < (MAX_EVENTS-1)) {
                    // Capture the frame name (although we
                    // may not save it):
                    EventsFrame[NumEvents]=event_val.string;
                    AIframe frame2 = new AIframe("fetch_2");
                    frame2.put("service", new AIframedata("fetch"));
                    frame2.put("name", new AIframedata(event_val.string));
                    AIframe response2 = client.GetService(frame2);
                    if (response2!=null) {
                        AIframedata event_name_slot =
                                        response2.get("description");
                        if (event_name_slot!=null) {
                            if (event_name_slot.type==AIframedata.STRING) {
                                Events[NumEvents] =
                                    new String(event_name_slot.string);
                                NumEvents++;
                            }
                        }
                    }
                }
```

```
                }
              }
            }
        } else {
            P("No response from server\n");
        }
    }

    public void finalize() {
        if (client!=null) client.CloseConnection();
    }

}


//
//      Extend the base class mwa.ai.nlp.Parser to
//      add a few new verbs and object names:
//

class HistoryParser extends Parser {

  final static int WHEN =1;
  final static int WHERE=2;
  final static int WHAT =3;
  final static int WHO  =4;
  int Wtype=0;

  private String synonyms[][] = {
      {"birth", "born"},
      {"die", "death", "died"}
  };
  private int num_synonyms=2;
  private int num_per_syn[] = {2, 3};

  private int synonymIndex(String s) {
      for (int i=0; i<num_synonyms; i++) {
          for (int j=0; j<num_per_syn[i]; j++) {
              if (synonyms[i][j].equals(s))       return i;
          }
      }
      return -1;
  }

  // Utilities for fuzzy matching:
```

```
private int NumFuzzy = 0;
private final int MAX_FUZZY = 20;
private float FuzzyValues[] = new float[MAX_FUZZY];
private AIframe FuzzyPersonFrames[] = new AIframe[MAX_FUZZY];
private AIframe FuzzyEventFrames[]  = new AIframe[MAX_FUZZY];

private void SortFuzzy() {
    for (int i=0; i<NumFuzzy; i++) {
        for (int j=i; j<NumFuzzy-1; j++) {
            if (FuzzyValues[j] < FuzzyValues[j+1]) {
                float temp = FuzzyValues[j];
                AIframe ftemp = FuzzyPersonFrames[j];
                FuzzyValues[j] = FuzzyValues[j+1];
                FuzzyValues[j+1] = temp;
                FuzzyPersonFrames[j] = FuzzyPersonFrames[j+1];
                FuzzyPersonFrames[j+1] = ftemp;
                ftemp = FuzzyEventFrames[j];
                FuzzyEventFrames[j] = FuzzyEventFrames[j+1];
                FuzzyEventFrames[j+1] = ftemp;
            }
        }
    }
}

private void AddFuzzy(AIframe person_frame,
                      AIframe event_frame,
                      float value) {
    int index = -1;
    for (int i=0; i<NumFuzzy; i++) {
        String name;
        if (person_frame==null) name = new String("");
        else                    name = person_frame.getName();
        String event = event_frame.getName();
        if (name.equals(FuzzyPersonFrames[i].getName()) &&
            event.equals(FuzzyEventFrames[i].getName())) {
            MyGUI.P("Fuzzy match for old frame at " + i +
                    ", value=" + value + "\n");
            FuzzyValues[i] += value;
            return;
        }
    }
    MyGUI.P("Fuzzy: adding frame at " + NumFuzzy +
            ", value=" + value + "\n");
    FuzzyPersonFrames[NumFuzzy] = person_frame;
```

```java
    FuzzyEventFrames[NumFuzzy]  = event_frame;
    FuzzyValues[NumFuzzy] = value;
    if (NumFuzzy < (MAX_FUZZY - 1)) NumFuzzy++;
}

private int MaxFuzzy() {
    int max=-1;
    float val = -9999;
    for (int i=0; i<NumFuzzy; i++) {
       if (FuzzyValues[i] > val) {
          val = FuzzyValues[i];
          max = i;
       }
    }
    return max;
}

private boolean noiseWord(String s) {
    if (s.equals("a"))  return true;
    if (s.equals("an"))  return true;
    if (s.equals("the")) return true;
    if (s.equals("that")) return true;
    return false;
}

static private String goodness[] = {
      "Best", "Second best", "Third best", "Fourth best",
      "Fifth best", "Sixth best"};

public void Parse(String sentence) {

    NumFuzzy = 0;
    Words = new String[20];
    try {
      GetWords(sentence);
    } catch (Exception E) {
       System.out.println("cannot process sentence:" + sentence);
    }
    DoWHwords();
    DoVerb();
    DoActor();
    DoObject();
    DoTime();
```

```
// Special cases for the WH words:
if (Wtype==WHO) {
    MyGUI.P("Processing WHO...\n");
    for (int i=0; i<NumWords; i++) {
        if (noiseWord(Words[i]))  continue;
        int s_index = synonymIndex(Words[i]);
        if (s_index==-1) {
          GetPersonFromEventDescription(Words[i]);
        }  else {
          // loop over all synonyms:
          for (int j=0; j<num_per_syn[s_index]; j++) {
             GetPersonFromEventDescription(synonyms[s_index][j]);
          }
        }
    }
}

if (Wtype==WHAT) {
    MyGUI.P("Processing WHAT...\n");
    for (int i=0; i<NumWords; i++) {
        if (noiseWord(Words[i]))  continue;
        int s_index = synonymIndex(Words[i]);
        if (s_index==-1) {
          GetPersonFromEventDescription(Words[i]);
        }  else {
          // loop over all synonyms:
          for (int j=0; j<num_per_syn[s_index]; j++) {
             GetPersonFromEventDescription(synonyms[s_index][j]);
          }
        }
    }
}

if (Wtype==WHERE) {
    MyGUI.P("Processing WHERE...\n");
    for (int i=0; i<NumWords; i++) {
        if (noiseWord(Words[i]))  continue;
        int s_index = synonymIndex(Words[i]);
        if (s_index==-1) {
          GetPersonFromEventDescription(Words[i]);
        }  else {
          // loop over all synonyms:
          for (int j=0; j<num_per_syn[s_index]; j++) {
             GetPersonFromEventDescription(synonyms[s_index][j]);
```

```java
                }
            }
        }
    }

    SortFuzzy();

    for (int i=0; i<NumFuzzy; i++) {
        if (FuzzyValues[i] < 0.3f) break;
        if (i<6) MyGUI.P("\n" + goodness[i] + " answer:\n");
        else     MyGUI.P("\nAnother answer:\n");
        if (Wtype==WHERE && FuzzyEventFrames[i]!=null) {
            AIframedata place = FuzzyEventFrames[i].get("place");
            if (place!=null) {
                if (place.type==AIframedata.AIFRAME) {
                    AIframe p =
                            History.GetFrameFromServer(place.aiframe);
                    if (p!=null) {
                        MyGUI.P("Where:\n");
                        p.PP(MyGUI);
                    }
                }
            }
        }
        FuzzyPersonFrames[i].PP(MyGUI);
        if (Wtype==WHAT || Wtype==WHERE) {
            MyGUI.P("Did:\n");
            FuzzyEventFrames[i].PP(MyGUI);
        }
    }

    for (int i=0; i<20;i++)  Words[i]=null; // garbage collection

    num_sentences++;
}
private void DoWHwords() {
    Wtype=0;
    for (int i=0; i<NumWords; i++) {
        if (Words[i].equals("When") || Words[i].equals("when"))
            Wtype=WHEN;
        if (Words[i].equals("Where") || Words[i].equals("where"))
            Wtype=WHERE;
        if (Words[i].equals("What") || Words[i].equals("what"))
            Wtype=WHAT;
```

```
          if (Words[i].equals("Who") || Words[i].equals("who"))
            Wtype=WHO;
      }
  }

  protected void GetPersonFromEvent(AIframe event, float value) {
    AIframedata fd = event.get("person");
    boolean save_event = true;
    if (fd!=null) {
        if (fd.type==AIframedata.AIFRAME) {
            AIframe frm = History.GetFrameFromServer(fd.aiframe);
            if (frm != null) {
                AddFuzzy(frm, event, value);
                save_event = false;
            }
        }
    }
    if (save_event) {
        AddFuzzy(null, event, value);
    }
  }

  protected float FuzzyMatch(String ss1, String ss2) {
    if (ss1.length() < 3)  return 0.0f;
    String s1 = " " + ss1 + " ";
    String s2 = " " + ss2 + " ";
    if (ss2.indexOf(ss1) > -1) {
        if (s2.indexOf(s1) > -1) return 0.99f;
        else                     return 0.52f;
    }
    if (ss1.length() > 5) {
        String no_first_char = ss1.substring(1);
        if (ss2.indexOf(no_first_char) > -1)  return 0.7f;
        String no_last = s1.substring(0, s1.length()-1);
        if (ss2.indexOf(no_last) > -1) return 0.7f;
        String no_first_last = no_last.substring(1);
        if (ss2.indexOf(no_first_last) > -1) return 0.55f;
    }
    return 0.0f;
  }

  protected void GetPersonFromEventDescription(String description) {
    float match_value=0f;
    for (int i=0; i<History.NumEvents; i++) {
```

```
      match_value = FuzzyMatch(description, History.Events[i]);
      if (match_value > 0.5f) {
          AIframe event =
            History.GetFrameFromServer(History.EventsFrame[i]);
          if (event != null) {
            MyGUI.P("event frame match:\n");
            event.PP(MyGUI);
            GetPersonFromEvent(event, match_value);
          }
      }
    }
  }
  return;
}

protected void DoVerb() {
  super.DoVerb();  // FIRST CALL SUPERCLASS FUNCTION
  for (int i=0; i<NumWords; i++) {
      if (Words[i].equals("move") || Words[i].equals("drive")) {
          sentences[num_sentences].put("tense",
                             new AIframedata("present"));
          sentences[num_sentences].put("action",
                             new AIframedata("ptrans"));
          if (MyGUI!=null) {
            MyGUI.P("Action: " + "ptrans\n");
          }
          if (i>0) {
              if (Words[i-1].equals("will")) {
                sentences[num_sentences].put("tense",
                                   new AIframedata("future"));
                if (MyGUI!=null) {
                  MyGUI.P("  (future tense)\n");
                }
              }
          }
      }
      if (Words[i].equals("moved") || Words[i].equals("drove")) {
          sentences[num_sentences].put("tense",
                                 new AIframedata("past"));
          sentences[num_sentences].put("action",
                                 new AIframedata("ptrans"));
          if (MyGUI!=null) {
            MyGUI.P("Action: " + "ptrans (past tense)\n");
          }
      }
```

```
    }
  }

  protected boolean ProperName(String name) {
    if (super.ProperName(name)) return true;
    boolean ret = false;
    int num=History.NumPeople;
    for (int i=0; i<num; i++) {
        if (name.equals(History.PeopleLast[i])) {
          ret=true;
          if (MyGUI!=null) {
              MyGUI.P("  proper name: " + name);
              if (History.PeopleFirst[i]!=null)
                  MyGUI.P(", " + History.PeopleFirst[i]);
              MyGUI.P("\n");
          }
        }
    }
    return ret;
  }

  protected boolean Place(String name) {
    boolean ret = false;
    int num=History.NumPlaces;
    for (int i=0; i<num; i++) {
        if (name.equals(History.Places[i])) {
          ret=true;
          if (MyGUI!=null) {
              MyGUI.P("  place: " + name);
              if (History.Places[i]!=null)
                  MyGUI.P(", " + History.Places[i]);
              MyGUI.P("\n");
          }
        }
    }
    return ret;
  }

  protected boolean Event(String name) {
    if (name.length() < 4) return false; // arbitrary. no short words.
    boolean ret = false;
    int num=History.NumEvents;
    for (int i=0; i<num; i++) {
        int pos = History.Events[i].indexOf(name);
```

```
        if (pos > -1) {
            ret=true;
            if (MyGUI!=null) {
                MyGUI.P("  (possible) event match: " + name +
                        ": " + History.Events[i] + "\n");
            }
        }
    }
    return ret;
}

static String objects[] = {"car", "money", "ball"};
static int num_objects=3;
protected void DoObject() {
    super.DoObject();   // FIRST CALL SUPERCLASS FUNCTION
    for (int i=0; i<NumWords; i++) {
        if (InList(Words[i], objects, num_objects)) {
            AIframedata fd = sentences[num_sentences].get("object");
            if (fd.string.equals("?")) {
                sentences[num_sentences].put("object",
                                    new AIframedata(Words[i]));
                if (MyGUI!=null) {
                    MyGUI.P("Object: " + Words[i] + "\n");
                }
                break;
            }
        }
    }
}
```

Figure 13.7 shows the client-side application implemented with the classes **mwa.ai.nlp.History** and **mwa.ai.nlp.HistoryParser**.

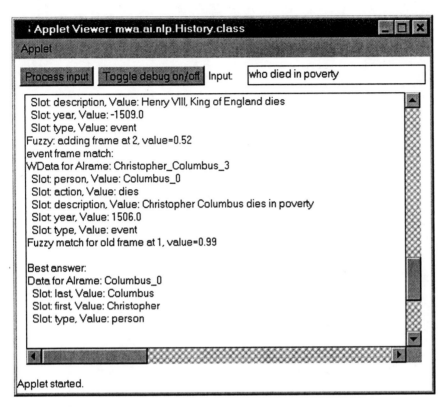

Figure 13.7 The Java class **mwa.ai.nlp.History**

Using Java-Based Data Collection Agents 14

This chapter provides the design and implementation of a complete agent-based information retrieval program for the Internet. The program designed and implemented in this chapter uses two sources of information: HTML documents on the World Wide Web and electronic mail.

Another great source of information on the Internet is newsgroups. The messages in many newsgroups are replicated in Web pages, so effectively searching HTML documents on the Web will often provide the same information as going directly to newsgroups.

Information sources are specified as arguments to the Java search agent application that supply the following information:

- Depth of search for following links in HTML Web documents
- URL addresses of Web pages to start searching from
- E-mail host, address, and password for connection to a POP electronic mail server

These arguments can be specified in an HTML document that references the search agent applet as seen in Listing 14.1 or as command line arguments if the search agent is run as a stand-alone application. The topic of Internet search agents is open-ended. The example program developed in this chapter is intended as both an example of using the utility libraries in the package **mwa.agent** and as an extensible example that you can use to build a customized search agent.

14.1 Requirements for the Java-based data collection agent example program

Everyone who browses the World Wide Web has their own unique interests. There are several new programs on the market that help automate finding information on the Internet. The example program developed in this chapter meets some of my personal search requirements:

- I have a (fairly constant) list of Internet World Wide Web sites that have information dealing with artificial intelligence, Java programming, object-oriented methodology, and so on. The example program allows me to easily set up multiple search sites by setting arguments in my Web page that serves as a starting point for my searches.
- The example program performs a breadth-first search of linked World Wide Web documents (see Section 14.2 for a discussion of how this works).
- The example program collects a potentially very large number of documents and stores them in a local disk directory on my PC. These documents can be searched repeatedly for different keywords.
- I often like to join low-volume Internet newsgroups; the articles in these newsgroups are E-mailed directly to a separate E-mail account. The example program developed in this chapter can also access the POP mail server (see Chapter 7) to automatically retrieve these articles.

I believe that general-purpose Internet search agents will improve quickly. Still, as programmers, we have the luxury of customizing our own information search tools. Since the example search agent developed in this chapter builds on tools developed in Chapter 7, the program itself is fairly short and easy to customize. Figure 14.1 shows the flow of information between a local computer running a search agent and information sources on the Internet. The example search agent developed in this chapter uses one remote POP mail server and multiple remote World Wide Web servers as sources of data.

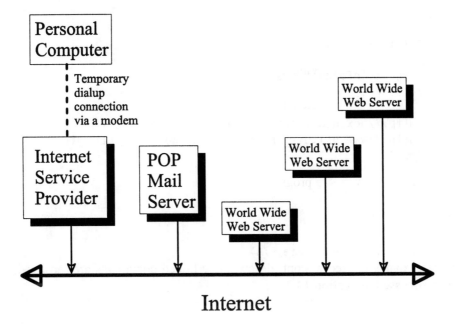

Figure 14.1   Retrieving information from the Internet

Listing 14.1 shows a sample HTML document for starting the search agent. Specified World Wide Web documents serve as the starting points for searching for information. The argument names are constructed by concatenating the string "page_" with any number between 0 and 499. If you want the search agent to also retrieve E-mail from a remote POP mail server, then the following arguments must be specified:

- E-mail
- passwd
- host

I replaced my password with the string "*******" in Listing 14.1, which shows the contents of the file **InfoAgent.html**. The file **InfoAgent2.html** (not shown) does not specify E-mail information.

Listing 14.1

```
<title>InfoAgent</title>
<hr>
<applet code=mwa.agent.InfoAgent.class
        width=530 height=370
        depth=2
        page_1="http://box.dcs.warwick.ac.uk:1080/agents.html"
        page_2="http://www.gsi.dit.upm.es/~jcg/AI-hotlist.html"
        E-mail="mwa"
        passwd="*******"
        host="netcom.com"
>
</applet>
<hr>
<a href="InfoAgent.java">The source.</a>
```

The parameter **depth** is used to control how many linked documents are retrieved; this parameter is discussed in Section 14.2.

14.2 Design of Java-based data collection agents

Most textual information on the Internet is stored using HTML. HTML is a reasonable format for structured text data, with one notable defect being the lack of extensibility; that is, HTML documents cannot define their own new format codes (or tags). Anyone writing HTML documents is certainly free to invent their own new format codes, but they will be ignored by the popular World Wide Web browsers like Netscape Navigator and Microsoft's Internet Explorer.

Figure 14.2 shows a Booch diagram of the **mwa.agent.InfoAgent** class. The **mwa.agent.InfoAgent** class uses the class **mwa.agent.URLdata** to fetch HTML documents from remote servers on the World Wide Web. Data retrieved from a remote server is stored internally in an instance of class **mwa.agent.URLdata**; this data can be stored in a local disk file as either plain ASCII text or in the original HTML format. It is easier to read data stored as ASCII text, but saving to HTML format maintains hypertext links to other related documents on the World Wide Web; the mouse pointer can be used to "cut and paste" URL addresses displayed in the application window to Netscape Navigator or the Microsoft Internet Explorer. The class **mwa.agent.HTMLdata** is used to access the retrieved data as a Java **String**. The search agent uses a parameter **depth** to control how many linked documents are returned. The search agent uses a breadth-first search to retrieve information.

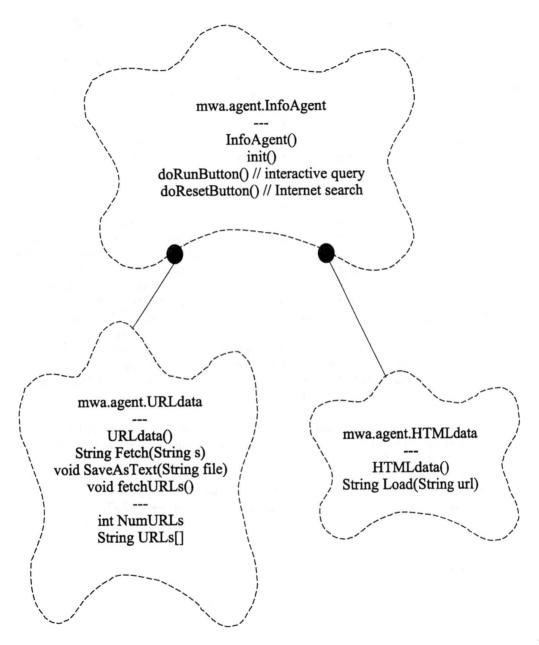

Figure 14.2   Booch diagram of the **mwa.agent.InfoAgent** class. Only the public interface elements of classes **URLdata** and **HTMLdata** that are used by class **Info-Agent** are shown. See Chapter 7 for a complete discussion of the classes **URLdata** and **HTMLdata**.

Depth-first and breadth-first search

Search involves starting in some initial state, applying one or more operators to generate new states, and continuing the search process on these new states. For the example program in this chapter, the operator for finding new states is the process of following a World Wide Web document link to another World Wide Web document.

In following hypertext links in World Wide Web documents, the *depth* of a search refers to the maximum number of links followed without backtracking from the initial set of documents. There are two ways to backtrack in following document links (this example assumes a depth of three):

1. Choose a single link in an initial document. Follow that link to the second document. Follow the first link in the second document to the third document. We have now reached our maximum depth of three, so we back up to the second document, find the second link and follow it. We will back up to the second link in the initial document only after exploring all of the links in the second document searched. This search technique is called *depth-first search*.
2. Make a list of all links in the initial document. Visit each of these links by finding the linked document and adding each new link to the end of the original list of links. We have now searched to a depth of two (the original document is depth one, and all of the linked documents are at depth two). We go back to our original list of links, now augmented with the links found in the documents for depth equals two. We follow these new links to the documents for depth equals three. We now stop the search process because we have reached the maximum depth of three. This search technique is called *breadth-first search*.

It is often possible to use heuristic rules to make breadth-first searches much more efficient than depth-first searches. The disadvantage of breadth-first search is the requirement of storing more data in order to conduct the search.

Both depth-first and breadth-first searches increase the number of states (or World Wide Web documents in our example) exponentially as the depth parameter increases. For example, assume that on the average each World Wide Web document that we are processing has 10 links to other Web documents. Table 14.1 shows the number of documents processed as the depth parameter increases.

Table 14.1

Depth	Number of documents processed
1	1
2	11
3	111
4	1,111
5	11,111
6	111,111
7	1,111,111

| 8 | 11,111,111 |

We see from Table 14.1 that if we set the depth parameter to eight, then we might expect to process over 11 million documents. In the example search agent developed in this chapter, I usually specify three or four starting documents, and specify a search depth of two or three.

14.3 Implementation of Java-based data collection agents

The implementation of the **mwa.agent.InfoAgent** class is fairly simple because we build on the behavior of the utility classes in the package **mwa.agent** that were developed in Chapter 7. Figure 14.3 shows the application window for the class **InfoAgent**.

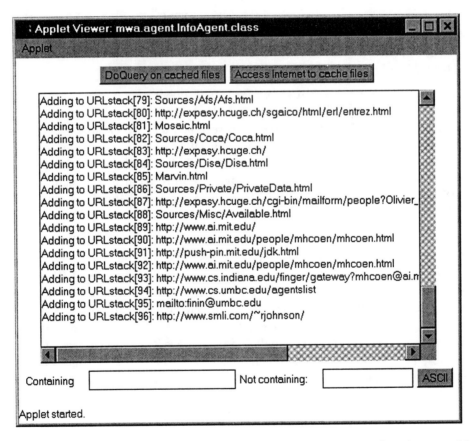

Figure 14.3   Application in Listing 14.2. The search parameters have been read from HTML parameter tags and printed in the text window. All documents referenced in the original search document have also been retrieved.

Listing 14.2 shows the implementation of the Java-based data collection agent example program. The class **mwa.agent.InfoAgent** is derived from **mwa.gui.GUI**. The method **InfoAgent.init( )** sets the following data values defined in the base class **GUI**:

- **NoGraphics = 1**
- **NoInput = 1**
- **RunLabel = "DoQuery on cached files"**
- **ResetLabel = "Access Internet to cache files"**
- **BigText = 3** (creates a very large scrolling output text field)

It then calls the base class **GUI.init()** function **super.init()**.

The applet parameter **depth** is retrieved from the HTML file that references this applet to set the search depth. The method **InfoAgent.init( )** defines two new text input fields for setting keywords for searching locally cached files and defines a command button to set the cache file save mode to ASCII text or HTML text.

In order to perform a breadth-first search for HTML documents on the Internet, the **InfoAgent** class uses an array of **String** objects **URLstack** to remember which documents (as specified by a URL address) have been searched and which still need to be searched. The method **SearchAgent.init( )** adds any URL addresses specified by parameter (e.g., **page_0**, **page_10**, **page_102**, etc.) in the HTML document that references this class as seen in Listing 14.1. The method **SearchAgent.init()** also (optionally) gets the login name, POP mail host, and password from the parameters **E-mail**, **passwd**, and **host**.

The method **SearchAgent.doResetButton( )** is called when the user clicks the reset button, which is labeled "Access Internet to cache files." The integer variable **URLstack_index** is used to count the number of URLs stored in the array **URLstack**. The variable **num** is used to keep track of which entries in the array **URLstack** have already been processed. URL entries at indices from zero to the value of the variable **num** have been searched; entries at indices greater than the value of variable **num** and less than the value of the variable **URLstack_index** still need to be searched. As the search continues, new URLs are added to the stack, and the value of the variable **URLstack_index** is increased. The method **doResetButton( )** uses instances of class **URLdata** to fetch remote World Wide Web HTML documents. Instances of the class **HTMLdata** are used both to store the retrieved documents locally and to enumerate all URL addresses contained inside of retrieved documents.

The method **SearchAgent.relevance( )** is used to determine how relevant a retrieved document is to a list of keywords and a list of avoidance keywords (which we do not want to see in retrieved documents).

The method **SearchAgent.doRunButton( )** is called when the user clicks the run button, which is labeled "DoQuery on cached files." A list of keywords and avoidance keywords is fetched from the input text fields in the applet's window. The method **SearchAgent.relevance( )** is called for each retrieved document to rank the document relative to the current keywords. Relevant documents are copied to the applet's scrolling output text field.

Listing 14.2

```
// InfoAgent class
//
// Copyright 1996, Mark Watson.

package mwa.agent;

import java.awt.*;
import java.applet.Applet;
import java.lang.*;
import java.util.*;
import java.net.*;
import java.io.*;

import mwa.gui.GUI;

public class InfoAgent extends GUI {

    public String getAppletInfo() {
        return "InfoAgent class test application. By Mark Watson";
    }

    private int Depth;
    private int URLstack_index;
    private String URLstack[];
    static final int MAX_STACK=500;

    TextField KeyWordText;
    TextField NotKeyWordText;

    String EmailAddress = null;
    String EmailHost = null;
    String EmailPassword = null;

    // Add a toggle button for selecting either ASCII
```

```java
// or HTML saved document format:
private Button toggleButton;
final static private int ASCII = 1;
final static private int HTML  = 2;
private int textType;


public void init() {
  // Disable graphics and input areas of standard GUI display:
  NoGraphics = true;
  NoInput=true;
  RunLabel   = new String("DoQuery on cached files");
  ResetLabel = new String("Access Internet to cache files");

  String param = getParameter("depth");
  if (param==null) Depth=2;
  else Depth = Integer.parseInt(param);

  BigText=3;

  super.init();

  // Add two extra input fields for search parameters:
  Panel panel2 = new Panel();
  panel2.setLayout(new FlowLayout());

  KeyWordText = new TextField("", 24);
  panel2.add(new Label("Containing"));
  panel2.add(KeyWordText);
  NotKeyWordText = new TextField("", 14);
  panel2.add(new Label("Not containing:"));
  panel2.add(NotKeyWordText);

  toggleButton = new Button("ASCII");
  textType = ASCII;
  panel2.add(toggleButton);

  add(panel2);

  P("Starting the InfoAgent applet\n");
  P("Search depth=" + Depth + "\n");

  URLstack = new String[MAX_STACK];
```

```java
    // Start to fill the URL stack with web page addresses
    // specified as applet parameters, like:
    //     page_1=http://www.nec.com
    //     page_9=http://www.apple.com

    for (int i=0; i<MAX_STACK; i++) {
       String temp = new String("page_" + i);
       param = getParameter(temp);
       if (param!=null) {
          URLstack[URLstack_index++] = new String(param);
          P("Adding resource URL " + param + "\n");
       }
    }

    // Get the optional EMAIL address and password:
    EmailAddress  = getParameter("email");
    EmailPassword = getParameter("passwd");
    EmailHost     = getParameter("host");
}

// extend the action method defined in
// class mwa.gui.GUI:

public boolean action(Event e, Object o) {
   if (e.target == toggleButton) {
      if (textType==ASCII) {
         textType = HTML;
         toggleButton.setLabel("HTML");
         P("Now saving documents in HTML\n");
         return true;
      } else {
         textType = ASCII;
         toggleButton.setLabel("ASCII");
         P("Now saving documents in ASCII\n");
         return true;
      }
   }
   return super.action(e, o);
}

public void doResetButton() {
   // Fetch EMAIL messages:
   if (EmailAddress!=null &&
       EmailPassword!=null &&
```

```
        EmailHost!=null)
{
    GetMail mailer = new GetMail(EmailHost,
                                 EmailAddress,
                                 EmailPassword);
    P("Number of EMAIL messages = " + mailer.NumMessages + "\n");
    for (int i=0; i<mailer.NumMessages; i++) {
        // Save to a file:
        String s = new String(mailer.Messages[i]);
        HTMLdata hd = new HTMLdata(s);
        // Save this document to the ../Data directory:
        String out_file =
            new String("." + File.separator + "Data" +
                        File.separator + "file_" + i);
        if (textType==ASCII) {
            hd.SaveAsText(out_file);
        } else {
            hd.Save(out_file);
        }
    }
    mailer=null;
}

// process all documents on the URLstack:
int num = URLstack_index;
int start = 0;
for (int d=0; d<Depth; d++) {
    for (int i=start; i<num; i++) {
        if (URLstack[i].endsWith("/") ||
            URLstack[i].endsWith("html") ||
            URLstack[i].endsWith("HTML") ||
            URLstack[i].endsWith("HTM") ||
            URLstack[i].endsWith("htm"))
        {
            URLdata ud = new URLdata();
            // fetch the input file as text and
            // treat as a URL address:
            String s = ud.fetch(URLstack[i]);
            HTMLdata hd = new HTMLdata(s);
            // Save this document to the ../Data directory:
            String out_file =
                new String("." + File.separator + "Data" +
                            File.separator + "file_" + i);
            hd.SaveAsText(out_file);
```

```
                hd.fetchURLs();
                for (int j=0; j<hd.NumURLs; j++) {
                    URLstack[URLstack_index++] = new String(hd.URLs[j]);
                    P("Adding to URLstack[" + (URLstack_index - 1) + "]: "
                        + hd.URLs[j] + "\n");
                }
                hd=null;
            }
        }
        start = num;
        num=URLstack_index;
    }
}


// Calculate the relevance of a file's data:
private int relevance(String data,
                      String keywords[],int num_key,
                      String not_keywords[], int num_not_key)
{
    int start;
    int len = data.length();
    int count=0;
    for (int i=0; i<num_key; i++) {
        start = 0;
        while (start<(len-2)) {
            start = data.indexOf(keywords[i],start);
            if (start==-1)  break;
            start++;
            count++;
        }
    }
    for (int i=0; i<num_not_key; i++) {
        start = 0;
        while (start<(len-2)) {
            start = data.indexOf(not_keywords[i], start);
            if (start==-1)  break;
            start++;
            count--;
        }
    }
    return count;
}

public void doRunButton() {
```

```java
// get a list of strings for the keywords
// and the not_keywords:
String keywords[] = new String[10];
String not_keywords[] = new String[10];
int num_key=0, num_not_key=0;
StringTokenizer sk =
  new StringTokenizer(KeyWordText.getText());
while (sk.hasMoreTokens() && num_key<19) {
    keywords[num_key++] = new String(sk.nextToken());
    P("keyword:" + keywords[num_key-1] + "\n");
}
sk = new StringTokenizer(NotKeyWordText.getText());
while (sk.hasMoreTokens() && num_not_key<19) {
    not_keywords[num_not_key++] = new String(sk.nextToken());
    P("not_keyword:" + not_keywords[num_not_key-1] + "\n");
}
sk=null;
int fitness[] = new int[MAX_STACK];
for (int i=0; i<MAX_STACK; i++) {
    fitness[i] = -9999;
    String input_file =
        new String("." + File.separator + "Data" +
                    File.separator + "file_" + i);
    showStatus("Processing file" + input_file + "....");
    HTMLdata hdata = new HTMLdata();
    if (hdata==null) continue;
    String data = hdata.Load(input_file);
    if (data==null) continue;
    if (data.compareTo("no document") != 0) {
        fitness[i] = relevance(data,
                              keywords, num_key,
                              not_keywords, num_not_key);
        P("fitness[" + i + "]=" + fitness[i] + "\n");
        showStatus("Processing file" + input_file +
                   " fitness=" + fitness[i]);
    }
}
// Find the best few documents:
int used=0;
int used_flag[] = new int[10];
int best_fitness = 1;
showStatus("Searching for best documents...");
while (best_fitness>0 && used < 10) {
    best_fitness=-9999;
```

```
        int index=-1;
        int ok=1;
        for (int i=0; i<MAX_STACK; i++) {
            // see if index i has been used:
            for (int j=0; j<used; j++)
                if (i == used_flag[j])  ok=0;
            if (ok == 1 && fitness[i] > best_fitness) {
                best_fitness=fitness[i];
                index=i;
            }
        }
        if (index>=0) {
            String input_file =
                new String("." + File.separator + "Data" +
                            File.separator + "file_" + index);
            HTMLdata hdata = new HTMLdata();
            if (hdata!=null) {
                String data = hdata.Load(input_file);
                P("\nFile: " + input_file + " has relevance " +
                  best_fitness + "\n");
                P(data + "\n\n- - - - - -\n\n");
                used_flag[used++] = index;
            }
        }
    }
  }
}
```

Figure 14.4 shows a screen shot of the example program after the user has retrieved HTML documents and selected E-mail from the Internet; the user requested a listing of all documents containing the keywords "AI" and "DAI."

Figure 14.5 shows the search agent application set in HTML save-file mode. The button in the lower right corner of the application toggles between "ASCII" and "HTML" when you click it. The button defaults to ASCII save-file mode; clicking the button to HTML save-file mode before accessing the Internet to cache files causes the search agent applet to save files in HTML format.

Figure 14.4   Application in Listing 14.2. Documents of interest have been automatically retrieved from the Internet, and the program user has searched the locally cached documents using the keywords "AI DAI."

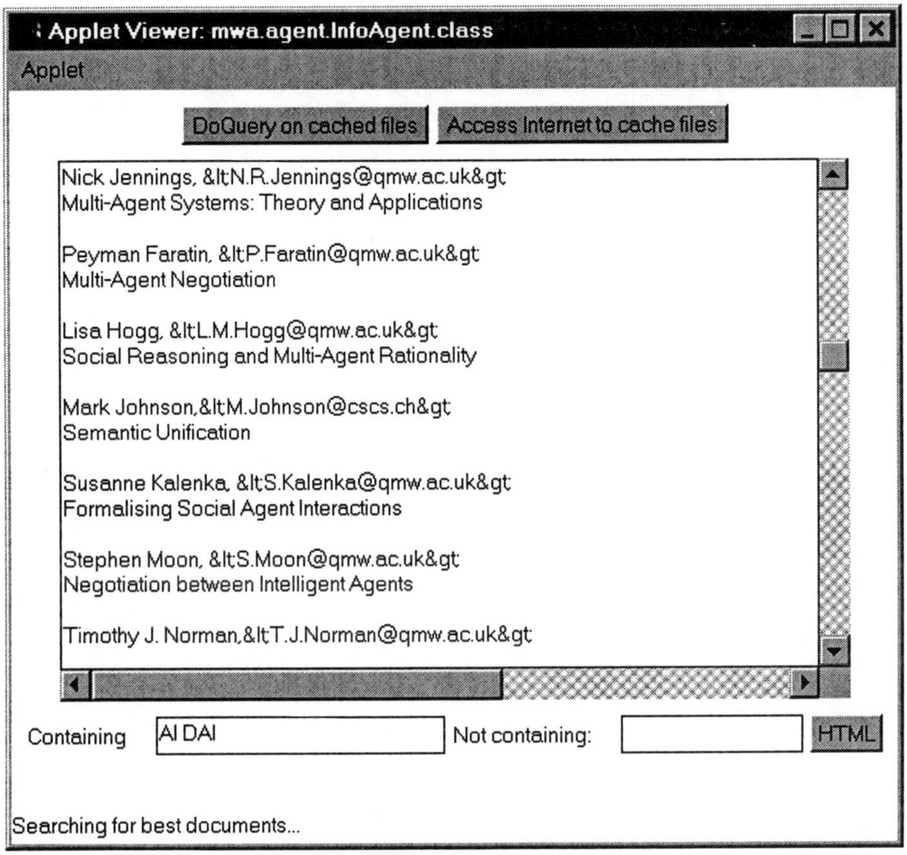

Figure 14.5 Using the search agent applet in HTML mode

Introduction to Java Programming

Java programs can be written to run inside World Wide Web pages as applets or as stand-alone applications. We will see how to write Java classes that serve as applets, stand-alone applications, and as both.

The Java language has created a lot of excitement. Indeed, no new computer technology since the World Wide Web has excited so many people. Sure, Java is great for adding process to the data usually found on the World Wide Web. We no longer need to constrain ourselves to the software components built into our favorite Web browsers. Java is also great for stand-alone application development.

This appendix is meant to be a quick tutorial for learning to program in Java. It should easily suffice for readers with programming experience in C or C++. For nonprogramming readers, I recommend augmenting this appendix with either an introductory Java programming book or one of the excellent Java tutorials available on the World Wide Web (search for "Java tutorial" using your favorite Internet search engine).

A.1 Data types

Most programming languages distinguish different types of data. Java is remarkable in its adherence to the object-oriented programming model. Java has eight primitive data types that are not considered to be objects:

- **int**—32-bit signed integer
- **short**—16-bit signed integer
- **long**—64-bit signed integer
- **float**—32-bit floating point
- **double**—64-bit floating point
- **boolean**—true or false
- **char**—16-bit character
- **byte**—8-bit signed integer

Everything else is a class, a method belonging to a class, or an instance of a class. An instance of any class is referred to as an object. In a strong sense, creating new classes is like adding to the primitive types of the language, with one notable exception: primitive data types have predefined operators like multiplication and addition that can operate on these data types. We usually do not think of using operators on instances of classes. (One notable exception that we will see in Section A.3 is the + operator used with the **String** class.) Part of the work of writing classes is defining methods that do operate on objects.

A.2   Methods

For those familiar with other programming languages (especially C, Pascal, FORTRAN, C++, etc.), one of the most surprising things about the Java language is that it does not contain any functions. In most cases, we write methods for classes; the execution of a method usually requires a class instance. As with so many things in life, however, there is an exception to this rule: static methods. Static methods can execute without declaring any instances of a class. This section uses two simple examples that show how to write and call static and normal methods.

Listing A.1 shows the standard "hello world" application program, often used to illustrate the most simple type of program in a new programming language. A similar Java class that implements an applet is shown in Listing A.3.

Listing A.1

```
public class HelloWorld {
  public static void main (String args[]) {
    System.out.println("Hello world.");
    for (int i=0; i<args.length(); i++) {
        System.out.println("command line argument #" +
                          i + " is " + args[i]);
    }
  }
}
```

Actually, this simple program that defines a new Java class **HelloWorld** can be used to introduce many Java programming techniques. For those with no previous programming experience, there are several mysteries in Listing A.1. The first mystery might be the heavy use of curly brackets. Briefly, Java is a *block-structured* language. Blocks are set off by inclusion in opening and closing curly brackets. The basic syntax for defining a new class is

```
class <class name> {
}
```

You can substitute any name for **<class name>**. Every method defined inside of a class definition is also a block:

```
class <class name> {
    <method qualifier(s)> <return type> <function name>
                                    (<zero or more arguments>) {
    }
}
```

The example in Listing A.1 uses two method qualifiers: **static** and **public**. The fact that the method **main** is **static** allows us to execute **HelloWorld.main( )** without creating a class instance. The method **main** is declared to be **public**; this means that this method can be accessed by any other method in a program that is not part of the same class. A method that is declared **private** cannot be accessed except by other methods in the same class. A method that is declared **protected** can be accessed by any method in this class or any class that is derived from this class (we will see an example of this in Section A.5). Data declarations inside a class can also be declared **public**, **private**, or **protected**.

The return type of the function **main** in class **HelloWorld** is **void**, which means that the method does not return a value. Other possible return type values are primitive data types (e.g., **int** or **float**) or class name. Let us look more carefully at the block that defines method **main** in Listing A.1:

```
public static void main (String args[]) {
    System.out.println("Hello world.");
    for (int i=0; i<args.length(); i++) {
        System.out.println("command line argument #" +
                        i + " is " + args[i]);
    }
}
```

The argument list of function main is **String args[]**. **String** is a Java class name; we will see several examples of using instances of class **String** in Section A.3. The square brackets indicate that the argument is an array of **String** objects. The characters **args** are a formal parameter of the function. The Java array class has a public method **length**, which can always be used to determine how many elements are stored in the array. The **for** statement is used to iterate or loop over a range of values. A simple example of a **for** statement is

```
    for (int v=0; v<4; v++) {
        System.out.println("v=" + v);
    }
```

The first thing that this **for** statement does is to declare the variable **v** to be of type **int** and assign it an initial value of zero. The next part of this **for** statement is a limit check; in this case, the iteration, or looping, will repeat as long as the value of the variable **v** is less than five. The third part of the **for** statement, **v++**, increases the value of **v** by one each time through the **for** loop. The fourth part of the **for** statement is a block of code that will be executed in each iteration of the **for** statement. In this example, the following will be printed out:

```
v=0
v=1
v=2
v=3
```

Another thing to note in this example is that the method **System.out.println** takes a **String** argument. As we will see in Section A.3, the operator + concatenates a **String** with another **String**, or a primitive data type to form a new string. The example in Listing A.1 concatenates the following terms into a single **String** value:

- `"command line argument #"`   (a **String**)
- `i`   (an **int**)
- `" is "`   (a **String**)
- `args[i]`   (an element of a **String** array)

The program in Listing A.1 must be stored in a file named **HelloWorld.java**. The Java compiler insists that there can only be one public class defined in a file, and that the root file name must exactly equal the class name. We could compile and run the program in Listing A.1 by typing

```
javac HelloWorld.java
java HelloWorld  Mark Carol Sammy
```

The Java compiler **javac** creates a compiled file **HelloWorld.class** from the source file **HelloWorld.java**. The Java runtime system treats a public static method named **main** specially. The second command instructs the Java runtime system to do the following:

- Find the file **HelloWorld.class** in the current directory or **CLASSPATH**.
- Execute the public static function **HelloWorld.main**; the formal parameter of function **main**, an array of **Strings**, is set to the array of **Strings**:
    "Mark"
    "Carol"
    "Sammy"

Listing A.2 is similar to the example in Listing A.1, except that a new (private) class is included. When the method **HelloWorld.main( )** is run, it creates an instance of the second class **DoubleString**.

Listing A.2

```
public class HelloWorld {
  public static void main (String args[]) {
    System.out.println("Hello world.");
    DoubleString s = new DoubleString("test!");
    System.out.println("DoubleString value: " + s.MyValue());
    for (int i=0; i<args.length(); i++) {
        System.out.println("command line argument #" +
                              i + " is " + args[i]);
    }
  }
}
class DoubleString {
  DoubleString() {
    myString = new String("");
  }
  DoubleString(String s) {
   myString = new String(s + s);
  }
  String myValue() {
    return myString;
  }
  private myString;
}
```

Listing A.3 shows the definition of a simple applet. The **import** statement is discussed in Section A.4.

Listing A.3

```
import java.applet.Applet;
import java.awt.*;

public class HelloApplet extends Applet {
    public void init() {
      System.out.println("init() method called " +
```

```
                        "automatically at startup");
    }
    public void paint(Graphics g) {
        g.drawString("Hello world…", 40, 20);
    }
    public boolean mouseDown(Event e, int x, int y) {
        System.out.println("Mouse down at: " + x + ", " + y);
    }
}
```

The class **java.applet.Applet** defines the methods **paint( )** and **mouseDown( )**, which the class **HelloApplet** overrides (see Section A.5 for discussion of extending Java classes). The class **java.applet.Applet** provides the behavior of calling the method **paint( )** when the applet's window needs to be redrawn and calls the method **mouseDown( )** when there is a mouse down event inside of the applet's window.

Listing A.4 shows an HTML file that references the applet defined in Listing A.3.

Listing A.4

```
<HTML>
<APPLET CODE="HelloApplet.class" width=110 height=35>
</APPLET>
</HTML
```

A.3   Strings

The **String** class is defined in the package **java.lang** (see Section A.4 for a discussion of Java packages). Objects belonging to the class **String** are *immutable*; once they are created, they cannot be changed. The class **StringBuffer** is similar to the class **String**, except that objects belonging to the class **StringBuffer** may be modified (e.g., removing or adding characters anywhere in the string).

The following example shows the creation and use of instances of both classes:

```
String s1 = new String("This is a test");
StringBuffer sb1 = new StringBuffer(s1);
if (s1.equals("This is a test") {
  System.out.println("String matched: " + s1);
}
sb1.append("! Wow!");
System.out.println("The length of string: " + s1 + " is "
                   + s1.length());
```

```
String s2 = new String(sb1);
```

There are seven constructors for class **String** and three constructors for class **StringBuffer**. The following are the specific constructors for both classes that are used in this book:

- **String(String s)**
- **String(StringBuffer sb)**
- **StringBuffer(String s)**

The following methods for class **String** are used in this book:

- **boolean endsWith(String another_string)**
- **boolean equals(String another_string)**
- **int indexOf(String another_string)**
- **int indexOf(String another_string, int starting_location)**
- **int length()**
- **boolean startsWith(String another_string)**
- **void trim()**

Character locations in strings start with an index value of zero. It is important to use the method **equals( )** for comparing strings:

```
String s1 = new String("abc");
String s2 = new String("abc");
if (s1==s2) { } // Wrong!
If (s1.equals(s2)) {}  // Correct way to compare 2 strings
                       // for equality
```

The method **trim( )** is useful for removing leading and trailing space characters from a string.

The following methods in class **StringBuffer** are used in this book:

- **StringBuffer append(String s)**
- **StringBuffer insert(int index_to_insert_at, String s)**
- **int length( )**
- **String toString( )**

The methods **append** and **insert** return a reference to themselves as their value after the indicated operation.

A.4   Packages

Ideally, programmers around the world will develop useful Java classes that will be made available either for free or for a small cost. It is much easier to build complex programs if we can use the work of other programmers. One potential difficulty with the large-scale sharing of Java class libraries is *name collision*, which occurs when two or more programmers use the same Java class name.

The solution to this problem is the use of Java *packages*. The Java language has two keywords to use packages: **package** and **import**.

For example, in Chapter 2, we see a reusable Java class for simplifying the task of creating a Java applet with standard components like buttons, text input and output fields, and so on. I named this class **GUI** (for graphic user interface). It is almost certain that other programmers will also use this class name, so I decided to create a separate package for all Java classes developed in this book: **mwa**. The name **mwa** stands for Mark Watson Associates (a company name that I have used since 1979, when I started selling a Go-playing program for the Apple II computer). The source file for the Java class **GUI** includes the following statements:

```
package mwa.gui;
import java.awt.*;
import java.applet.Applet;
```

The **package** statement names the package that contains all classes defined in a source file. The **import** statements specify which classes can be referenced without specifying a complete package name. All classes in the package **java.awt** are imported, while only the class **Applet** is imported from the package **java.applet**. For example, the **GUI** class (which has a complete package name of **mwa.gui.GUI**) uses the Sun Microsystem's utility class **Button**. The complete class name for **Button** is **java.awt.Button**.

A new command button could be created using the complete package name:

```
java.awt.Button aButton = new java.awt.Button("click me!");
```

However, the statement

```
import java.awt.*;
```

indicates to the Java compiler that we want to be able to reference all classes in the package **java.awt** without specifying the entire package name. For example,

```
Button aButton = new Button("click me!");
```

In order to make it clear where classes are defined, I will occasionally specify the complete package name for a class, even when it is not necessary because of the use of an **import** statement.

The class **mwa.gui.GUI** is used in most example programs in this book. For example, it is referenced in the handwriting recognition program developed in Chapter 12:

```
package mwa.ai.neural;

import java.awt.*;
import java.applet.Applet;
import java.lang.*;
import java.util.*;
import java.lang.*;

import mwa.gui.GUI;
```

As a matter of style, I always import the names of classes that I write after importing other classes.

A.5 Extending Java classes with inheritance

Data and methods in Java classes can be private, protected, or public. Private data and methods can only be referenced from inside the class. Public data and methods of a class can be referenced anywhere in a program that uses the class. Protected data and methods are similar to private data and methods except that they are accessible in classes derived from (or extended from) a class. If data and methods are not defined using the keywords **private**, **protected**, or **public**, then they are accessible like public data and methods to any classes defined in the same package and are private to all other classes.

Java classes can be extended to create new Java classes. Extended classes inherit all protected and public data and methods from the *base class* that they are derived from. For example, in the handwriting recognition program developed in Chapter 12, the class **testHand** is derived from the class **mwa.gui.GUI**:

```
package mwa.ai.neural;

import java.awt.*;
import java.applet.Applet;
import java.lang.*;
import java.util.*;
```

```
import java.lang.*;

import mwa.gui.GUI;

public class testHand extends GUI {
  ...
}
```

All of the behavior of class **mwa.gui.GUI** (i.e., initializing an applet and supporting scrolling output text, input text, command buttons, and graphics) is available to the derived (or extended) class **mwa.ai.neural.testHand**. Methods in derived classes can reference methods in the base class by using the keyword **super**. For example, the method **testHand.init( )** overrides the base class method **GUI.init( )**, but it is easy to call the base class **init()** method inside the extended class **init( )** method:

```
public void init() {
        NoInput = 1;  // we do not need an input text field
        BigText=1;
        NoRunButton=1;
        NoResetButton=1;

        network = new Neural("hand_4.dat");

        super.init();
    }
```

Here, the public variables in the base class **mwa.gui.GUI**

- **GUI.NoInput**
- **GUI.BigText**
- **GUI.NoRunButton**
- **GUI.NoResetButton**

are set before calling the base class method **mwa.gui.GUI.init( )**

```
        super.init();
```

A.6   Multithreaded Java applications

The interface **java.lang.Runnable** is used with the thread class to create multithreaded applets and multithreaded stand-alone programs. The public interface for **Runnable** is

```
public abstract interface Runnable {
    public abstract void run();
}
```

Any class that supports the **Runnable** interface must define the method **run( )**. This method is called by a thread that is usually created in a method called **start( )**, which is called when the application starts. For example, a class might define a thread **workThread**:

```
Thread workThread = null;
```

The **start( )** method would initialize the thread:

```
public void start() {
    workThread = new Thread(this);
    workThread.start();
}
```

The **stop()** method is called automatically when an application terminates. This is a good place to stop any threads that are still active. For example,

```
publc void stop) {
    if (workThread != null) {
        workThread.stop();
    }
    workThread = null;
}
```

While any thread is active, the method **run( )** is automatically called periodically.

A.7   Exception handling in Java

The Java exception-handling capability is used to prevent Java programs from terminating from error conditions. An exception occurs when a runtime error (for example, an IO error) occurs. Java provides two statements for trapping and dealing with runtime errors: **try** and **catch**.

A **try** statement contains a block of code, which can contain other code blocks, method calls, and so on. A **try** statement has a corresponding **catch** statement, which specifies what processing should occur to deal with the runtime error, or exception.

For example, from the class **mwa.ai.neural.NNfile**,

```
String input_file = new String("test1.dat"); // not in class
FileInputStream is = null;
try {
    is = new FileInputStream(input_file);
} catch (Exception E) {
    System.out.println("cannot open file " + input_file);
}
```

The Java **Exception** class can be extended. For example,

```
class FileFormatException extends Exception {
  public FileFormatException(String str) {
    super(str);
  }
}
```

Now a method can throw an instance of class **FileFormatException**. For example, from the class **mwa.ai.neural.NNfile**,

```
void ReadFile(InputStream inp)
        throws IOException, FileFormatException {

  // if any error occurs in this method, or any method called
  // in this method, then a FileFormatException can be thrown:
  // << exception code goes here >>

  if (st.ttype!=StreamTokenizer.TT_EOF)
    throw new FileFormatException(st.toString());

}
```

Using the CD-ROM

The examples developed in this book and included in complete source code form on the CD-ROM that accompanies this book have been tested using the following Java compilers:

- Sun Microsystem's JDK 1.0 final
- Sun Microsystem's JDK 1.02 final
- Sun Microsystem's JDK 1.1 final
- Symantec Café 1.5
- Borland Java IDE 5.0
- Microsoft J++ 1.0

The Web site **www.markwatson.com** contains updates to the examples provided in this book for new versions of the Java language.

While I almost always work using an integrated Java development environment (IDE), the files on the CD-ROM are set up for building with Sun Microsystem's JDK using a command line interface.

The software developed in this book is organized using the Java language package system. The package structure used (with classes italicized) is shown on the following page.

Java packages for software on CD-ROM

MWA
    Agent
                                  Server
                                  Client
    AI
        Neural
                                  Neural
                                  NNfile
        Genetic
                                  Genetic
        NLP
                                  Parser
                                  ParseObject
    Data
                                  AIframe
                                  AIframedata
    GUI
                                  GUI
                                  GUIcanvas

The CD-ROM is set up with the following directory structure:

```
class               ; compiled Java class files for mwa.* packages
src                 ; source code tree
src\mwa             ; source for mwa packages
src\mwa\gui         ; source for the mwa.gui package
src\mwa\data        ; source for the mwa.data package
src\mwa\agent       ; source for the mwa.agent package
src\mwa\ai          ; source for the mwa.ai packages
src\mwa\ai\genetic  ; source for the mwa.ai.genetic package
src\mwa\ai\neural   ; source for the mwa.ai.neural package
src\mwa\ai\nlp      ; source for the mwa.ai.nlp package
jess                ; source and class files for Jess
game                ; source and class files for game
```

In order to ensure that long file names are preserved for UNIX system users, the source code is stored as both ZIP files (for Windows 95 and Windows NT) and in TAR form for UNIX systems on the CD-ROM:

- **src.zip**
- **src.tar**

- **jess.zip**
- **jess.tar**
- **game.zip**
- **game.tar**
- **class.zip**
- **class.tar**

B.1 For Windows 95 or Windows NT users

1. Copy the contents of this CDROM to your **c:** drive. Make sure that long file names are intact in the new directory **c:\JavaAI**.
2. Set your CLASSPATH environment variable to include `c:\JavaAI\class`. Note: Some Java systems (e.g., Symantec) ignore the **CLASSPATH** environment variable! Make sure that both the command line programs **java** and **javac** are searching the **c:\JavaAI\class directory** for *.class files.
3. Every source directory that contains Java source files contains a batch file **c.bat** to compile the contents of that directory and place the class files in the directory **c:\JavaAI\class**.
4. All source directories are precompiled into **c:\JavaAI\class** for your convenience.

B.2 For UNIX users

1. You will probably want to use either the four ZIP or the four TAR files to load the contents of the CDROM onto your hard disk. The DOS-style **c.bat** files can be re-named as **sh** or **csh** files and edited appropriately for compiling the source directories.
2. Make sure that your **CLASSPATH** environment variable references the location of the class directory created from either the **class.zip** or **class.tar** file.
3. After running the example programs, make sure that you can build all of the class directory files from the source code.

Javadoc Documentation

Listing C.1 shows the index of all classes in the packages

- **mwa.data**
- **mwa.agent**
- **mwa.ai.genetic**
- **mwa.ai.neural**
- **mwa.ai.nlp**

Listing C.1 also shows all classes directly referenced in these packages.

Listing C.1

```
Class Hierarchy

   * class java.lang.Object
       o class mwa.data.AIframe
           + class mwa.ai.nlp.ParseObject
       o class mwa.data.AIframedata
       o interface java.applet.AppletContext
       o interface java.applet.AppletStub
       o interface java.applet.AudioClip
       o class java.util.BitSet
         (implements java.lang.Cloneable)
       o class java.awt.BorderLayout
         (implements java.awt.LayoutManager)
       o class java.lang.Character
       o class java.lang.Class
```

```
o class mwa.agent.Client
o class java.awt.Component (implements
  java.awt.image.ImageObserver)
      + class java.awt.Canvas
      + class java.awt.Container
            + class java.awt.Panel
                  + class java.applet.Applet
                        + class mwa.gui.GUI
                              + class mwa.ai.nlp.History
                              + class
                                mwa.ai.nlp.HistoryAIframeServer
                              + class mwa.agent.InfoAgent
                              + class mwa.data.testAIframe
                              + class mwa.agent.testAIframeServer
                              + class mwa.agent.testClient
                              + class mwa.gui.testGUI
                              + class mwa.ai.neural.testGenNeural
                              + class mwa.agent.testGetMail
                              + class mwa.ai.neural.testGreedy
                              + class mwa.ai.neural.testHand
                                (implements java.lang.Runnable)
                              + class mwa.ai.neural.testHand_2
                                (implements java.lang.Runnable)
                              + class mwa.ai.neural.testHand_3
                              + class mwa.ai.neural.testHand_4
                                (implements java.lang.Runnable)
                              + class mwa.ai.nlp.testNLP
                              + class mwa.ai.nlp.testNLP2
                              + class mwa.ai.neural.testNeural
                                (implements java.lang.Runnable)
                              + class mwa.ai.neural.testNeuralFile
                              + class mwa.agent.testObjectClient
                              + class mwa.agent.testSendMail
                              + class mwa.agent.testServer
                              + class mwa.agent.testURLdata
            + class java.awt.Window
o interface java.awt.peer.ComponentPeer
o interface java.awt.peer.ContainerPeer (extends
  java.awt.peer.ComponentPeer)
o class java.util.Date
o class java.util.Dictionary
      + class java.util.Hashtable
        (implements java.lang.Cloneable)
            + class java.util.Properties
```

```
o class java.awt.Dimension
o class java.awt.Event
o class java.io.File
o class java.awt.FlowLayout (implements java.awt.LayoutManager)
o class mwa.ai.genetic.Genetic
o class mwa.agent.GetMail
o class java.awt.Graphics
o class mwa.agent.HTMLdata
o interface java.awt.image.ImageObserver
o class java.io.InputStream
    + class java.io.FileInputStream
    + class java.io.FilterInputStream
        + class java.io.BufferedInputStream
o class java.awt.Insets (implements java.lang.Cloneable)
o interface java.awt.LayoutManager
o class java.lang.Math
o class mwa.ai.neural.NNfile
o class mwa.ai.neural.NNgreedy
    + class mwa.ai.neural.GenNeural
o class java.lang.Number
    + class java.lang.Double
    + class java.lang.Integer
    + class java.lang.Long
o class java.io.OutputStream
    + class java.io.ByteArrayOutputStream
    + class java.io.FilterOutputStream
        + class java.io.BufferedOutputStream
        + class java.io.PrintStream
o class mwa.ai.nlp.Parser
o class java.awt.Point
o class java.awt.Polygon
o class java.util.Random
o class java.awt.Rectangle
o interface java.lang.Runnable
o class java.lang.Runtime
o class java.lang.SecurityManager
o class mwa.agent.SendMail
o class java.net.ServerSocket
o class java.net.Socket
o class java.net.SocketImpl
o class java.lang.String
o class java.lang.StringBuffer
o class java.lang.System
o interface mwa.data.TextFileConstants
```

```
o class mwa.data.TextFileIn
o class mwa.data.TextFileOut
o class java.lang.Thread (implements java.lang.Runnable)
    + class mwa.agent.Server
        + class mwa.agent.AIframeServer
o class java.lang.ThreadGroup
o class java.lang.Throwable
    + class java.lang.Error
        + class java.awt.AWTError
        + class java.lang.LinkageError
            + class java.lang.IncompatibleClassChangeError
                + class java.lang.NoSuchMethodError
            + class java.lang.UnsatisfiedLinkError
        + class java.lang.ThreadDeath
        + class java.lang.VirtualMachineError
            + class java.lang.InternalError
    + class java.lang.Exception
        + class java.lang.CloneNotSupportedException
        + class java.io.IOException
            + class java.io.FileNotFoundException
            + class java.net.MalformedURLException
            + class java.net.UnknownHostException
        + class java.lang.InterruptedException
        + class java.lang.RuntimeException
            + class java.lang.IllegalArgumentException
                + class
                  java.lang.IllegalThreadStateException
                + class java.lang.NumberFormatException
            + class java.lang.IndexOutOfBoundsException
                + class
                  java.lang.ArrayIndexOutOfBoundsException
                + class
                  java.lang.StringIndexOutOfBoundsException
            + class java.lang.NullPointerException
o class java.awt.Toolkit
o class java.net.URL
o class java.net.URLStreamHandler
o interface java.net.URLStreamHandlerFactory
o class mwa.agent.URLdata
o class java.util.Vector (implements java.lang.Cloneable)
o class mwa.ai.genetic.testGenetic
```

Listing C.2 shows a complete cross-reference index of the classes developed in this book.

Listing C.2

Index of all Fields and Methods

A

action(Event, Object). Method in class mwa.gui.GUI
action(Event, Object). Method in class mwa.agent.InfoAgent
AddSpecial(float). Method in class mwa.ai.neural.NNfile
AddTraining(float[], float[]). Method in class mwa.ai.neural.NNfile
aiframe. Variable in class mwa.data.AIframedata
AIFRAME. Static variable in class mwa.data.AIframedata
AIframe(String). Constructor for class mwa.data.AIframe
AIframe(String, AIframe). Constructor for class mwa.data.AIframe
AIframedata(float). Constructor for class mwa.data.AIframedata
AIframedata(int). Constructor for class mwa.data.AIframedata
AIframedata(String). Constructor for class mwa.data.AIframedata
AIframeServer(). Constructor for class mwa.agent.AIframeServer
AIframeServer(int). Constructor for class mwa.agent.AIframeServer
AIframeServer(int, GUI). Constructor for class mwa.agent.AIframeServer

B

BaseIndex. Variable in class mwa.ai.neural.NNfile
BigText. Variable in class mwa.gui.GUI

C

CalcFitness(). Method in class mwa.ai.genetic.Genetic
ClearOutput(). Method in class mwa.gui.GUI
Client(). Constructor for class mwa.agent.Client
Client(int, String). Constructor for class mwa.agent.Client
Client_Helper(int, String). Method in class mwa.agent.Client
close(). Method in class mwa.data.TextFileOut
CloseConnection(). Method in class mwa.agent.Client

D

data. Variable in class mwa.agent.HTMLdata
DEFAULT_HOST. Static variable in class mwa.agent.Client
DEFAULT_PORT. Static variable in class mwa.agent.Client

DEFAULT_PORT. Static variable in class mwa.agent.Server
DoActor(). Method in class mwa.ai.nlp.Parser
DoCrossovers(). Method in class mwa.ai.genetic.Genetic
doMouseDown(int, int). Method in class mwa.gui.GUI
doMouseDown(int, int). Method in class mwa.ai.neural.testHand
doMouseDown(int, int). Method in class mwa.ai.neural.testHand_2
doMouseDown(int, int). Method in class mwa.ai.neural.testHand_4
DoMutations(). Method in class mwa.ai.genetic.Genetic
DoObject(). Method in class mwa.ai.nlp.Parser
doResetButton(). Method in class mwa.gui.GUI
doResetButton(). Method in class mwa.ai.nlp.History
doResetButton(). Method in class mwa.agent.InfoAgent
doResetButton(). Method in class mwa.agent.testClient
doResetButton(). Method in class mwa.ai.neural.testGenNeural
doResetButton(). Method in class mwa.ai.neural.testHand
doResetButton(). Method in class mwa.ai.neural.testHand_2
doResetButton(). Method in class mwa.ai.neural.testHand_3
doResetButton(). Method in class mwa.ai.neural.testNeural
doResetButton(). Method in class mwa.ai.neural.testNeuralFile
doResetButton(). Method in class mwa.ai.nlp.testNLP
doResetButton(). Method in class mwa.ai.nlp.testNLP2
doRunButton(). Method in class mwa.gui.GUI
doRunButton(). Method in class mwa.ai.nlp.History
doRunButton(). Method in class mwa.agent.InfoAgent
doRunButton(). Method in class mwa.data.testAIframe
doRunButton(). Method in class mwa.agent.testClient
doRunButton(). Method in class mwa.ai.neural.testGenNeural
doRunButton(). Method in class mwa.agent.testGetMail
doRunButton(). Method in class mwa.ai.neural.testGreedy
doRunButton(). Method in class mwa.gui.testGUI
doRunButton(). Method in class mwa.ai.neural.testHand
doRunButton(). Method in class mwa.ai.neural.testHand_2
doRunButton(). Method in class mwa.ai.neural.testHand_3
doRunButton(). Method in class mwa.ai.neural.testNeural
doRunButton(). Method in class mwa.ai.neural.testNeuralFile
doRunButton(). Method in class mwa.ai.nlp.testNLP
doRunButton(). Method in class mwa.ai.nlp.testNLP2
doRunButton(). Method in class mwa.agent.testObjectClient
doRunButton(). Method in class mwa.agent.testSendMail
doRunButton(). Method in class mwa.agent.testURLdata
DoTime(). Method in class mwa.ai.nlp.Parser
DoVerb(). Method in class mwa.ai.nlp.Parser
DoWork(AIframe). Method in class mwa.agent.AIframeServer
DoWork(AIframe). Method in class mwa.agent.Server

init(). Method in class mwa.ai.neural.testHand_3
init(). Method in class mwa.ai.neural.testHand_4
init(). Method in class mwa.ai.neural.testNeural
init(). Method in class mwa.ai.neural.testNeuralFile
init(). Method in class mwa.ai.nlp.testNLP
init(). Method in class mwa.ai.nlp.testNLP2
init(). Method in class mwa.agent.testObjectClient
init(). Method in class mwa.agent.testSendMail
init(). Method in class mwa.agent.testServer
init(). Method in class mwa.agent.testURLdata
init(int, int). Method in class mwa.ai.genetic.Genetic
InitialInput. Variable in class mwa.gui.GUI
InList(String, String[], int). Method in class mwa.ai.nlp.Parser
instanceCount. Static variable in class mwa.ai.nlp.ParseObject

L

listen_socket. Variable in class mwa.agent.Server
Load(String). Method in class mwa.agent.HTMLdata

M

main(String[]). Static method in class mwa.ai.neural.NNfile
main(String[]). Static method in class mwa.ai.genetic.testGenetic
MAX_EVENTS. Static variable in class mwa.ai.nlp.History
MAX_PEOPLE. Static variable in class mwa.ai.nlp.History
Messages. Variable in class mwa.agent.GetMail
Mode. Variable in class mwa.ai.neural.testHand
Mode. Variable in class mwa.ai.neural.testHand_2
MyObjects. Variable in class mwa.agent.AIframeServer

N

NAN. Static variable in interface mwa.data.TextFileConstants
NeuralFile. Variable in class mwa.ai.neural.NNgreedy
NNfile(). Constructor for class mwa.ai.neural.NNfile
NNfile(String). Constructor for class mwa.ai.neural.NNfile
NNgreedy(). Constructor for class mwa.ai.neural.NNgreedy
NNgreedy(String). Constructor for class mwa.ai.neural.NNgreedy
NoGraphics. Variable in class mwa.gui.GUI
NoInput. Variable in class mwa.gui.GUI
NoOutput. Variable in class mwa.gui.GUI
NoResetButton. Variable in class mwa.gui.GUI
NoRunButton. Variable in class mwa.gui.GUI

num_sentences. Variable in class mwa.ai.nlp.Parser
NUMBER. Static variable in class mwa.data.AIframedata
number. Variable in class mwa.data.AIframedata
NumChrom. Variable in class mwa.ai.genetic.Genetic
NumEvents. Static variable in class mwa.ai.nlp.History
NumGenes. Variable in class mwa.ai.genetic.Genetic
NumHidden. Variable in class mwa.ai.neural.NNfile
NumInput. Variable in class mwa.ai.neural.NNfile
NumLayers. Variable in class mwa.ai.neural.NNfile
NumMessages. Variable in class mwa.agent.GetMail
NumNeuronsPerLayer. Variable in class mwa.ai.neural.NNfile
NumObjects. Variable in class mwa.agent.AIframeServer
NumOutput. Variable in class mwa.ai.neural.NNfile
NumPeople. Static variable in class mwa.ai.nlp.History
NumTraining. Variable in class mwa.ai.neural.NNfile
NumURLs. Variable in class mwa.agent.HTMLdata

P

P(float). Method in class mwa.gui.GUI
P(int). Method in class mwa.gui.GUI
P(String). Method in class mwa.gui.GUI
paint(Graphics). Method in class mwa.gui.GUI
paintGridCell(Graphics, int, int, int, float, float, float). Method in
class mwa.gui.GUI
paintToDoubleBuffer(Graphics). Method in class mwa.gui.GUI
paintToDoubleBuffer(Graphics). Method in class mwa.gui.testGUI
paintToDoubleBuffer(Graphics). Method in class mwa.ai.neural.testHand
paintToDoubleBuffer(Graphics). Method in class mwa.ai.neural.testHand_2
paintToDoubleBuffer(Graphics). Method in class mwa.ai.neural.testHand_4
paintToDoubleBuffer(Graphics). Method in class mwa.ai.neural.testNeural
paintToDoubleBuffer(Graphics). Method in class
mwa.ai.neural.testNeuralFile
paintToDoubleBuffer(Graphics). Method in class mwa.ai.nlp.testNLP
panel. Variable in class mwa.gui.GUI
Parent. Variable in class mwa.data.AIframe
Parse(String). Method in class mwa.ai.nlp.Parser
Parser(). Constructor for class mwa.ai.nlp.Parser
PeopleFirst. Static variable in class mwa.ai.nlp.History
PeopleFrame. Static variable in class mwa.ai.nlp.History
PeopleLast. Static variable in class mwa.ai.nlp.History
port. Variable in class mwa.agent.Server
PP(). Method in class mwa.data.AIframe
PP(GUI). Method in class mwa.data.AIframe

ProperName(String). Method in class mwa.ai.nlp.Parser
put(String, AIframedata). Method in class mwa.data.AIframe
PutChar(). Method in class mwa.ai.neural.testHand
PutChar(). Method in class mwa.ai.neural.testHand_2
PutChar(). Method in class mwa.ai.neural.testHand_4

R

readFloat(). Method in class mwa.data.TextFileIn
remove(String). Method in class mwa.data.AIframe
RemoveTraining(int). Method in class mwa.ai.neural.NNfile
repaint(). Method in class mwa.gui.GUI
ResetLabel. Variable in class mwa.gui.GUI
ReverseVerb. Variable in class mwa.ai.nlp.ParseObject
run(). Method in class mwa.agent.AIframeServer
run(). Method in class mwa.agent.Server
run(). Method in class mwa.ai.neural.testHand
run(). Method in class mwa.ai.neural.testHand_2
run(). Method in class mwa.ai.neural.testHand_4
run(). Method in class mwa.ai.neural.testNeural
RunLabel. Variable in class mwa.gui.GUI

S

Save(String). Method in class mwa.ai.neural.GenNeural
Save(String). Method in class mwa.agent.HTMLdata
Save(String). Method in class mwa.ai.neural.NNfile
Save(String). Method in class mwa.ai.neural.NNgreedy
SaveAsText(String). Method in class mwa.agent.HTMLdata
SendMail(String, String, String, String, String). Constructor for class
mwa.agent.SendMail
sentences. Variable in class mwa.ai.nlp.Parser
Server(). Constructor for class mwa.agent.Server
Server(int). Constructor for class mwa.agent.Server
Server(int, GUI). Constructor for class mwa.agent.Server
Server_helper(int, GUI). Method in class mwa.agent.Server
SetGene(int, int, boolean). Method in class mwa.ai.genetic.Genetic
SetGene(int, int, int). Method in class mwa.ai.genetic.Genetic
SetInputText(String). Method in class mwa.gui.GUI
SetW1(int, int, float). Method in class mwa.ai.neural.NNfile
SetW2(int, int, float). Method in class mwa.ai.neural.NNfile
Sort(). Method in class mwa.ai.genetic.Genetic
SpecialFlag. Variable in class mwa.ai.neural.NNfile
STRING. Static variable in class mwa.data.AIframedata

string. Variable in class mwa.data.AIframedata

T

testAIframe(). Constructor for class mwa.data.testAIframe
testAIframeServer(). Constructor for class mwa.agent.testAIframeServer
testClient(). Constructor for class mwa.agent.testClient
testGenetic(). Constructor for class mwa.ai.genetic.testGenetic
testGenNeural(). Constructor for class mwa.ai.neural.testGenNeural
testGetMail(). Constructor for class mwa.agent.testGetMail
testGreedy(). Constructor for class mwa.ai.neural.testGreedy
testGUI(). Constructor for class mwa.gui.testGUI
testHand(). Constructor for class mwa.ai.neural.testHand
testHand_2(). Constructor for class mwa.ai.neural.testHand_2
testHand_3(). Constructor for class mwa.ai.neural.testHand_3
testHand_4(). Constructor for class mwa.ai.neural.testHand_4
testNeural(). Constructor for class mwa.ai.neural.testNeural
testNeuralFile(). Constructor for class mwa.ai.neural.testNeuralFile
testNLP(). Constructor for class mwa.ai.nlp.testNLP
testNLP2(). Constructor for class mwa.ai.nlp.testNLP2
testObjectClient(). Constructor for class mwa.agent.testObjectClient
testSendMail(). Constructor for class mwa.agent.testSendMail
testServer(). Constructor for class mwa.agent.testServer
testURLdata(). Constructor for class mwa.agent.testURLdata
TextFileIn(). Constructor for class mwa.data.TextFileIn
TextFileIn(String). Constructor for class mwa.data.TextFileIn
TextFileOut(). Constructor for class mwa.data.TextFileOut
TextFileOut(String). Constructor for class mwa.data.TextFileOut
TopIndex. Variable in class mwa.ai.neural.NNfile
toString(). Method in class mwa.data.AIframe
toString(). Method in class mwa.data.AIframedata
toString(). Method in class mwa.agent.HTMLdata
train(). Method in class mwa.ai.neural.testHand
train(). Method in class mwa.ai.neural.testHand_2
train(). Method in class mwa.ai.neural.testNeural
type. Variable in class mwa.data.AIframedata

U

update(Graphics). Method in class mwa.gui.GUI
URLdata(). Constructor for class mwa.agent.URLdata
URLs. Variable in class mwa.agent.HTMLdata

W

WeightFlag. Variable in class mwa.ai.neural.NNfile
writeComment(String). Method in class mwa.data.TextFileOut
writeFloat(float). Method in class mwa.data.TextFileOut

Bibliography

Brownston, Lee, Robert Farrell, Elaine Kant, and Nancy Martin. 1985. *Programming Expert Systems in OPS5*. Reading, MA: Addison-Wesley.

Flanagan, David. 1996. *Java in a Nutshell*. Sebastapol, CA: O'Reilly & Associates, Inc.

Goldberg, David E. 1989. *Genetic Algorithms*. Reading, MA: Addison-Wesley.

Hayes-Roth, Frederick, Donald A. Waterman, and Douglas B. Lenat. 1983. *Building Expert Systems*. Reading, MA: Addison-Wesley.

Hofstadter, Douglas. 1995. *Fluid Concepts and Creative Analogies*. New York: Basic Books.

Jamsa, Kris, and Ken Cope. 1995. *Internet Programming*. Las Vegas, NV: Jamsa Press.

Negroponte, Nicholas. 1995. *Being Digital*. New York: First Vintage Books.

Schank, Roger C., and Christopher K. Riesbeck. 1981. *Inside Computer Understanding*. Hillsdale, NJ: Lawrence Erlbaum Associates.

Watson, Mark. 1991. *Common LISP Modules. Artificial Intelligence in the Era of Neural Networks and Chaos Theory*. New York: Springer-Verlag.

Watson, Mark. 1995. *C++ Power Paradigms.* New York: McGraw-Hill.

Watson, Mark. 1996a. *Programming in Scheme. Learn Scheme through Artificial Intelligence Programs.* New York: Springer-Verlag.

Watson, Mark. 1996b. *Programming Intelligent Agents for the Internet.* New York: McGraw-Hill.

Index

+ (plus sign) concatenation operator, 25

N

About the CD-ROM

CUSTOMER NOTE: PLEASE READ THE FOLLOWING BEFORE OPENING THE CD-ROM PACKAGE.

SYSTEM REQUIREMENTS: PC with WINDOWS NT or WINDOWS 95. UNIX users can use the sample programs on the CD-ROM by copying either the *.zip or *.tar files to their disk and using an unzip or tar utility.

For more information regarding the CD-ROM, see the *Introduction* and *Appendix B: Using the CD-ROM.*